LISTENING/DVD	SPEAKING	
listen to people introduce themselves	introduce yourself and others	
	identify objects	
understand people in tourist situations	make requests	
Fawlty Towers: watch an extract from a sitcom about a hotel	check into a hotel	complete a registration form at a hotel
	talk about activities and groups	link sentences with *and*, *but* and *or*
listen to people talk about their daily routines	talk about your daily routine and people's jobs	
listen to people at a tourist information centre; check when you don't understand	ask questions at a tourist information centre	
Tribal Wives: watch an extract from a programme about living with tribes	talk about good guests and bad guests	write an email asking a friend for a place to stay
	talk about your family	
listen to people talk about their friends	describe someone you know and say why you like them	improve your use of apostrophe *'s*; write about your family and friends
learn to show interest when you listen	make arrangements to meet friends	
Diwali: watch an extract from a BBC programme showing the traditions of Diwali	talk about a special occasion	write a description of a special event
listen to a woman describing her apartment	describe a room in your home	improve your use of commas; write a description of your home
	talk about things you can do in your town	
understand conversations in shops	have a conversation in a shop	
50 Places To See Before You Die: watch an extract from a documentary about some amazing places	talk about a favourite place	write a blog about your favourite place
listen to a photographer talk about food	talk about your eating and drinking habits	
	conduct a class food survey	use paragraphs to write a short report about your class
listen to people ordering in a restaurant; learn to understand fast speech	order a meal in a restaurant	
Ainsley Harriott's Beach Barbecue: watch an extract from a cookery programme with a famous chef	describe your favourite special dish	write an email with a recipe
hear interesting facts about famous people's lives	describe your favourite chidhood things	
	talk about past events in your life	link sentences with *because* and *so*; write your life story in 100 words
listen to people talking about their weekends	talk about how your weekend was	
Nelson Mandela: The Fight For Freedom: watch an extract from a documentary about a great leader	interview a special person	write a profile about a special person

CONTENTS

LISTENING/DVD	SPEAKING	WRITING
listen to people talk about how they like to travel	talk about holidays	
listen to a conversation with a traveller	plan and talk about a long journey	check and correct information about a holiday
understand directions	give directions	
BBC **Going Local: Hong Kong**: watch an extract from a travel show about Hong Kong	describe part of a town/city you know	write a short travel article about a town/city
	talk about what people are doing	improve your use of pronouns; write comments on a photo
listen to people talk about actors	talk about what you wear	
listen to conversations about films	ask for and give recommendations	
BBC **Robert Peston Goes Shopping**: watch an extract from a BBC programme about shopping trends	talk about a survey on trends	write a summary of a survey
	talk about transport in different cities	
listen to a man talk about travelling for free	talk about types of transport	
listen to a woman talk about her problems getting to work	apologise for being late	write a story using linkers
BBC **Airport**: watch an extract from a documentary about a day at Heathrow airport	deal with problems when flying	write a website entry about problems when flying
listen to a radio interview with lottery winners	talk about your future plans/wishes	
	make predictions about situations	improve your use of linkers and write a short story
	make and respond to suggestions for a day out	
BBC **Wild Weather**: watch an extract from a documentary about the wettest place in Europe	describe unusual weather	write a message forum notice about your city
listen to a radio programme about colds and flu	talk about what to do when you don't feel well	
	talk about ways of reducing stress	make your stories more interesting with adverbs
listen to situations where people offer to help	offer to help someone	
BBC **Horizon: Sugar Versus Fat**: watch an extract from a documentary about fat and sugar	talk about diets	write some advice for a health forum
listen to people talking about their experiences	ask and answer questions about life experiences	write an email using linkers
	describe how you feel about different situations	
listen to phone conversations	make telephone calls and say telephone numbers	
BBC **Shark Therapy**: watch an extract from a documentary about sharks	talk about an exciting or frightening experience	write a story about an exciting or frightening experience

COMMUNICATION BANK page 161 AUDIO SCRIPTS page 169

LEAD-IN

OBJECTS AND COLOURS

1 A Look at the words in the box. Which objects are in your classroom?

chair bag notebook table whiteboard pen book CD player pencil noticeboard projector picture

B Work in pairs and take turns. Student A: point to objects in the classroom. Ask your partner. Student B: name the objects.

A: What is it?
B: It's a book.

C Write the colours.

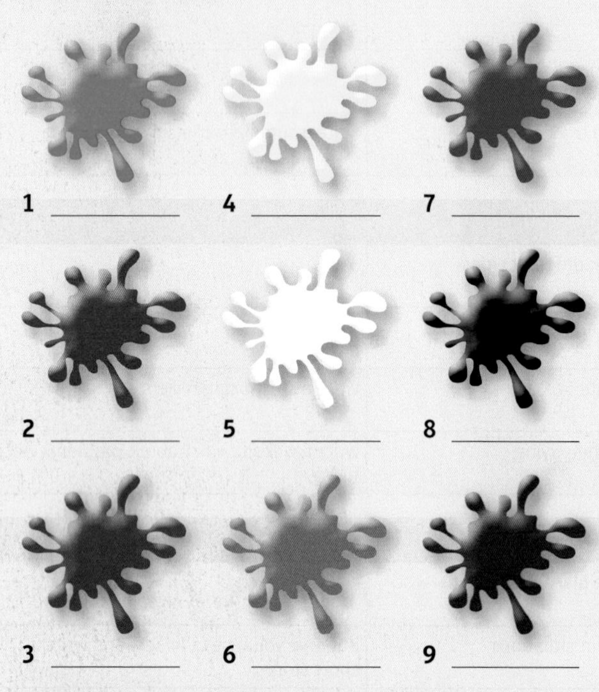

1 ________ 4 ________ 7 ________
2 ________ 5 ________ 8 ________
3 ________ 6 ________ 9 ________

D Work in pairs. Ask and answer *What's your favourite colour?*

THE ALPHABET

2 A L.1 Listen and write the letters in the correct column. Each column has the same vowel sound.

~~A~~ ~~B~~ ~~C~~ D E ~~F~~ G H ~~I~~ J K L M N ~~O~~ P ~~Q~~ ~~R~~ S T U V W X Y Z

A	B	F	I	O	Q	R
	C					

B Listen and repeat.

C Work in pairs and take turns. Student A: spell an object or colour. Student B: say it.

A: b-l-u-e
B: Blue!

QUESTION WORDS

3 A Underline the correct question word.

1 *How/What* 's your name?
2 *Who/Where* are you from?
3 *How/When* are you today?
4 *What/Who* 's your favourite actor?
5 *When/Where* 's your birthday?
6 *What/Why* are you here?
7 *Which/What* spelling is correct: c-h-i-a-r or c-h-a-i-r?

B Work in pairs. Ask and answer the questions above.

CLASSROOM LANGUAGE

4 A Complete the questions with a word from the box.

~~mean~~ repeat don't that could page

1 **A:** What does 'capital' *mean*?
B: It means capital city, for example, London or Tokyo.
2 **A:** 'Work in pairs'? I ________ understand.
B: It means 'Work together'. So, you two …
3 **A:** Could you ________ that?
B: Yes. Page ninety-five.
4 **A:** Could you spell ________?
B: Yes, m-e-e-t.
5 **A:** ________ you write it?
B: Yes, of course.
6 **A:** Which ________ is it?
B: Thirty-five.

B L.2 Listen and check. Then listen and repeat.

NUMBERS

5 A Write the numbers.

1	one	____	twelve	____	fifteen
____	three	____	eight	____	thirteen
____	nine	____	two	____	fifty
____	four	____	seven	____	thirty
____	ten	____	eleven	____	a hundred
____	six	____	five	____	twenty

B L.3 Listen and repeat the numbers.

C Work in pairs. Student A: say five numbers. Student B: write the numbers.

1 welcome

SPEAKING **1.1** Introduce yourself and others **1.2** Identify objects **1.3** Make requests **1.4** Check into a hotel

LISTENING **1.1** Listen to people introduce themselves **1.3** Understand people in tourist situations **1.4** Watch an extract from a sitcom about a hotel

READING **1.2** Read about travelling light

WRITING **1.1** Improve your use of capital letters **1.4** Complete a registration form at a hotel

BBC
INTERVIEWS

What's your name?

1.1 NICE TO MEET YOU

G present simple: *be*
P word stress
V countries and nationalities

SPEAKING

1 A Put the conversation in the correct order (A–D).

1 Nice to meet you, Nick.
2 Hi, Susanna, I'm Nick.
3 You too.
4 Hello, my name's Susanna. *A*

B Work with other students and practise the conversation. Use your own names.

C Work in pairs. What are the names of the other students in the class?

A: His name's Juan.
B: Yes. And her name's Ana, I think.
A: No, her name's Anya, not Ana.

LISTENING

2 A 1.1 Listen to three conversations. Which conversations are in the photos?

B Listen again and underline the correct alternative.

1 a Jenny and Omar *are/aren't* friends.
  b Omar *is/isn't* a student.
2 a Chris *is/isn't* from the UK.
  b It *is/isn't* his first time in Hong Kong.
3 a Andrea *is/isn't* an Italian name.
  b Andrea *is/isn't* from Italy.

C Look at these expressions from the listening. Write N (a new person) or F (a friend or someone you know).

1 How are you? *F*
2 How are things?
3 Great. / Fine. / Good. / OK. / All right. / Not bad.
4 Nice to meet you.
5 Good to see you.
6 Pleased to meet you.

GRAMMAR

PRESENT SIMPLE: *BE*

3 A 1.2 Work in pairs and complete the table. Then listen and check.

Positive and negative statements		
I He We	*'m* _____ _____	Dave. here from the UK. friends.
I	_____ not	a student.

Questions and short answers			
_____	you	friends from school?	Yes, we _____.
_____	your name	Andrew?	No, it _____.

▷ page 128 LANGUAGEBANK

B Complete the conversation.

A: Hi, Muhammed. Good to see you. This [1]_____ Zofia. She [2]_____ in my class.
B: Hi, Zofia. Nice to meet [3]_____.
C: You too. [4]_____ you a student?
B: Yes, I [5]_____.

C Work in groups. Take turns to introduce people.

VOCABULARY

COUNTRIES AND NATIONALITIES

4 A Complete the table with the nationalities.

Country	Nationality
Poland, Spain, Turkey, the UK	*Polish,*
Italy, Argentina, Russia, the USA	
China, Japan	

B Circle your country and nationality above or add them to the table.

C 1.3 **WORD STRESS** Listen and underline the stressed syllable.

Poland, Polish

D Work in pairs and take turns. Student A: say a country. Student B: say the nationality.

speakout TIP

Write new vocabulary in your notebook. Underline the stressed syllables to help you with the pronunciation.

▷ page 152 **PHOTOBANK**

5 A 1.4 Work in pairs and do the quiz below.

A: *I think it's from Australia.*
B: *I think it's Brazilian, from Brazil.*

B Check your answers on page 163.

WRITING

CAPITAL LETTERS

6 A Tick the correct information in the box below.

Use capital letters for the first letter of:

countries ✓ all nouns famous places jobs cities names of people nationalities food languages the first word in a sentence

B Correct the sentences.

1 the eiffel tower is in france.
2 'buenos días!' is spanish for 'hello'.
3 sake is japanese.
4 spaghetti is food from italy.

C Work in pairs. Student A: spell your name or the name of a famous person. Student B: write it. Then check your spelling with Student A.

A: *De Luca: D, e, new word, L, u, c, a.*
B: *Vanessa Mae: V, a, n, e, s, s, a, new word, M, a, e.*

SPEAKING

7 A Write the names of four countries. Add information about a place, food/drink and a famous person.

India – Taj Mahal, curry …

B Work in pairs and take turns. Student A: read out your information. Student B: guess the country.

A: *The Taj Mahal, curry.*
B: *Is it India?*
A: *Yes, it is.*

HEAR IT SEE IT TASTE IT!

1 **Listen and match the countries to the music (A–E) you hear.**

1 Russia ______ 2 Ireland ______ 3 Turkey ______ 4 Brazil ______ 5 Australia ______

2 **Look at the maps and match the countries to the shapes you see.**

A 
B 
C 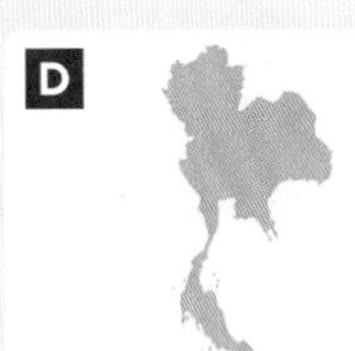
D 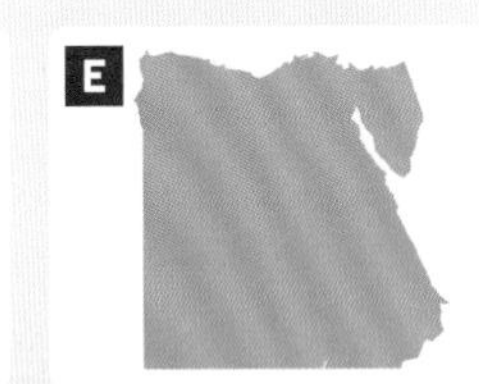

1 France __ 2 Egypt __ 3 Peru __ 4 Thailand __ 5 New Zealand __

3 **Look at the pictures and match the food with the nationalities.**

A 
B 
C 
D 
E 

1 Italian __ 2 Japanese __ 3 Indian __ 4 Spanish __ 5 Chinese __

G *this/that, these/those*; possessives
P word stress; *this, that, these, those*
V objects

VOCABULARY

OBJECTS

1 A Match the words in the box with objects A–P in the picture. Which object isn't in the picture?

a camera *J* a mobile (phone) keys a diary a passport a magazine a credit card an MP3 player and earphones a newspaper a toothbrush a sweater sunglasses a watch a purse a ticket a laptop shampoo

B 1.5 **WORD STRESS** Listen and underline the stressed syllable in the words.

camera

C Work in pairs and take turns. Student A: point to an object in the picture. Student B: name the object.

A: *What's this?*
B: *It's a camera.*

D Work in pairs and discuss. What five things are always in your bags?

A: *I always have a laptop in my bag.*
B: *Me too.*

READING

2 A Look at the picture again. Work in pairs and discuss. What five things are always in your carry-on bag on a plane?

A: *I think a laptop is important.*
B: *Yes. Sunglasses? No. Take sunglasses in your pocket.*

B Read the information and circle the correct number.

Take *9 / 10 / 11 / 12* things in your carry-on bag.

C Read the text again and write the names of objects 1–5.

1 ________ 2 ________ 3 ________

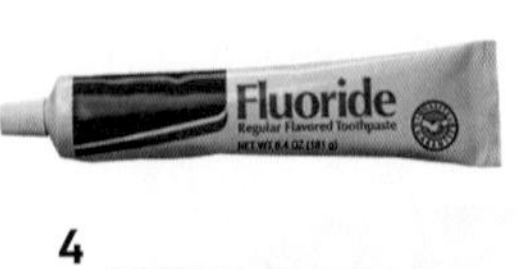

4 ________

5 ________

D Read the text again and put a tick (✓) next to two good ideas and a cross (✗) next to two bad ideas. Then work in pairs and discuss.

Take it or leave it!

With only 10 kilograms for your carry-on bag, what's important to take?

Electrical Things

- **MP3 PLAYER** good for music and audiobooks – put it in your bag.
- **MOBILE PHONE** put it in your pocket, but take the charger in your bag.
- **CAMERA** is your mobile a camera too? Then leave your camera at home.
- **EARPHONES** good for watching DVDs on your laptop. Put them with your mobile phone.
- **LAPTOP** in your bag, with an adaptor, of course.

Practical Things

- **DIARY** with all your important travel and contact information. Put it in your bag.
- **KEYS** put them in the bag so they're easy to find.
- **PASSPORT AND TICKET** these are important so have them in a pocket on your bag.
- **PURSE** coins are a problem at security. Put them in a purse in your bag – yes, men too.

Other Things

- **MAGAZINES AND NEWSPAPERS** leave them at home; they're free on the plane.
- **SHAMPOO** most hotels have shampoo or buy it in town.
- **SUNGLASSES** go in your pocket or on your head, not in the bag!
- **SWEATER** wear it. It's good for the plane if it's cold.
- **TOOTHBRUSH AND TOOTHPASTE** max 100 ml in your carry-on bag.

GRAMMAR

THIS/THAT, THESE/THOSE; POSSESSIVES

3 A 1.6 **Listen to three conversations. Where are the people? Write the number of the conversation under the picture.**

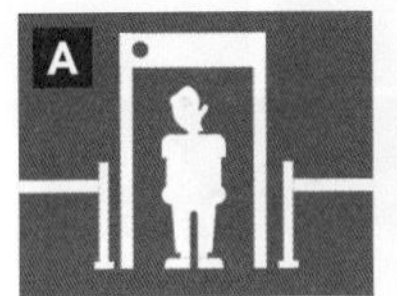
A

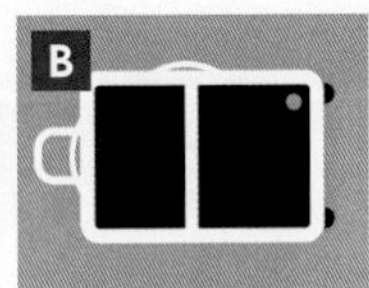
B

C

B 1.7 **Underline the correct alternative in the extracts below. Then listen and check.**

1 **S:** Is [1]*this/these* your bag?
W: Yes, it is.
S: Could you open it, please?
W: What's the problem?
S: [2]*This/Those* is the problem.
W: [3]*These/That's* my shampoo.

2 **S:** What's [4]*that/those* in your pocket?
M: Ah, sorry, [5]*these/those* are my keys.
S: OK, go ahead.

3 **M:** Excuse me, [6]*that's/those are* my [7]*friend/friend's* bags. Can I ...?
W: Sorry, [8]*this is/that's* my bag. The black one. In your hand.
M: No, [9]*this/these* is my [10]*friend's/friend*.
W: Look, my name's on it. It's [11]*my/mine*.
M: Oh, sorry, you're right. It's [12]*your/yours*.

4 A **Write** ***this, that, these*** **or** ***those*** **under the pictures below.**

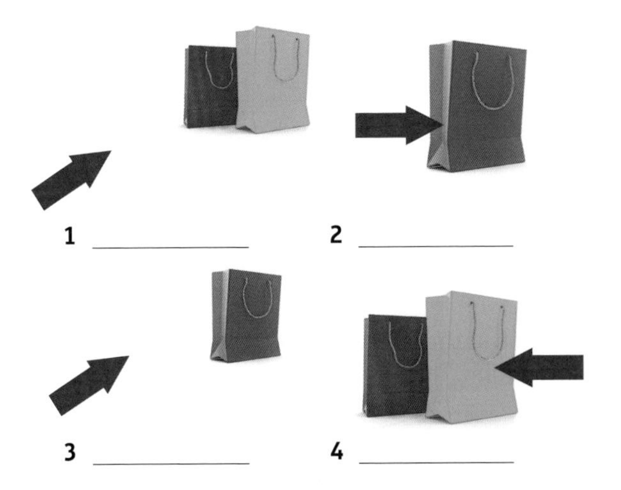

1 ____________ 2 ____________

3 ____________ 4 ____________

B 1.8 **WEAK FORMS:** ***this, that, these, those***
Listen to the pronunciation. Then listen and repeat.

1 Is this /ðɪs/ your bag?
2 Are these /ðiːz/ your bags?
3 Is that /ðæt/ your bag?
4 Are those /ðəʊz/ your bags?

5 A **Correct the sentences. Use Exercise 3B to help.**

1 That's the bag of my friend. ✗
That's my ___*friend's*___ bag. ✓
2 This is the mobile of John. ✗
This is ____________ mobile. ✓
3 That's mine bag. ✗ That's ____________ bag. ✓
4 It's my. ✗ It's ____________. ✓
5 They're yours bags. ✗ They're ____________ bags. ✓
6 They're your. ✗ They're ____________. ✓
7 This bag is Sally. ✗ This bag is ____________. ✓

B **Complete the conversation. Use the words in brackets to help.**

A: Is that [1]___*my*___ book? (I)
B: No, it isn't. It's [2]____________. (Maria)
A: Where's [3]____________? (I)
B: Is this [4]____________? (you)
A: Yes, thanks. Is this [5]____________bag? (you)
B: No, it isn't [6]____________. (I)
A: Maybe it's [7]____________. (Ali)

▷ page 128 **LANGUAGEBANK**

SPEAKING

6 **Work in pairs. Student A: point to an object in the classroom and ask your partner what it is. Student B: name the object.**

A: *What's* ***this*** *in English?*
B: *It's a dictionary.*
A: *What are* ***those*** *in English?*
B: *They're windows.*

7 A **Work in groups. Put two objects from your bag/ pocket on a table. Identify the objects.**

Silvia's bag, Cheng's keys, my watch ...

B **Work with a partner from another group. Look at their objects. Ask and answer questions.**

A: *Is that your pen?*
B: *No, it isn't. It's Bruno's.*
A: *Are these Jack's glasses?*
B: *No, they aren't. They're Veronika's.*

▷ page 152 **PHOTOBANK**

1.3 CAN I HAVE A COFFEE?

(F) making requests
(P) polite intonation; sentence stress
(V) tourist places

VOCABULARY

TOURIST PLACES

1 A Match photos A–C with these places.

1 a tourist shop ______
2 a snack bar ______
3 a train station ______

B Write the words from the box in the word webs below. Add one more word to each place.

~~a postcard~~ an apple juice a battery a single ticket a return ticket a coffee a sandwich a platform a souvenir

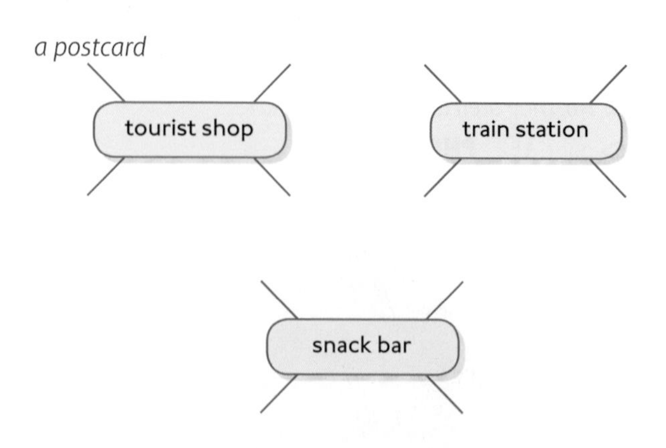

C 1.9 Listen and check. Then listen and repeat.

D Work in pairs. Student A: say a place from Exercise 1B. Student B: say three things you can buy there.

FUNCTION

MAKING REQUESTS

2 A 1.10 Listen to three conversations. Where are the people?

1 ______________________
2 ______________________
3 ______________________

B Listen again. What does each tourist buy?

1 ______________________
2 ______________________
3 ______________________

3 A 1.11 Listen and complete the requests.

1 *Can* *I* *have* a sandwich, please?
2 ______ ______ ______ one of those batteries, please?
3 ______ ______ ______ a single to Sydney, please?

B Look at the question. Listen to the polite intonation. Then listen and repeat.

Can I have a sandwich, please?

▷ page 128 **LANGUAGEBANK**

4 A 1.12 **POLITE INTONATION** Listen to the speakers. Are they polite (P) or not very polite (N)?

B Work in pairs. Student A: you are in one of the places in the photos. Make requests. Student B: only answer if Student A is polite.

A: *Could I have one of those postcards, please?*
B: *Yes. Here you are.*

LEARN TO

LISTEN FOR KEY WORDS

5 A SENTENCE STRESS **Read the conversation. Underline the key words in each sentence.**

A: Can I have a sandwich and an apple juice, please? (3 words)
B: That's six euros. (2 words)
A: Ah, I only have five euros. How much is the sandwich? (3 words)
B: Four euros fifty, and the apple juice is one fifty. (7 words)
A: OK. Could I have the sandwich, but no juice? (3 words)
B: That's four fifty. (2 words)

B 1.13 **Listen to the conversation and check your answers. Then listen and repeat.**

speakout TIP

Key words are the important information words in a sentence. These words are stressed and are l o n g e r, **LOUDER** and higher.

6 1.14 **Listen to three conversation extracts and circle the correct prices.**

Extract 1

	a)	b)	c)
1 an apple juice	a) €2.00	b) €2.10	c) €2.20

Extract 2

	a)	b)	c)
2 a single ticket	a) €4.20	b) €4.50	c) €4.80
3 a taxi	a) €13	b) €23	c) €30

Extract 3

	a)	b)	c)
4 a coffee	a) €2.15	b) €2.50	c) €3.50
5 a sandwich	a) €2.25	b) €2.75	c) €3.75
6 a bottle of water	a) €1.30	b) €1.40	c) €1.60

7 Work in pairs and take turns. Student A: look at page 162. Student B: look at page 164.

SPEAKING

8 A Work in pairs. Complete the menu with prices.

B Role-play the conversation. Student A: look at the menu. Choose and order your food and drink. Student B: take your partner's order. Say the price.

A: Could I have a coffee and a cheese sandwich, please?
B: A coffee and a cheese sandwich? That's four euros fifty.

the HUB

menu

drinks

Coffee	*€1.50*
Tea	____
Hot chocolate	____
Mineral water	____
Juice	____

sandwiches

Cheese	*€3.00*
Egg	____
Chicken	____

cakes

Chocolate cake	____
Coffee cake	____

FAWLTY TOWERS

DVD PREVIEW

1 Look at the photo and read the programme information. Who are the people in the photo?

Fawlty Towers
BBC
Fawlty Towers is a hotel in a BBC TV comedy. The manager's name is Basil Fawlty and he's married to Sybil. Polly and Manuel work at the hotel. Polly is British and Manuel is Spanish. Manuel speaks a little English but he sometimes has problems! The hotel is terrible and Basil often gets angry with his staff and guests!
A
B
C
D

2 A Match the words in the box with pictures A–H.

a lift *A*	a restaurant	stairs	air-conditioning
reception	free WiFi	room service	parking

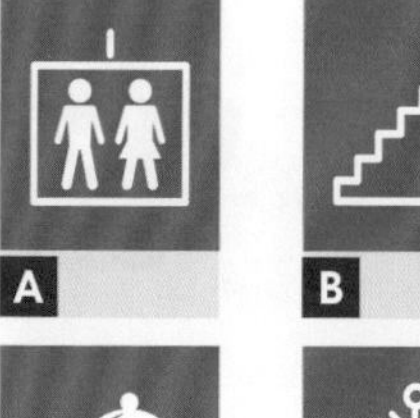
A

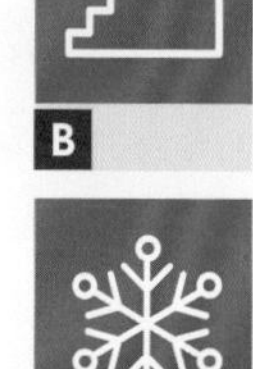
B

C

D

E

F

G

H

B What do you remember? Close your books and write a list of the words. Underline the stressed syllables.

C Discuss. What five things are important for you in a hotel?

A: *Parking's important for me. Free parking.*
B: *Yes, and a friendly person in reception.*
A: *Yes, for me too.*

DVD VIEW

3 A Watch the DVD. How funny is it? Put a cross on the line.

1	2	3	4	5
not funny				funny

B Work in pairs. Are the sentences true (T) or false (F)?

1 Manuel speaks English.
2 The animal speaks English.
3 The Major is surprised.
4 Mr Fawlty is surprised.

C What do the people say? Work in pairs and underline the correct alternative.

1 *How/Who* are you, Sir?
2 I speak English *good/well*.
3 I learn it from a *book/cook*.
4 Hello, Major. How are you *OK/today*?
5 I'm *tired/fine*, thank you.
6 That's a remarkable *animal/apple* you have there, Fawlty.
7 Er … *£20/£12*, I think.
8 *Canadian/American*, I think, Major.

D Watch again and check your answers.

speakout at a hotel

4 A Look at the key phrases below. Who says them? Write guest (G) or receptionist (R) next to each phrase.

KEYPHRASES

Good evening. Can I help you? *R*
Yes, I have a reservation.
For two nights?
What's your surname?
Could you spell that?
You're in room 407.
This is your keycard.
What's the WiFi code?
What time's breakfast?

B 1.15 Listen and check.

C Listen again and complete the information. Write the guest's name and telephone number and the WiFi code.

Name: ______
Phone number: ______
WiFi code: ______

5 Work in pairs and take turns. Student A: you are the receptionist. Welcome the guest and complete the information. Student B: you are the guest. Answer the receptionist's questions.

Surname: ______
First name: ______
Address: ______
______
Phone: ______
Email: ______
Number of nights: ______

A: *Good evening, can I help you?*
B: *Yes, I have a reservation. My name's Pirez.*
A: *Ah, yes. Could you spell that?*
B: *Yes. It's P-i-r-e-z.*

writeback a form

6 A Look at the hotel booking form below and answer the questions.

1 How many times do you write your name?
2 How many dates do you write?
3 Which of these are not correct for this form? a) JOHN, b) *John*, c) John

B Complete the form. Write N/A (= not applicable) for information you don't know.

(Please write in BLOCK CAPITALS)

Surname: (Family name)
First name:
Address:

City:
Country:
Post code:

Passport/ID number:
Tel no:
Fax:
Email:

No of rooms: Single Double
Arrival date:
Departure date:

Credit card type:
Name of card holder as it appears on card:

Number:
Expiry date:
Signature:
Date:

FAWLTY TOWERS

G PRESENT SIMPLE: *BE*

1 A Complete sentences 1–5 with the correct form of *be*.

1 Where'_______ Kuala Lumpur?
2 Where _______ these people from: Angela Merkel, Daniel Radcliffe, Lang Lang, Cristiano Ronaldo?
3 Where'_______ the Blue Mosque?
4 What _______ the names of four countries in South America beginning with A, B or C?
5 I'_______ the President of the USA. What _______ my name?

B Work in pairs and answer the questions.

G QUESTIONS WITH *BE*

2 Work in pairs. Student A: choose a famous person. Student B: ask questions to identify him/her.

B: Is it a man?
A: Yes, it is.
B: Is he French?
A: No, he isn't.
B: Is he on TV?
A: Yes, he is.

V COUNTRIES, NATIONALITIES AND CAPITAL LETTERS

3 A Unjumble the letters and find six countries.

aanpj = Japan
1 isusar
2 typeg
3 isnap
4 dtalhani
5 omicxe
6 diain

B Write five new words from Unit 1.

____
____
____
____
____

C Work in pairs. Student A: say one of your words. Student B: spell it.

A: sandwich
B: s-a-n-d-w-i-c-h

V OBJECTS, *THIS/THAT THESE/THOSE*

4 A Write the name of each object.

1 _______

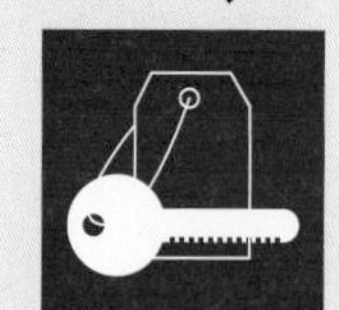

4 _______

2 _______

5 _______

3 _______

6 _______

B Underline the correct alternatives.

1 A: Which newspaper is *that/those*?
B: It's *The New York Times*.
2 A: What are *this/these*?
B: They're my new sunglasses.
3 A: What are *that/those*?
B: They're English magazines.

C Work in pairs. Student A: give your partner an object from your bag/pocket. Student B: close your eyes and guess the object.

A: What's this? / What are these?
B: It's a … / They're …

G POSSESSIVES

5 A Work in pairs. Complete the poems with words from the box.

~~my~~ your my mine yours hands fine Ann's

A: This is [1] *my* book.
B: No, it's [2]_______.
A: Here's [3]_______ name. Look!
B: Oh! That's [4]_______.

B: Are these [5]_______ pens?
A: No, they're [6]_______.
B: Where are [7]_______ then?
A: In my [8]_______!

B Read the poems together.

V WORD GROUPS

6 A Write five words from Unit 1 for the three groups below:

1 electrical objects
a mobile phone, …
2 two-syllable words
a passport, …
3 places
a tourist shop, …

B Work in pairs. Student A: read out the words but don't say which group. Student B: guess the group.

F MAKING REQUESTS

7 A Complete the conversation with the words in the box.

~~could~~ is return there you it

A: Hello, *Could* I have a ticket to Rome, please?
B: A single or?
A: A return, please. How much is?
B: Twenty-five euros.
A: And which platform it?
B: Platform three. Over.
A: Thank.

B Write down twelve key words from the conversation.

C Work in pairs. Compare your key words and practise the conversation.

A: Good evening, can I help you?
B: Yes, I have a reservation. My name's Pirez.
A: Ah, yes. Could you spell that?
B: Yes. It's P-i-r-e-z.

2 lifestyle

SPEAKING 2.1 Talk about activities you do 2.2 Talk about your daily routine and people's jobs 2.3 Ask questions at a tourist information centre 2.4 Talk about good guests and bad guests

LISTENING 2.2 Listen to people talk about their daily routines 2.3 Listen to people at Tourist Information; Check when you don't understand 2.4 Watch an extract from a programme about living with tribes

READING 2.1 Read about local groups

WRITING 2.1 Link sentences with *and, but* and *or*
2.4 Write an email asking a friend for a place to stay

BBC INTERVIEWS

What's your daily routine?

G present simple: *I/you/we/they*
P linking: *do you*
V activities

READING

1 A Work in pairs and discuss. What's a good way to meet people in a new city?

B Read the information from a website about meeting people in Dublin. Which group is good for these people?

1 'I'm from Italy and I want to improve my English, but it's difficult to meet people.'
2 'I like doing things in the evenings, going to restaurants and the cinema.'
3 'I work at home all day and I want to meet people at the weekends. I like walking and going to cafés.'

C Work in pairs and discuss. Which group is good for you? Why?

VOCABULARY

ACTIVITIES

2 A Complete phrases 1–8 below with words from the box. Use the website extracts to help you.

~~have~~ read listen to do eat play go watch

1 *have* a coffee/fun
2 ________ films/TV
3 ________ tennis/computer games
4 ________ running/to a restaurant
5 ________ newspapers/magazines
6 ________ music/an MP3 player
7 ________ exercise/sport
8 ________ pasta/junk food

B Add these words to phrases 1–8.

~~a drink~~ the teacher DVDs swimming a sandwich football a book nothing

1 *have a coffee/fun/a drink*

C Work in pairs. Student A: say a noun from Exercise 2A or 2B. Student B: say the verb that goes with it.

A: *football*
B: *play football*

speakout TIP

Look for words that go together (collocations). When you write new words in your notebook, write the words that go with them, e.g. *do exercise/sport/nothing*. Look at the website extracts. In your notebook, write the words that go with *meet* and *get*.

Group-meet Dublin

ABOUT MEMBERS PHOTOS EVENTS

Dublin film group

This group is open to all film lovers. We go to see different kinds of films, including new Hollywood movies and old black and white films. We watch films in members' homes and at cinemas in the city centre. We meet about 30 minutes before the start time and have a coffee or tea. Then after the film we have a drink or go to a restaurant and talk about the film. We're a very friendly group and welcome new members.

Join Us **Charlotte** Members: 128

English Italian group

Do you study English or Italian? Do you like meeting new people? Then join us. Every week we meet in a café for conversation: one hour in Italian and one hour in English. We also read newspapers and magazines in Italian, listen to Italian music and eat pasta. We welcome all nationalities (especially Italian speakers) and all levels, from beginner to advanced.

Join Us **Miguel** Members: 73

Get fit group

Is this you? You work on a computer all day, and in the evening you play computer games or watch TV. You don't eat well, you eat junk food, you don't do exercise, but you want to get fit. Well, join our group. We aren't all fit, but we like being outside, we love walking and we do all kinds of sport. Every Saturday we play tennis or football, or go walking or running. Join us, get fit and have fun!

Join Us **Sandy** Members: 64

GRAMMAR

PRESENT SIMPLE: *I/YOU/WE/THEY*

3 A Complete the table with words from the website extracts.

Positive and negative statements		
We	______	films.
You	______ ______	well.

Questions and short answers						
______	you	study	English?	Yes,	I	do.
				No,		don't.

B Underline the correct word(s) to complete the rule.

RULES	Use the present simple for activities we do *regularly/at the moment of speaking.* Make the negative with *no* + verb/*don't* + verb. Make the question with *do you* + verb/verb + *you.*

▷ page 130 **LANGUAGEBANK**

4 Cover the website extracts on page 18. Complete the information below. Use a verb in the positive or negative form.

In the English Italian Group they [1] *don't speak* Italian all the time. They [2] ______ English half the time. In the Dublin Film Group they [3] ______ to cinemas and people's homes. They [4] ______ before the film but they go to a restaurant after the film. In the Get Fit Group they [5] ______ being inside all the time and they [6] ______ all kinds of sport. On Saturdays they [7] ______ computer games all day, they [8] ______ running.

5 A ▶ 2.1 Listen and underline the stressed words.

1 Do you want to practise your English? Yes, I do.
2 Do you like meeting new people? No, I don't.

B LINKING: ***do you*** Look at the pronunciation of *do you*. Then listen and repeat.

do‿you /dəjə/
/dəjə/ like meeting new people?

C Work in pairs. Write three questions for each Group-meet group. Use the website extracts to help.

Film group – Do you like films? Do you watch films on TV or online? Do you go to the cinema a lot?

D Work with another pair. Ask them your questions. Which is the right group for the other students? Do they agree with your idea?

SPEAKING

6 A Work in pairs. Start a new Group-meet group. Choose one of the groups below or think of another. Then write answers to the questions.

1 What do people in your group do? (three activities)
2 What don't you do? (two activities)

Concert group — Photography group
Coffee group — Book club
Women's group — Men's group
Cooking group — Salsa dancing group
Football group

B Talk to other students. Tell them about your group, but don't look at your notes. Find out about their group. Which group do you like the most?

Our group is a Concert group. We love rock music. We …

WRITING

AND, BUT, OR

7 A Read the sentences. Which Group-meet group are they about?

1 We speak English for one hour. It's not easy ______ we know it's good for us.
2 Do you play football on Saturday, ______ do you play tennis?
3 Do you like meeting people ______ watching movies with them?

B Complete the sentences above with *and*, *but* and *or*.

C Complete each sentence in three different ways. Use *and*, *but* and *or*.

1 I like listening to English …
2 At the weekend, I go running …

D Work in pairs and compare your answers. Which sentences are true for both of you?

E Work in groups. Write a Group-meet website page for your group. Use the website extracts to help.

Ⓖ present simple: *he/she/it*
Ⓟ third person *'s'*
Ⓥ daily routines; jobs

VOCABULARY

DAILY ROUTINES

1 A Match the phrases in the box with photos A–H below. Which phrase is not in the photos?

get up *A*	go to bed	have breakfast
get home	have lunch	start work/school
leave home	finish work/school	have dinner

B Cover the vocabulary box in Exercise 1A and complete the questions.

1 Do you *get* up early?
2 Do you ______ breakfast at home?
3 What time do you ______ home?
4 When do you ______ work/school?
5 Where do you ______ lunch?
6 When do you ______ home after work/school?
7 Do you ______ to bed late?

C Work in pairs. Ask and answer the questions above. Find three things in common.

A: Do you get up early?
B: Yes, I do. I get up at 6. How about you?
A: I get up at 7.30.

LISTENING

2 Work in pairs and look at the photos on page 21. What's one good and one bad thing about each job?

3 A ▶ 2.2 Listen to a radio programme about two of the people and answer the questions.

1 Do the people like their jobs?
2 Do their families think the jobs are good?

B Listen again. Is the information true (T) or false (F)?

	Gonzales	Emma
1 I leave home	at 5. *F*	on Monday morning.
2 For lunch, I have	2 sandwiches.	a sandwich on the plane.
3 I get home	at 3p.m.	on Thursday.
4 One good thing about the job is	it's quiet.	the mountains are quiet.

GRAMMAR

PRESENT SIMPLE: *HE/SHE/IT*

4 A Look at audio script 2.2 on page 169 and complete the table and the rules.

Present simple positive statements		
He	______	on bridges.
	______	a great job.
She	______	the money.
	______	animal programmes on TV.

Present simple negative statements		
Alice	doesn't ______	flying.

RULES

To make the present simple with *he/she/it*, add ______ or ______ to the verb.
To make the negative, use *he/she/it* + ______ + verb.
To make the present simple of *have*, use *he/she/it* + ______.

B ▶ 2.3 **THIRD PERSON *'S'*** Listen and write the verbs in the correct group below.

/s/ *works*
/z/
/ɪz/

C ▶ 2.4 Listen to other verbs. Write them in the correct group. Then listen and repeat.

▷ page 130 **LANGUAGEBANK**

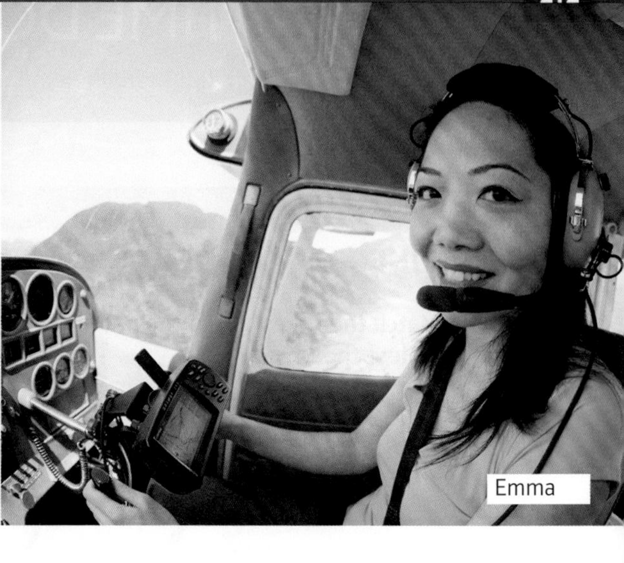

5 Complete the text about Gagan. Use the verbs in brackets in the positive or negative form.

Gagan [1] _gets up_ (get up) at four in the morning. He [2]______ (not have) a big breakfast, usually a piece of fruit and a cup of tea. He [3]______ (leave) home at five, [4]______ (go) to the guest house and [5]______ (meet) his tourist group. He helps them with their bags, and he [6]______ (put) extra food and water on his horse. They [7]______ (walk) all morning and [8]______ (stop) for lunch at about twelve. Gagan [9]______ (make) lunch for the group; he [10]______ (not eat) meat so they have a simple vegetable dish. Then they [11]______ (walk) all afternoon to a new guest house before dark. Sometimes Gagan [12]______ (not go) home for two to three days.

6 A Write two true and two false sentences from Exercise 1C about your partner's daily routine.

B Check with your partner and write T (true) or F (false).

A: Pilar gets up early.
B: True. I get up at six.

C Work with a new partner. Student A: read the sentences about your first partner. Student B: guess which are true and which are false.

GRAMMAR

PRESENT SIMPLE: *HE/SHE/IT*

7 A Look at the sentences in the table and complete the rule.

Present simple questions and short answers						
What	does	your family	think?			
	Does	she	want to be a pilot?	Yes, No,	she	does. doesn't.

RULES	
RULES	Make the question with ______ + *he/she/it* + verb. Make the short answer with *Yes, he/she/it* ______ and *No, he/she/it* ______.

B 2.5 Listen and underline the stressed words. Then listen again and repeat.

1 Does she want to be a pilot?
2 What does your family think?

8 Work in pairs. Student A: look at page 162. Student B: look at page 166.

▷ page 130 LANGUAGEBANK

VOCABULARY

JOBS

9 A 2.6 Listen and write the names of the jobs.

A ______ C ______ E ______
B ______ D ______ F ______

B Work in pairs. How many other jobs do you know in English?

▷ page 153 PHOTOBANK

SPEAKING

10 Work in groups. One student: choose a person from the photo bank on page 153. The other students: ask ten questions to find the job.

B: Is it a woman?
A: Yes, it is.
C: Does she work with food?

2.3 WHAT TIME DOES IT START?

F asking for information
P sentence stress; polite intonation
V the time

VOCABULARY
THE TIME

1 A Match the times 1–6 to the photos A–F. Then complete the times.

1 four o'clock *C*
2 _______ past eight
3 ten fifteen OR quarter past _______
4 one thirty OR _______ past one
5 seven forty-five OR _______ to eight
6 five _______ six

B Work in pairs and take turns. Student A: point to a photo. Ask the time. Student B: say the time.

A: *What's the time?*
B: *It's …*

C 2.7 Listen and circle the correct times below.

1	10:30	12:30	2:30
2	3:15	3:45	4:15
3	6:40	7:20	7:40
4	4:25	4:35	5:25

D Work in pairs. Student A: look at page 161. Student B: look at page 166.

E Work in pairs and take turns. Ask and answer the questions below.

At the weekend, what time do you …
- get up?
- have breakfast?
- have lunch?
- go to bed?

On Saturday I get up at eight, but on Sunday I …

FUNCTION
ASKING FOR INFORMATION

2 A Work in pairs. Look at the photos and leaflets from San Francisco. Answer the questions.

1 What tours can people take?
2 Which tours have **a)** eating or drinking **b)** a famous bridge **c)** shopping?
3 Which tour do you like?

B 2.8 Listen and answer the questions.

1 Which tour do the tourists want?
2 Do they book the tour?
3 What's the problem?

3 A Put the questions about the bus tour in the correct order.

1 it / does / what / time / start?
2 leave / where / from? / does / it
3 when / the tour / finish? / does
4 much / cost? / it / how / does
5 take / do / credit cards? / you

B 2.9 SENTENCE STRESS Listen and check. Then listen again and underline the stressed words in the questions above.

C Look at the pronunciation of *does it*. Listen again and repeat the questions.

does‿it /dəzɪt/
What time /dəzɪt/ start?

D 2.10 Listen and answer the questions in Exercise 3A.

▷ page 130 LANGUAGEBANK

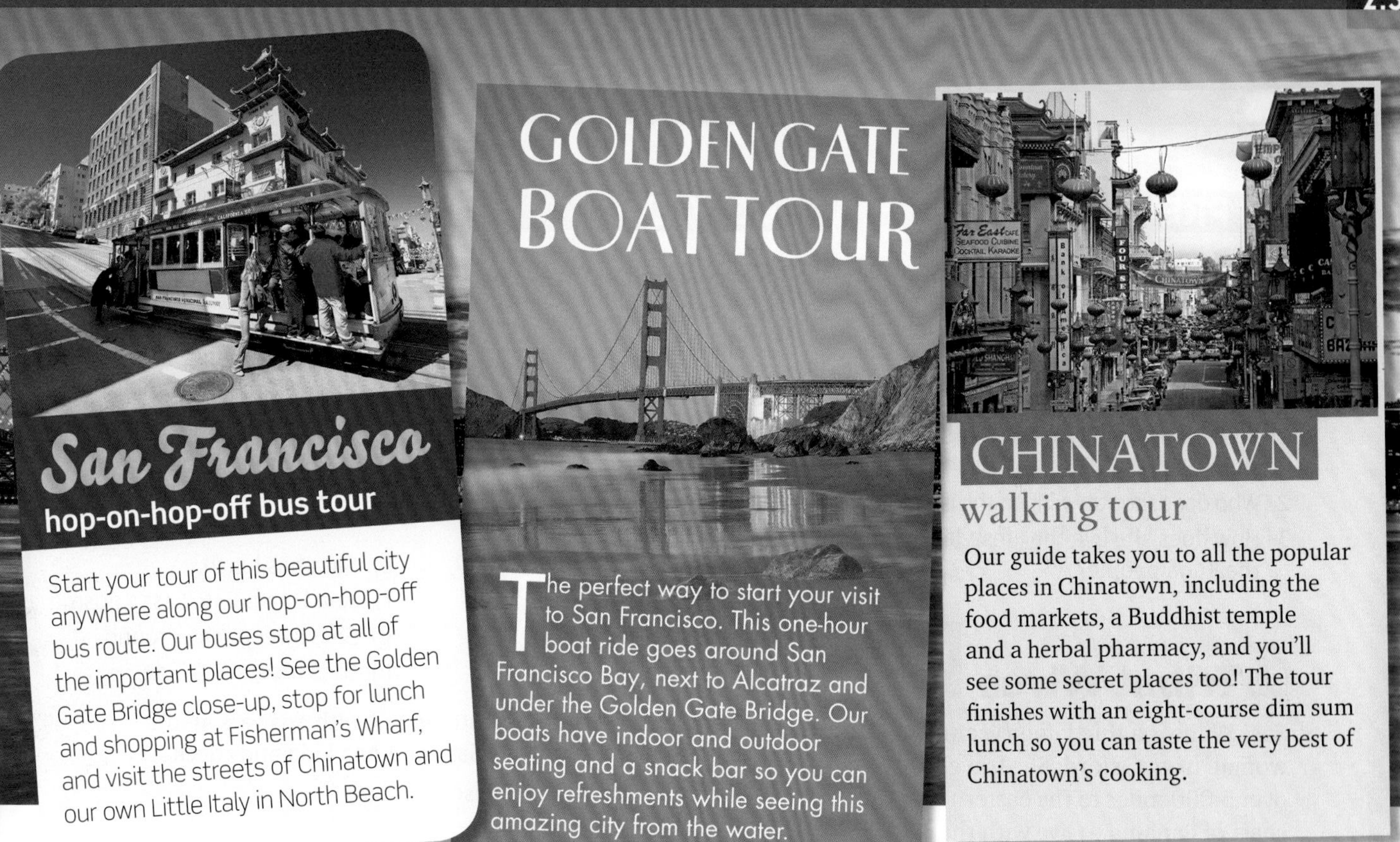

San Francisco
hop-on-hop-off bus tour
Start your tour of this beautiful city anywhere along our hop-on-hop-off bus route. Our buses stop at all of the important places! See the Golden Gate Bridge close-up, stop for lunch and shopping at Fisherman's Wharf, and visit the streets of Chinatown and our own Little Italy in North Beach.
GOLDEN GATE BOAT TOUR
The perfect way to start your visit to San Francisco. This one-hour boat ride goes around San Francisco Bay, next to Alcatraz and under the Golden Gate Bridge. Our boats have indoor and outdoor seating and a snack bar so you can enjoy refreshments while seeing this amazing city from the water.
CHINATOWN
walking tour
Our guide takes you to all the popular places in Chinatown, including the food markets, a Buddhist temple and a herbal pharmacy, and you'll see some secret places too! The tour finishes with an eight-course dim sum lunch so you can taste the very best of Chinatown's cooking.

LEARN TO

SHOW YOU DON'T UNDERSTAND

4 A 2.11 **Read and listen to part of the conversation again. Underline three expressions the woman uses when she doesn't understand.**

A: Hello. We're back.
C: Hello again! So, do you want the Golden Gate boat tour?
A: Er. Could you speak more slowly, please?
C: Of course. Would you like the Golden Gate boat tour?
A: Yes. Tomorrow.
C: Would you like the morning or afternoon tour?
A: Tomorrow morning. What time does it start?
C: At ten o'clock exactly.
A: Excuse me, ten o'clock … ?
C: Yes, at ten.
A: And where does it leave from?
C: From Pier 43. Or the minibus to the boat leaves from the front gate at nine forty-five.
A: Sorry, could you repeat that?
C: The minibus to the boat leaves from the front gate.

B 2.12 **POLITE INTONATION Listen again to the three expressions. Then repeat and practise the polite intonation.**

C Work in groups. Ask each student for an address and telephone number. Use the expressions from Exercise 4A to check the information.

SPEAKING

5 A Work in pairs. Student A: you work at the Tourist Information Centre. Look at page 163.
Student B: You are a tourist in San Francisco. Ask Student A questions and complete the notes below.

Excuse me. Can you give me some information about the … ? What time does it … ?

	Start time	Finish time	Place	Price
Boat tour				
Bus tour				

B Change roles. Student B: now you work at the Tourist Information Centre. Look at the information below. Answer Student A's questions.

	Start time	Finish time	Place	Price
Walking tour	10a.m.	1p.m.	Leaves from Chinatown Gateway	$30
Rock concert	8p.m.	11.30p.m.	The Fillmore	$75

A VISIT TO PANAMA

DVD PREVIEW

1 **Look at the photos and find a hut, a boat, a palm tree and the sea.**

2 **Read the programme information and answer the questions.**

1 Who is Sass Willis and where does she go?
2 Who does she stay with on the island?
3 How does she live the lifestyle of the Kuna people?

Tribal Wives

Sass Willis is a thirty-four-year-old woman from Oxford. She travels over 5,000 miles to the eastern coast of Panama to live with the Kuna Indians on the island of Niadup. On the island she stays at the home of fifty-five-year-old Ana Lida and her husband Diego. In her time on Niadup, Sass lives the lifestyle of the Kuna people: she lives in a hut, she sleeps in a hammock, she wears Kuna clothes and helps with jobs around the home. Another woman, Ana Lina, helps by painting her face in the traditional way.

DVD VIEW

3 **A** **Watch the DVD. Why does Sass cry at the end? Tick all the true sentences.**

1 She's sad/unhappy.
2 She wants to go home.
3 She's thankful to Ana Lida.
4 She's ill and wants a doctor.
5 She's happy.
6 She doesn't like the work.

B **What do you remember? Number the activities in the correct order. Which activity is not in the programme? Watch again and check.**

a) Sass makes coffee.
b) Sass mends clothes.
c) Sass flies to Niadup.
d) Sass puts on a Kuna shirt.
e) Sass has lunch.
f) Ana Lina paints Sass's nose.
g) Sass sweeps the ground.
h) Sass meets Ana Lida.

C **Work in pairs. Match questions 1–4 with answers a)–d). Watch the first meeting of Sass and Ana Lida and check.**

1 'And who lives in this house?'
2 'Is that, erm, the bed?'
3 'Hi, my name is Sass. And your name is … ?'
4 'And do you … do you live here, or do you live nearby?'

a) 'Ana Lina.'
b) 'I live here with my husband.'
c) 'I sleep in the hammock and my husband sleeps in the bed.'
d) 'Yes, I live in the hut opposite. The door is open.'

D **Work alone. For *you*, what things are good and bad about the family's lifestyle? Put a tick (✓) for good and cross (✗) for bad.**

1 They live on a small island.
2 They don't live in a city.
3 They are very friendly to visitors.
4 They don't have a lot of money.
5 They sleep in hammocks.

E **Work in pairs and compare your answers. Say why you put a ✓ or ✗.**

A: *Do you think number one is good or bad?*
B: *For me, it's good.*
A: *Why?*
B: *Because an island is beautiful and quiet.*

speakout a good guest

4 A Work in pairs and discuss.

1 Do you like having guests in your home?
2 What's good about having guests?
3 What don't you like?
4 What are three problems with bad guests?

B Work in pairs and complete the sentence: 'A good guest …' with three different endings. Give examples. Choose from the topics below.

A good guest brings a small gift, for example chocolates.

bring a big/small gift
bring food/drink
give money
arrive early/late
use the phone
help with cooking
speak in your/their language
stay a short/long time

5 A 2.13 Listen to two people talk about being a good guest. Which topics above do they talk about?

B Listen again and tick the key phrases you hear.

KEY PHRASES

What do you think?
What does a good guest do?
For example, he …
Yes, I agree. That's bad.
What do you mean?
A good guest doesn't …
I think it's important to …
I don't agree.
It depends.

C Work in groups and use the key phrases to help. Write five top tips for being a good guest in your country or in another country.

A good guest in Poland …
… brings flowers for the hostess and perhaps something to drink.
… arrives …

D Tell the rest of the class. Other students: listen and make notes. Then ask one or two questions about the ideas.

writeback an email

6 A Read the parts of the email below. What does the writer want?

INBOX

Dear Antonio, *1*
I'm in Barcelona
Best wishes,
How are you?
Can I come and stay with
Are you very busy?
for ten days next month
Do you know a good hotel in the city?
you for the last weekend?
Dom

B Number the phrases in the correct order.

C Write an email to another student using the phrases in Exercise 6A to help you. Give it to them.

D Answer the email that another student gives you.

2.5 LOOKBACK

V ACTIVITIES

1 A Complete the questions with a suitable verb.

1 Do you *read* magazines? Which ones?
2 Do you ______ sport on TV? Which sport?
3 Do you ______ a coffee every morning? Do you drink it black?
4 Do you ______ to music when you work or study? What kind?
5 Do you ______ exercise every week? What do you do?
6 Do you ______ a lot of junk food? What and when?
7 Do you ______ books in English? Which ones?
8 Do you ______ to restaurants a lot? Which ones?

B Work in pairs. Ask and answer the questions.

V DAILY ROUTINES

2 A On a piece of paper write:

- a place you like
- your job or study subject
- the time you get up
- two things you do in the evening

B Work in pairs. Exchange papers. Ask and answer questions.

A: Moonbucks. What's that?
B: A coffee bar.
A: Why do you like it?
B: Well, …

C Take your partner's paper. Work with a new partner and exchange papers. Ask and answer questions about your first partner.

Why does he get up at six?
What does he study?

G PRESENT SIMPLE

3 A Complete the sentences about your partner. Use the positive or negative form of the verbs in brackets.

1 He/She *doesn't like* (like) shopping.
2 He/She ______ (play) computer games.
3 He/She ______ (go) out a lot in the evenings.
4 He/She ______ (do) his/her homework every night.
5 He/She ______ (study) a lot at the weekend.
6 He/She ______ (watch) breakfast television.
7 He/She ______ (go) to bed very late.
8 He/She ______ (cook) every night.

B Work in pairs and check your answers.

A: Do you like shopping?
B: No, I don't.

C Work with a new partner and ask questions about your first partner.

A: Does she like shopping?
B: Yes, she does.
A: You're wrong. She doesn't like shopping.

V JOBS

4 A What are the jobs? Find and circle twelve jobs.

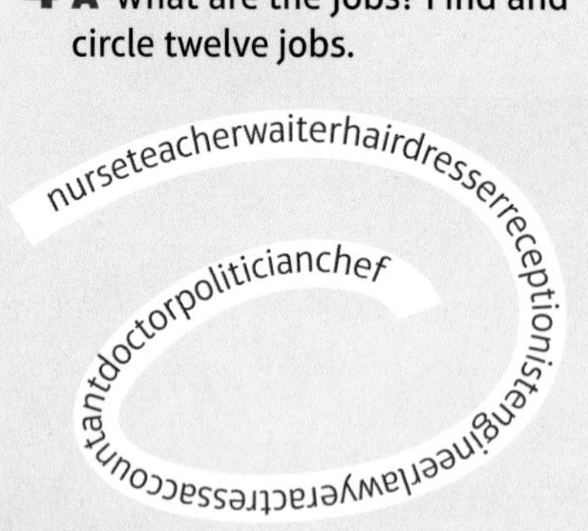

B Work in pairs. Which jobs are right for these people? Write two jobs for each person.

1 I like people.
______
______

2 I talk a lot.
______
______

3 I work well alone.
______
______

4 I love numbers.
______
______

5 I'm very active.
______
______

6 I like food.
______
______

F ASKING FOR INFORMATION

5 A Look at the leaflet below. Write questions to ask for the information in the leaflet.

SICILY FULL-DAY TOUR

Start time:	9.45a.m.
Finish time:	4.30p.m.
Leaves from:	Hotel lobby
Adult:	€20
Payment:	All major credit cards accepted.

B Work in pairs. Student A: you are a tourist. Ask questions about the Sicily tour. Student B: you work at the Tourist Information Centre. Answer your partner's questions.

A: What time does the tour start?
B: It starts at nine forty-five in the morning.

3 people

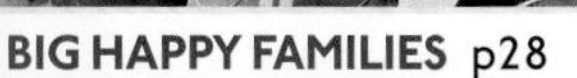

SPEAKING **3.1** Talk about your family **3.2** Describe a friend and why you like them **3.3** Make arrangements to meet friends **3.4** Talk about a special occasion

LISTENING **3.2** Listen to people talk about their friends **3.3** Learn to show interest when you listen **3.4** Watch an extract from a BBC programme showing the traditions of Diwali

READING **3.1** Read about an unusual family

WRITING **3.2** Improve your use of apostrophe *'s*; Write about your family and friends **3.4** Write a description of a special event

BBC INTERVIEWS

What do you like doing with friends/family?

3.1 BIG HAPPY FAMILIES

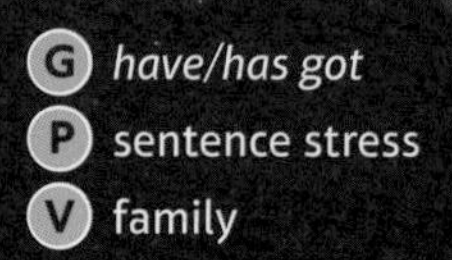

G have/has got
P sentence stress
V family

VOCABULARY

FAMILY

1 A Work in pairs. Look at the photo of the Bonell family. Can you find:

- the parents?
- the number of children?
- a son and a daughter?
- a brother and a sister?
- a husband and a wife?

B Circle the 'family' words above. Do you know any other family words?

▷ page 154 **PHOTOBANK**

READING

2 A Discuss. What do you think are the good/bad things about life in a big/small family?

B Work in pairs. Student A: look at page 167. Student B: read the text on this page. Circle the numbers in the box which are in your text. What do they refer to?

600	17	(16)	9	8	7	3	2	1

16 children in the Bonell family

C Work in pairs. Tell your partner about your text. Use your numbers to help.

D Work in pairs. Draw lines to complete the information. Use the texts to help.

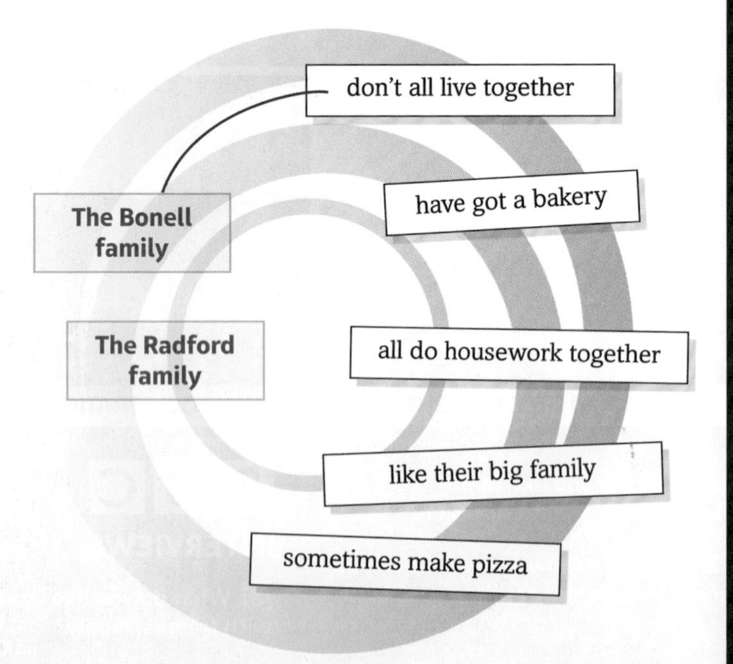

FAMILY WELCOMES BABY SIXTEEN

Baby Katelyn is the latest child of Jeni and Ray Bonell of Queensland, Australia. They have got sixteen children – seven girls and nine boys.

Life in the Bonell house is noisy, but they've got rules so things don't get too crazy. The house has got seven bedrooms but each child sleeps in his or her own bed. Jesse and Brooke, the two oldest kids, don't live with the family. They have got their own homes in the neighbourhood but they often visit.

Jeni says that having a big family is normal for them. Her day-to-day life is similar to the life of other mums, just with more washing to do and bigger meals to cook. Food shopping costs about $600 a week. Meals and house cleaning are big jobs, but all the children help from the age of eight. One of the Bonell's neighbours says, 'I've only got two children and I haven't got time for myself. I don't know how Jeni and Ray do it. And they love it. They're great parents!'

Giving each of their children enough time and attention isn't easy, but it's important for both parents. 'Jeni and Ray spend so much time with the kids,' says a family friend. 'The kids definitely feel loved and happy and the new baby is beautiful.'

GRAMMAR

HAVE/HAS GOT

3 A Look at the article on page 28 again and complete the sentences.

1 They ____________ sixteen children.
2 The house ____________ seven bedrooms.
3 I ____________ time for myself.

B Complete the table.

I/You/We/They	______	got	eight brothers.
He/She	______		
I	______n't		a sister.
He/She/It	______n't		

C 3.1 Listen and underline the alternative you hear.

1 Kate *'s/has* got five sisters.
2 I *'ve/have* got a sister and two brothers.
3 They *'ve/haven't* got a car.
4 He *'s/hasn't* got a big family.

D SENTENCE STRESS Listen again and underline the stressed words. Listen and repeat.

4 A Complete the text. Use the correct form of *have got* or *be*.

I [1] *'ve got* a brother and a sister. My sister, Lisa, [2] __________ thirty-five, my brother, Paul, [3] __________ thirty and I [4] __________ twenty-seven. My sister [5] __________ married to Andreas and they [6] __________ a daughter, Eva. Eva [7] __________ (not) any brothers or sisters. My brother [8] __________ (not) married, but he [9] __________ a girlfriend. I [10] __________ married to Marek. We [11] __________ two sons, Vlad and Henryk. They [12] __________ three and one.

B Use the information above to complete the family tree.

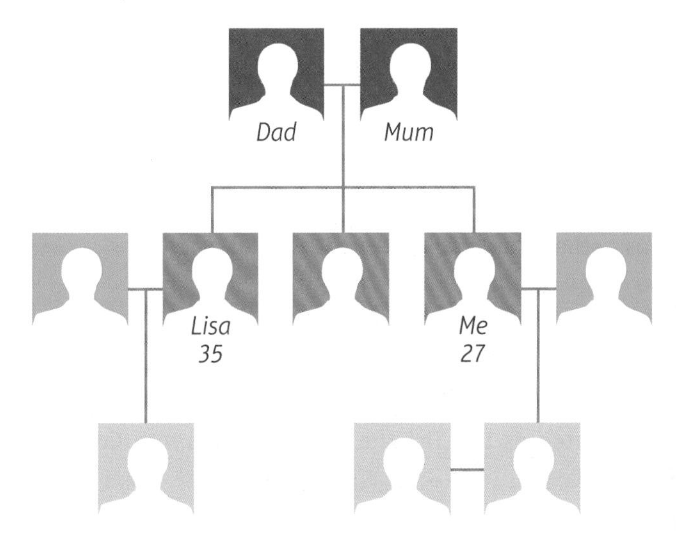

page 132 LANGUAGEBANK

SPEAKING

5 A Complete the questions.

1 ______ you ______ any brothers or sisters?
2 How many brothers ______ you ______?
3 ______ your brother ______ any children?
4 How many children ______ he ______?

B Look at Exercise 4B and draw an empty family tree for your family in your notebook. Write your name and two family members in your tree.

C Work in pairs. Exchange family trees with your partner. Ask and answer questions.

A: *How many brothers and sisters have you got?*
B: *I've got two brothers and one sister.*
A: *What are their names?*
B: *Joel, Santiago and Cecilia.*
A: *And how old is Joel?*
B: *He's twenty-five.*
A: *And has he got a job?*
B: *Yes, he works in a big hotel. He's the manager.*

D Look at your own family tree again. Check the information and correct any mistakes.

6 A Work in groups. Read people's answers to the question *What do you call your parents and grandparents?*

Jan, UK
I call my mother Mum. My daughter calls me Mummy.

Sylvia, USA
We call our parents Mom and Dad. Maybe some people call their dad Pop.

Chris Australia
My son calls me Dad and my grandchildren call me Grandpa.

B Discuss. What do you call people in your family?

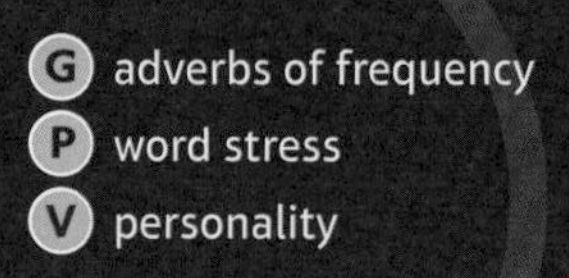

SPEAKING

1 A **Work in pairs. Look at the photos and discuss. What are the three types of friends? Give an example of each type of friend.**

B **Work in pairs and discuss the questions.**

1 Have you got a lot of online friends?
2 Have you got friends you see every week? What activities do you do with them?
3 Have you got one real best friend?

A 'Online' friends

B 'Have fun' friends

C 'Real' friends

LISTENING

2 A 3.2 **Listen to three people talking about their friends. Draw a line between the name and the topic.**

1 Hakim — **a)** talks about online friends.
2 Bridget — **b)** talks about a friend he/she does things with.
3 Jane — **c)** talks about his/her best friend.

B **Listen again and tick the correct answer.**

1 Hakim and Tomi *play tennis / go running ✓/ talk about personal things.*
2 Hakim *has got / wants / doesn't want* lots of friends.
3 Bridget has got *thirty / thirty-five / forty-five* online friends.
4 Mark *knows / doesn't know / meets* all his online friends.
5 Jane *talks to / visits / meets* her sister every day.
6 Jane *talks to / emails / doesn't see* her friend Julie every day.

C **Work in pairs and discuss. Which person, Hakim, Bridget, Mark or Jane, is similar to you? Why?**

GRAMMAR

ADVERBS OF FREQUENCY

3 A **Read the sentences and put the adverbs in bold in the correct place on the line below.**

1 At the weekends we **usually** play football or go running together.
2 Mark is **sometimes** on his computer for eight or ten hours.
3 We **often** visit each other or do things together.
4 We **hardly ever** see each other, maybe three or four times in the last five years.

never ——————————————————— **always**

0% 10% 40% 60% 80% 100%

B **Read the sentences again and underline the correct alternative in the rules below.**

RULES	
	The adverb goes *before/after* the verb *be*.
	The adverb goes *before/after* other verbs.

C **Put the words in the correct order.**

1 A / you / problems / often / with / friend / helps / real
A real friend often helps you with problems.
2 friends / other / understand / each / Real / always
3 friend / is / a brother or sister / real / sometimes / A
4 about / friends / ask / personal things / never / Real
5 disagree / Real / hardly ever / friends
6 are / age / the same / friends / Real / usually

D **Look at sentences 1–6. Tick the ones you agree with. Compare with a partner.**

▷ page 132 LANGUAGEBANK

VOCABULARY

PERSONALITY

4 A Match the adjectives in the box with pictures A–F.

interesting *D* intelligent kind talkative friendly funny

B Look at the adjectives in the box below. Complete the box with the opposite adjectives from Exercise 4A.

stupid *intelligent* serious boring unfriendly quiet unkind

C ▶ 3.3 **WORD STRESS** Listen and underline the stressed syllables. Then listen and repeat.

stupid

5 A Complete 1–4 with the correct phrases in the box.

~~very interesting~~ not very interesting interesting really interesting

1 ✓✓ = She's *very interesting*.
2 ✓✓ = She's ______.
3 ✓ = She's ______.
4 ✗ = She's ______.

B ▶ 3.4 Listen and repeat.

C Correct the words in bold in four of the sentences below. One sentence is correct.

1 I'm ~~**not very**~~ *really* friendly. I love being with people.
2 I'm **very** quiet. I speak all the time.
3 I'm **not** funny. People often laugh at my jokes.
4 I'm **really** kind. I always help my friends.
5 I'm **not very** serious. I like studying and I don't like doing nothing.

D Change the sentences above so that they are true for someone you know. Then work with a new partner and compare your answers.

My sister's very funny. People always laugh at her jokes.

speakout TIP

We often make words negative with *un-*. Write the negative of these words: *happy, usual, well, real.*

SPEAKING

6 A Complete the table with the names of three people you know.

Relationship	Name	Personality	Things we do together
Friend	*Carlos*		
Family member			
Online friend			
Classmate/ Colleague			

B Work in pairs. Cover the last two columns of the table. Ask and answer questions about the people.

A: *Who's Carlos?*
B: *He's an old friend of mine. He's intelligent and very funny. We sometimes watch DVDs together.*

C Which of your partner's friends or family would you like to meet?

WRITING

DESCRIPTIONS; APOSTROPHE 'S

7 A Read the description of Miguel. Underline six examples of apostrophe *'s*.

> Miguel's an online friend of mine. We're friends because we both like photography. Miguel's photos are fantastic. He's got a great camera. I don't know a lot about his family, but I know he lives in Bogotá and he's got three children. His wife's name's Angelica.

B Work in pairs. Which *'s* means *has, is* or possessive *'s*?

C Read the text. Put in seven missing apostrophes (').

> My best friends names Leo. Hes got a lovely wife, Klara, and they both work as actors in films and on television programmes. They live in an apartment in Moscow and have two children, Vera and Nikolay. Veras at school and she lives with them. Nikolay, Veras brother, is single and he lives and works in St Petersburg. Hes got a small apartment there. Leo likes talking, but Klaras a quiet person, and very kind.

D Write about two people, a friend and a family member. Write 45–65 words for each.

3.3 ARE YOU FREE TONIGHT?

Ⓕ making arrangements
Ⓟ intonation to show interest
Ⓥ time expressions

VOCABULARY

TIME EXPRESSIONS

1 A Match the time expressions 1–5 with the examples a)–e).

1 every day
2 once a week
3 once a month
4 twice a year
5 three times a day

a) on Fridays
b) in June and December
c) Sunday, Monday, Tuesday, etc.
d) at 8a.m., 1p.m. and 6p.m.
e) on the first Saturday of every month

B How often do you do these activities with friends?

- go to a café, a restaurant or a club
- go to the cinema or a concert
- go for a walk or do some sport

C Work in pairs and compare your answers.

I do sport with my friends once a week. We play football on Sunday morning.
Alicia and I go to a café every day after work.

LISTENING

2 A ▶ 3.5 Listen to a phone call between Ron and Max. Which thing in Exercise 1B do they talk about?

B Listen again. Are the sentences true (T) or false (F)? Correct the false sentences.

1 Ron doesn't like his new job.
F Ron likes his new job.
2 Ron likes all the people in his office.
3 Ron wants to meet Max tonight.
4 They agree to meet.

C Is Max a good listener? Why/Why not?

3 A ▶ 3.6 Listen to a phone call between Ron and Amy. Complete the note below with the information you hear.

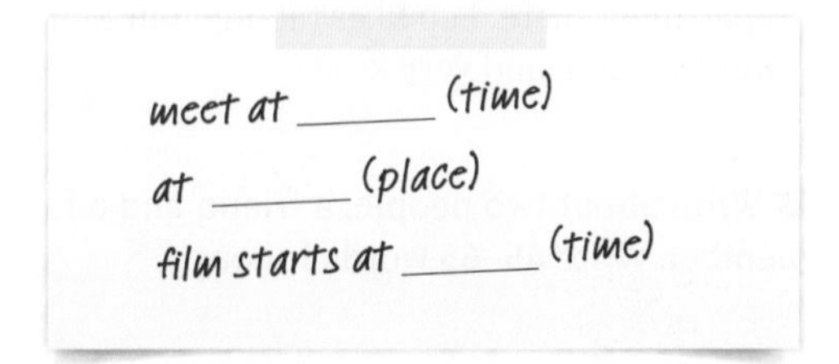

B Is Amy a good listener? Why/Why not?

LEARN TO

SHOW INTEREST

4 A Look at the extract. How does Amy show interest? Underline three of her phrases.

Amy: How's your new job?
Ron: Good. The people are very friendly …
Amy: Uh-huh.
Ron: … and the work's really interesting.
Amy: That's great!
Ron: It's not perfect. I haven't got my own office, and my manager isn't very friendly …
Amy: Oh, that's a shame!

B Which of the three phrases is positive (+), negative (-) or neutral (N)?

C Complete the phrases with the words in the box.

~~great~~ ~~a shame~~ terrible wonderful awful fantastic

Positive	Negative
That's *great* !	That's *a shame* !
_______	_______
_______	_______

D ▶ 3.7 INTONATION TO SHOW INTEREST Look at the intonation. Then listen and repeat.

That's great! *That's a shame!*

E ▶ 3.8 Listen to the sentences. Reply with a positive or negative phrase.

I've got a new job!
***You:** That's fantastic!*

SPEAKING

7 A You want to go to the cinema. Write down:

- the name of a film
- the name of the cinema
- two start times

B Work in pairs. Student A: ask your partner to see a film with you. Student B: ask about the film.

Student A	Student B
Say hi: *Hello, it's …*	
	Say hi. Ask about Student A: *How … ?*
Answer. Ask about Student B.	
	Answer. Give news.
Show interest. Ask if Student B is free.	
	Say yes.
Suggest a film.	
	Ask about time and place.
Answer.	
	Say yes.
Finish call.	
	Finish call.

FUNCTION

MAKING ARRANGEMENTS

5 A Underline the correct alternative.

1 *Do/Are* you free tonight?
2 What *you like/would you like* to do?
3 How about *go/going* to the cinema?
4 Where's it *film/showing*?
5 *When/What* time does it start?
6 The film's *at/on* six o'clock.
7 *What/Was* time's good for you?
8 How about *meeting/to meet* at half past five?

B 3.9 Listen and check. Then listen and repeat.

▷ page 132 **LANGUAGEBANK**

6 Work in pairs and take turns. Student A: say a number below. Student B: say the complete sentence/question.

1 free / tonight?
2 What / like / do?
3 How / going / cinema?
4 Where / showing?
5 What time / start?
6 The film / six
7 What / time / good / you?
8 How about / at half past five?

A: *Four*
B: *Where's it showing?*

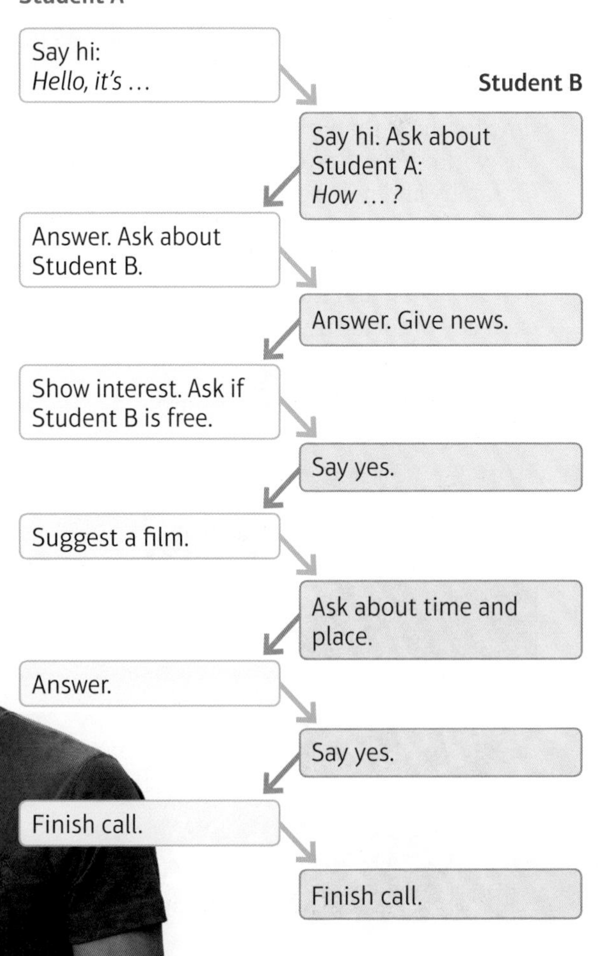

BBC DIWALI CELEBRATIONS

DVD PREVIEW

1 Discuss. What special occasions do people usually celebrate in your country? What do people usually do on these occasions?

2 A Match the verbs with the phrases they go with.

1 have	a) a restaurant
2 eat	b) fireworks
3 go to	c) new clothes
4 sing	d) presents/gifts to each other
5 give	e) a party
6 watch	f) to special music
7 invite	g) special food
8 decorate	h) 'Happy Birthday'
9 wear	i) guests
10 dance	j) your home

B Work in pairs. Add two more activities to the list above.

3 Read the programme information and answer the questions.

1 What is another name for Diwali? Why?
2 Which country is the programme about?
3 Is the festival one day or more?

Diwali

BBC

Diwali, the Festival of Light, is an important time for more than a billion Hindus all around the world. It's a time of colour and light, a time for family and new beginnings. This BBC programme joins Hindu families in the UK for Diwali, and looks at how they prepare for the five-day event and their different customs on each day of the festival.

DVD VIEW

4 A Watch the DVD. Which of the activities in Exercise 2A do you see? What other customs do you see?

B Work in pairs. Are sentences 1–8 true (T) or false (F)? Watch the DVD again and check your answers.

1 Diwali is always in October or November. *T*
2 It lasts for three days.
3 Men buy jewellery for their wives.
4 The woman throws a pakora* in two directions.
5 They make a picture out of coloured paints.
6 The Hindu New Year's Day is the third day.
7 People visit their parents and children.
8 Fireworks are only on the last day of Diwali.

*pakora = an Indian snack food

C Complete sentences 1–8 with words from the box. Then watch again and check.

before everywhere ~~full~~ long about time everyone back

1 Diwali is *full* of light and colour.
2 People start to prepare many weeks ______ the festival begins.
3 The Diwali festival is five days ______.
4 She walks forwards and she doesn't look ______.
5 Diwali is ______ new beginnings.
6 It's a very busy ______ for clothes shops.
7 For the five days of Diwali, light is ______.
8 It's a new beginning for ______.

speakout a special occasion

5 A **Work in pairs. Think of a special occasion, e.g. a birthday, a national holiday or a wedding. Use the questions below to make notes about it.**

- What's the name of the occasion?
- When and where does it happen?
- What do you usually do? Describe three or four activities.
- What's your favourite thing on that day?

B 3.10 **Listen to someone talking about Hogmanay. Number the pictures in order.**

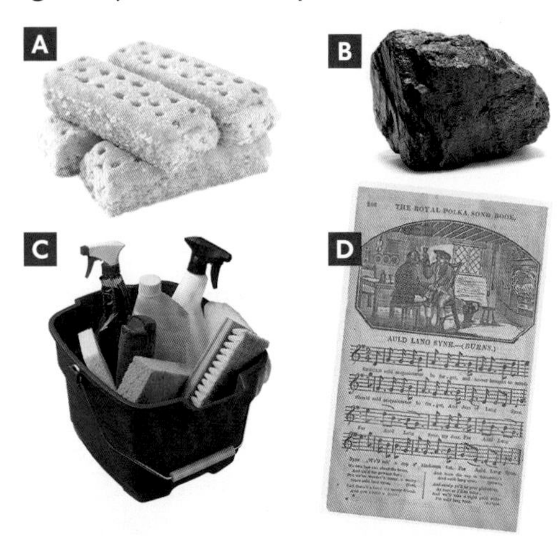

C **Look at the key phrases below. Listen again and tick the key phrases you hear.**

KEYPHRASES

I want to talk/Let me tell you about …
This/It happens in [place] on [date] …
On [this day/the day before], we [always/usually/often/…]
We have a special custom.
I like it because …

D **Work in groups and take turns. One student: talk about your special occasion. Use the key phrases to help. Other students: listen and make notes. Then ask two questions about the occasion.**

writeback describing an event

6 A **Read the description of Hogmanay below and underline the time expressions in the second paragraph.**

In Scotland we celebrate Hogmanay on New Year's Day in January every year. It's an important time for family and friends. It's a time to say 'goodbye' to the old year and welcome the new year.

In my family, before Hogmanay we always clean the house and then in the evening we have a big party. At midnight we stand in a circle and sing *Auld Lang Syne*. It's a song about friends, old friends and new friends. Then we have a special custom. After midnight, the first visitor to the house gives us presents, usually shortbread or coal for good luck.

I love Hogmanay because all our friends and family come together and it's a great start to the New Year!

B **Write a description of your special occasion from Exercise 5A. Write about 100 words.**

V FAMILY

1 A Complete the sentences with the correct family word.

1 My mother's father is my _______.
2 My brother's son is my _______.
3 My sister's daughter is my _______.
4 My father's sister is my _______.
5 My grandmother's son is my _______ or my _______.
6 My sister's mother and father are my _______.

B Write four more sentences to test your partner.

My mother's daughter is my …

C Work in pairs and take turns. Student A: read out your sentences. Student B: say the family word.

G *HAVE/HAS GOT*

2 A Work in pairs. Write questions to ask other students.

Find someone who …

1 has got a cat.
Have you got a cat?
2 has got a laptop.
3 hasn't got children.
4 has got brothers or sisters.
5 has got a job.
6 hasn't got a car.
7 has got a camera with him/her.
8 has got keys in his/her bag.
9 hasn't got a dog or a cat.
10 has got a birthday this month.

B Ask other students the questions. Then, write sentences using a different student's name for each one.

1 *Naomi has got a cat.*

G ADVERBS OF FREQUENCY

3 A Add the vowels to the adverbs of frequency.

1 _lw_ys
2 _s_ _lly
3 _ft_n
4 s_m_t_m_s
5 h_rdly _v_r
6 n_v_r

B Choose six events and write six sentences that are true about you. Use each adverb of frequency only once.

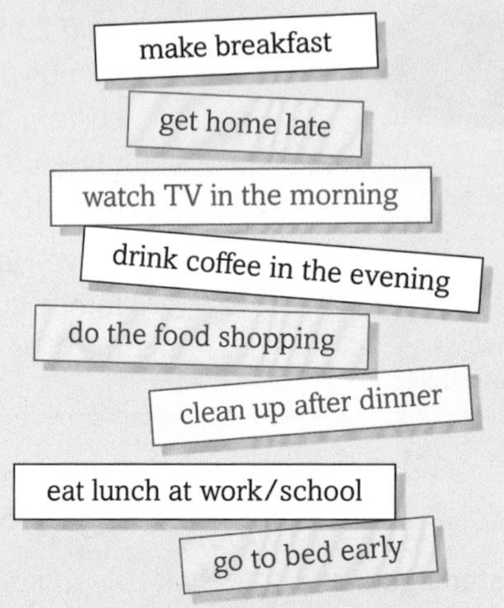

make breakfast
get home late
watch TV in the morning
drink coffee in the evening
do the food shopping
clean up after dinner
eat lunch at work/school
go to bed early

I always get home late.

C Work in pairs. Read out your six sentences. What things are the same/different?

V PERSONALITY

4 A Rearrange the letters to make adjectives. Then write the opposites.

1 itspud *stupid – intelligent*
2 alavetkit
3 relyfind
4 eurosis
5 dink
6 ingnitreest

B Complete the sentences below. It is important/not important that:

- a doctor is …
- a parent is …
- a TV presenter is …

C Work in pairs and discuss your answers.

A: *I think it's important that a doctor is intelligent and kind.*
B: *Yes, I agree./I don't agree.*

F MAKING ARRANGEMENTS

5 A Rewrite the text messages with spaces and punctuation.

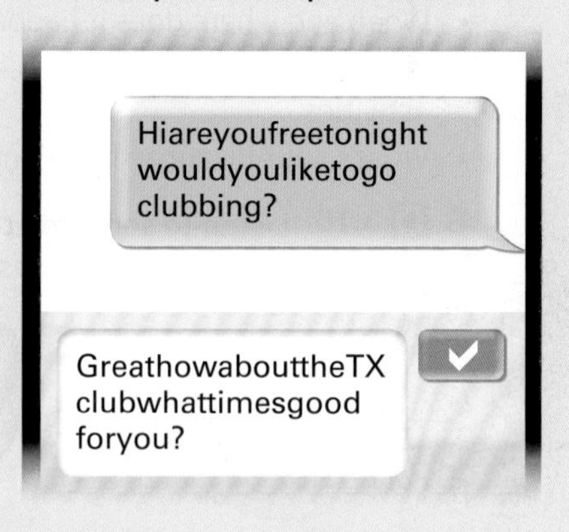

Hiareyoufreetonight wouldyouliketogo clubbing?
GreathowabouttheTX clubwhattimesgood foryou?

B Write a reply.

6 A Write three activities in the diary below. Leave three spaces empty.

Saturday
morning:
afternoon:
evening:

Sunday
morning:
afternoon:
evening:

B Invite other students to do the activities with you. When they accept, write their names and the activity in your diary.

A: *How about going shopping on Saturday morning?*
B: *Sorry, I'm busy./Great! I'm free.*

4 places

A PLACE TO STAY p38

AROUND TOWN p40

CAN I HELP YOU? p42

FAVOURITE PLACES p44

SPEAKING 4.1 Describe your home 4.2 Talk about things you can do in your town 4.3 Have a conversation in a shop 4.4 Talk about a favourite place

LISTENING 4.1 Listen to a woman describing her apartment 4.3 Understand conversations in shops 4.4 Watch an extract from a documentary about some amazing places

READING 4.2 Read about some unusual places in town

WRITING 4.1 Improve your use of commas; Write a description of your home 4.4 Write a blog about your favourite place

BBC INTERVIEWS

Where do you live?

G *there is/are*
P word stress; weak forms: *there's a, there are*
V rooms and furniture; prepositions

VOCABULARY
ROOMS AND FURNITURE

1 A Look at the website. Work in pairs and discuss. What does the website offer? Would you like to stay in a stranger's home?

B Read the information about two places in Malta. Which one would you like to stay in? Why?

Sunny room and sea views
€36 a night
A sunny double bedroom with a private bathroom in our apartment, only two minutes from the sea and with a roof terrace with great views. There are lots of restaurants, cafés and clubs nearby. The capital city Valletta is only thirty minutes away by bus. You are welcome to join us for dinner and evening walks along the seafront. Renée and George

Historic centre
€38 a night
Light, clean rooms in our apartment in the centre of historic Valletta, with a large bedroom with two beds, a sofa and a washbasin. There's also a living room with a big-screen television. We are happy to show you around the beautiful streets of Valletta. Franco and Janine

Start looking now
LOOK
LAST MINUTE
REGISTER
CONTACT US
No more expensive hotels!
Stay with people in hundreds of different countries. Have a friendly guide to show you around town.

2 A Read the texts again. Underline four rooms/places in an apartment and four items of furniture.

B Work in pairs. Think of two other rooms and two items of furniture for each room. Then check in the photo bank.

▷ page 155 **PHOTOBANK**

C 4.1 Listen and write down the words you hear.

D WORD STRESS Listen again and underline the stressed syllable. What do they all have in common? Listen and repeat.

E Work in pairs and take turns. Student A: say a room. Student B: say the furniture which is usually in that room.

A: Living room
B: A sofa, an armchair, …

speakout TIP

Write words on Post-its and put them around your home. Choose eight words for furniture. Label them in your home. When you look at the Post-its, say the words aloud.

LISTENING

3 A 4.2 Listen to the telephone conversation between Jamie and one of the apartment's owners. Which place in Exercise 1B do they talk about?

B Work in pairs and look at Jamie's plans for his visit. Listen again and tick the things that are possible in the apartment. Put a cross next to the things that are not possible and write why.

1 have lunch on the terrace. ✗
It's very hot in the middle of the day.
2 cook dinner for two
3 go to Valletta by bus
4 come back from Valetta by bus at 11p.m.
5 go to a restaurant near the apartment
6 go swimming in the sea

C Work in pairs and discuss. What's important for you in choosing a place to stay? Use Exercise 3B for ideas.

A: For me, it's important to have a place outside, maybe a balcony or a garden. I like sitting in the sun.

GRAMMAR

THERE IS/ARE

4 A Look at audio script 4.2 on page 171 and complete the table.

There	_'s_	a roof terrace.
	______	chairs and a table.
	______	a separate kitchen.
	______	any buses late at night.
Is	______	a kitchen?
Are	______	buses at night?

B 4.3 **WEAK FORMS:** ***there's a / there are*** **Listen and repeat. Notice the pronunciation of** ***there's a*** **/ðeəzə/ and** ***there are*** **/ðeərə/.**

5 A Read the email from Franco to Jamie. Is Franco a friend of Jamie's?

B Complete the email with *there 's/isn't, there are/aren't.*

Hi Jamie,

Here are answers to your questions. [1] _There isn't_ a separate kitchen, but [2]______ lots of great restaurants, cafés and bars in the city. Yes, bring your laptop. [3]______ free WiFi in the apartment and [4]______ a desk in the living room. We're often out in the evenings but [5]______ any neighbours, so it's no problem to play music or DVDs. [6]______ lots of DVDs in English in our living room. Sorry, [7]______ a balcony, but [8]______ a park by the sea only ten minutes' walk away.

Best wishes, Franco

6 Work in pairs and take turns. Ask your partner about his/her home. How are your homes different? How are your homes similar?

How many rooms? garage? garden? dishwasher? shower? balcony? WiFi? TV in the kitchen?

A: How many rooms are there? B: There are six. There's a ...

▷ page 134 LANGUAGEBANK

WRITING

COMMAS

7 A Look at the sentences below. How are they different? Which one is correct?

1 There are four rooms – a bedroom and a living room and a bathroom and a kitchen.
2 There are four rooms – a bedroom, a living room, a bathroom and a kitchen.

B Put commas in the sentences if necessary.

1 There are three bedrooms two bathrooms and a balcony.
2 We've got a bathroom and two bedrooms.
3 I get up at seven have a shower have breakfast in the kitchen and go to work.

C Write a text about your home for the website. Use the texts and the email in Exercise 5A to help. Check your use of commas.

D Read other students' descriptions. Where would you like to stay?

VOCABULARY

PREPOSITIONS

8 A Match the prepositions in the box with the pictures below.

in *A*	under	above	in front of
on	behind	between	next to

A B C D E F G H

B Work in pairs. Look at the picture on page 165 for fifteen seconds. Then correct the words in bold in sentences 1–6 below.

1 There are four books on the **shelves**.
2 There's a table in front of the **door**.
3 There's a **mirror** above the TV.
4 There's a **chair** next to the sofa.
5 There's a rug under the **armchair**.
6 There's a **plant** behind the lamp.

C Look at the room on page 165 again. Write three false sentences about where things are.

D Work in pairs and take turns. Correct your partner's sentences. Don't look at the picture.

SPEAKING

9 A In your notebook, draw the outline of your favourite room at home. Draw only the windows and door.

B Work in pairs. Exchange notebooks. Student A: describe the furniture in your room. Student B: draw the furniture in the room.

It is my living room. There's a table under the window.

4.2 AROUND TOWN

G *can* for possibility
P word stress; weak forms: *can/can't*
V places in towns; prepositions

READING

1 A Work in pairs. Look at the photos and discuss. What are the places? Why are they unusual?

B Read the text and check your ideas.

around town

Walk through any town in the world and you usually find a post office, a supermarket, a school, a bank, a cinema, a library and so on. But these places are different.

A tourist in Vanuatu (2,000 kilometres east of Brisbane, Australia) can send a postcard from a very unusual place: an underwater post office! You buy your plastic postcard on the beach, write it, and then swim down to the post office. But check the opening times – the post office is only open for one hour a day!

You can borrow a book in Pakistan and return it in Canada – that's the idea of the Little Free Library (LFL). This LFL is in Lakki Marwat, Pakistan, but there are over 12,000 of these libraries all over the world, in North and South America, Africa, Asia and Australia. They are usually simple, small wooden houses, big enough for twenty books, and the library is free for everyone.

The Sol Cinema is perhaps the smallest cinema in the world. It's often in South Wales, but it can travel anywhere. There's enough space for sixteen people, and they only show short films up to ten minutes long. When you go to see a film at Sol Cinema, you choose the type of film, get a ticket and a bag of popcorn, sit inside and enjoy the show. It's called Sol Cinema because it's solar powered.

C Work in pairs and match the sentences with the place. Write PO (post office), L (library) or C (cinema).

1 'They're plastic, not paper.' *PO*
2 'No, you don't pay. You can take one for free.'
3 'It's too long – the maximum is ten minutes.'
4 'Sorry, we're only open for a short time. You can send it tomorrow.'
5 'Twelve people? OK. Four more can come too.'
6 'There's one in your town. Take it back there.'

D Work in pairs and answer questions 1–6 below about Exercise 1C.

1 What is 'They' in number 1? *postcards*
2 What is 'one' in number 2?
3 What is 'It' in number 3?
4 What is 'it' in number 4?
5 What is 'one' in number 6?
6 What is 'it' in number 6?

E Discuss. Which place would you like to visit or use? Why?

VOCABULARY

PLACES IN TOWNS

2 A Work in pairs and look at the text again. How many words can you find for places in a town?

B Complete the sentences with the words in the box below.

~~an art gallery~~	a post office	a police station
a supermarket	a theatre	a sports centre
a pharmacy	a library	a museum	a cinema

1 You can look at paintings at *an art gallery*.
2 You can send a letter at ______.
3 You can borrow a book from ______.
4 You can buy food at ______.
5 You can watch films at ______.
6 You can see plays at ______.
7 You can play tennis and football at ______.
8 You can look at old objects at ______.
9 You can find a police officer at ______.
10 You can buy medicine at ______.

C 4.4 **WORD STRESS** Look at the place words in the box in Exercise 2B and underline the stressed syllables. Then listen and repeat.

D Look at the sentences in Exercise 2B again. Say which things you can do in your town/city.

GRAMMAR

CAN FOR POSSIBILITY

3 A Look at the sentence and underline the correct alternative.

You can send a postcard. = It's *possible/not possible* to send a postcard.

B Complete the sentences about the Little Free Library and the underwater post office. Use *can* or *can't*.

You	______	find books and magazines to read.
	______	send paper postcards.

C ▶ 4.5 **WEAK FORMS: *can/can't*** Listen and check. Then underline the correct alternatives below.

1 In sentences, *can* is usually *stressed/unstressed* and pronounced /kən/.
2 In sentences, *can't* is usually *stressed/unstressed* and pronounced /kɑːnt/.

D ▶ 4.6 Listen and write positive (+), negative (–) or question (?) for each sentence.

1 ______ 4 ______
2 ______ 5 ______
3 ______ 6 ______

E Listen again and repeat the sentences.

4 A Choose a place from the box in Exercise 2B. Write two sentences about what you can/can't do there.

Post office: You can buy stamps there. You can't play tennis there.

B Work in pairs and take turns. Student A: read your sentences. Student B: guess the place.

C Choose another place. Work with a new partner and take turns. Student A: ask questions with *Can you … ?* and guess the place. Student B: answer.

A: *Can you do exercise there?*
B: *No, you can't.*

▷ page 134 **LANGUAGEBANK**

VOCABULARY

PREPOSITIONS

5 A Match the sentences with the pictures.

1 The cat is in front of the dog. *a*
2 The cat is opposite the dog. __

3 The cat is near the dog. __
4 The cat is next to the dog. __

5 The cat is on the left of the dog. __
6 The cat is on the right of the dog. __

B Look at the map and find the art gallery, the shopping centre and the pharmacy.

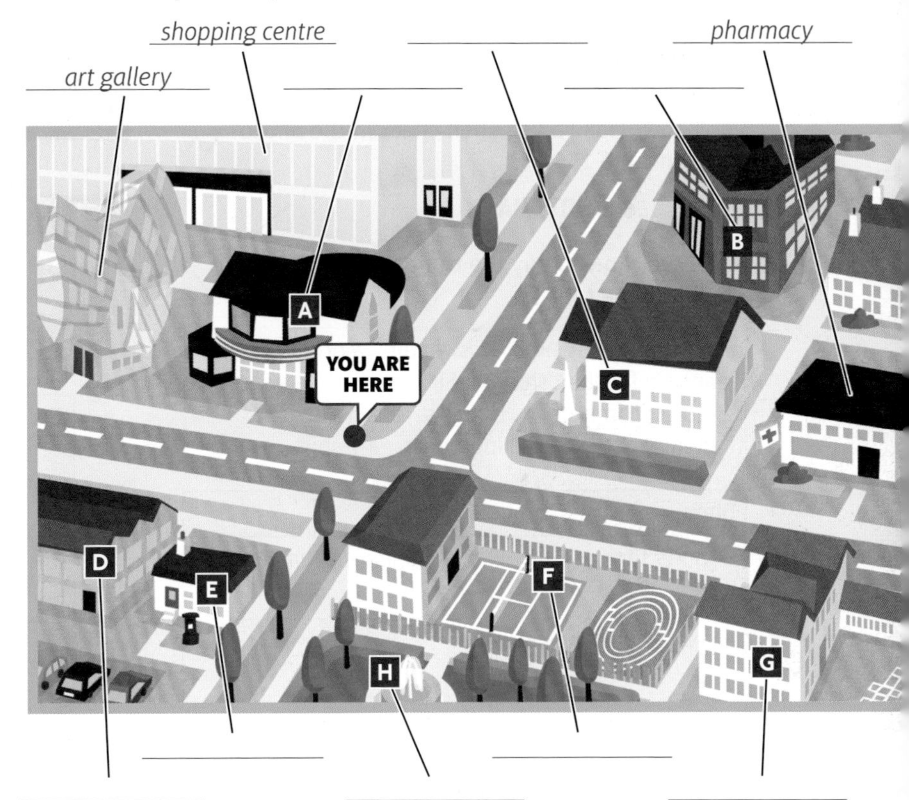

C ▶ 4.7 Find the 'You are here' sign on the map. Then listen and write the places on the map.

D Work in pairs. Student A: look at page 162. Student B: look at page 167.

SPEAKING

6 A Think of a favourite place in your town/city. Make notes about where it is and what you can do there.

B Work in groups. Tell each other about the places. Which places would you like to visit?

There's a good cinema called the Rialto. It's in the main square opposite the metro, next to a big pizza restaurant. It's got six screens, and you can also have a coffee there.

4.3 CAN I HELP YOU?

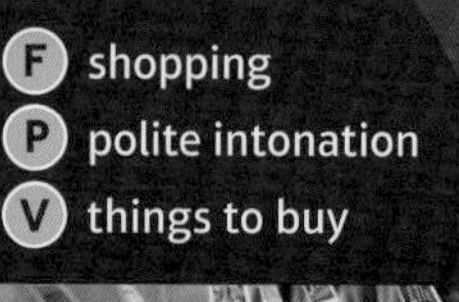

VOCABULARY
THINGS TO BUY

1 A Work in pairs and discuss.

1 Do you enjoy shopping? Why/Why not?
2 Is there a big shopping centre in your town/city? Do you like it? Why/Why not?
3 Where do you usually buy these things in your town/city? Do you buy any of these things online?

- food and drink
- clothes
- magazines, newspapers or books
- headphones or a charger for your mobile
- shampoo or medicine
- music or DVDs
- things for the home

B Work in pairs. What different kinds of shops do you know? Make a list. Then check in the photo bank on page 156.

▷ page 156 **PHOTOBANK**

2 A Where can you buy the things in the box? Complete the table.

~~a swimming costume~~ a sweater a printer jeans a football shirt a SIM card a tablet (computer) trainers a jacket a memory stick walking boots a T-shirt

Shop	Item
a sports shop	*a swimming costume*
an electronics shop	
a clothes shop	

B ▶ 4.8 Listen and check. Then listen and repeat.

C Work in pairs. Write two other things you can buy in each shop.

1 ______
2 ______
3 ______

D Work in pairs and take turns. Student A: say a shop. Student B: say three things you can buy there.

A: A newsagent's.
B: Newspapers, magazines and sweets.

FUNCTION
SHOPPING

3 A ▶ 4.9 Listen to the customers and complete A and B in the table.

Customer	A: Item	B: Does the customer buy it/them?	C: Price
1	*sweater*		
2			
3			
4			

B Listen again and complete C in the table with the price of each item.

C Look at audio script 4.9 on page 171 and complete the sentences below.

1 It's too *small*.
2 Have you got it in ______?
3 How much is ______?
4 That's fine. I'll ______ it.

D Use the words/phrases in the box below to complete sentences 1–4.

have long are they medium

1 It's too ______.
2 That's fine. I'll ______ this one.
3 Have you got it in ______?
4 How much ______?

▷ page 134 **LANGUAGEBANK**

4 A Look at the flowchart. Use the prompts to complete the customer's sentences.

Shop assistant

Can I help you?

Customer

Yes. Have you / this sweater / size forty-two?

Size forty-two in grey? Just a moment. Here you are.

Oh, it / big. / Have you / it / size forty?

Let me look. Ah yes. Here you are.

Have you / it / black?

No, sorry. We've only got size thirty-six in black.

That / too small. / I / have / the grey one.

B Work in pairs. Read your conversation aloud.

LEARN TO

SAY *NO* POLITELY IN A SHOP

5 A Look at the three conversation extracts. How does B say *no* politely? Underline six expressions.

1 **A:** Can I help you?
B: No, thanks. I'm just looking.

2 **B:** Have you got it in large?
A: Sorry, no. Only in medium.
B: Mmm. No, it isn't right. Thanks anyway.
A: No problem.

3 **B:** How much are they?
A: One hundred and twenty euros. Would you like to buy them?
B: One hundred and twenty euros! I'm not sure. I need to think about it.
A: Fine. No problem.

B 4.10 **POLITE INTONATION** Listen and check. Then listen and repeat. Copy the intonation to sound polite.

C 4.11 Cover Exercise 5A. Listen to the shop assistant. Say *no* politely.

SPEAKING

6 A Work in pairs. Student A: look at page 164. Student B: you are a customer in a sports shop. Try to buy the things below. When you buy something, write the price.

- a football
- trainers
- a swimming costume
- walking boots

B Student B: now you are a shop assistant in an electronics shop. Write a different price for the things below. Answer Student A's questions. Begin with: *Good morning. Can I help you?*

- a SIM card *€12.99*
- a memory stick
- headphones
- a tablet

BBC FAVOURITE PLACES

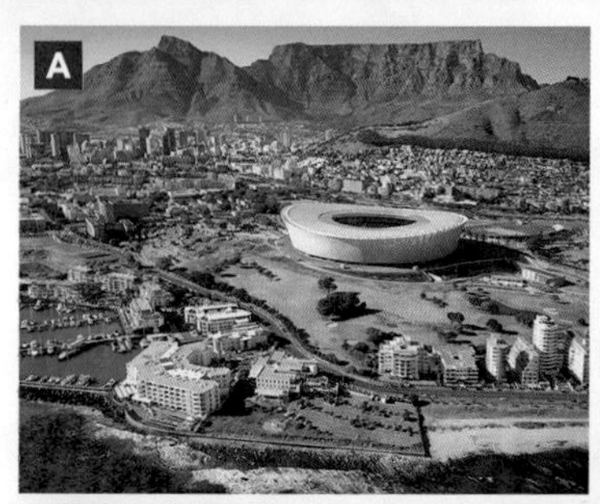

DVD PREVIEW

1 A Work in pairs. Look at photos A–F. Where are the places? Which countries are they in?

B Match the phrases 1–6 with photos A–F.

1 It's a romantic city with a lot of museums and art galleries. *D*
2 There are beautiful views of mountains and beaches.
3 You can visit hundreds of temples and the shopping and the nightlife are great.
4 The colours change all the time. It's awesome!
5 It's a fantastic place to watch animals. You can see zebras, elephants, antelope, hippos and lions.
6 There's so much water all around you.

2 Work in pairs. Read the programme information and answer the questions.

1 How many places does this programme look at?
2 Which place do you think is number one?

50 Places To See Before You Die

BBC

There are so many wonderful places to see in the world. When the BBC asked people to choose their fifty favourite places, thousands of people answered. In this BBC programme we look at six of the places: Bangkok, Cape Town, the Grand Canyon, the Iguaçu Falls, the Masai Mara and Paris. Watch the programme and find out which is the number one place to see!

DVD VIEW

3 A Watch the DVD and check your answers to Exercise 2. Which place is number one?

B Watch again and underline the words you hear in the sentences.

1 'It's got lots of clubs, bars, shops, food. Everything you *need/want*, really.'
2 'I just love the wide, *open/big* spaces. The animals are amazing, and the people are so *kind/warm* and friendly.'
3 'You stand next to them and feel very, very *small/little*.'
4 'To me, Paris is elegant, romantic and *expensive/exciting*.'
5 'We went there over New Year … Lovely, just a lovely, lovely *place/town*.'
6 'The colours are just so … *wonderful/amazing*.'

C Work in pairs and look at the positive adjectives in the box. Write three of the adjectives next to each correct stress pattern.

~~lovely~~ amazing wonderful romantic friendly awesome exciting popular interesting

1 Oo *lovely* 2 oOo 3 Ooo

D Work in pairs and discuss. Which three places in the world would you both most like to visit? Why?

speakout a favourite place

4 A Choose a favourite place: a place in the countryside, a town, a building or a room. Make notes on the questions below:

- Where is it?
- How often do you go there?
- What do you do there?
- Why do you like it?

B 4.12 Listen to a woman talk about her favourite place and answer the questions above.

C Listen again and tick the key phrases you hear.

KEY PHRASES

One of my favourite places is …
It's [in/near/between/ …]
I go there every [day/year/summer/weekend/ …]
When I'm there, I usually …
I like it because it's …
It's a great place to …
There's always something [different/interesting/ fun/ …] to do.

D Work in groups and take turns. Tell each other about your place. Use the key phrases to help. Which places would you like to visit?

writeback describing a place

5 A Read the description below and put the topics of the paragraphs in the correct order.

a) Why do you like it? ______

b) What's the name of the place and where is it? ______

c) How often do you go there and what do you do there? ______

B Write a description of your favourite place. Use three paragraphs. Write about 100 words.

Traveller
26-09-16 Posting 1

1 One of my favourite places is my aunt's apartment. It's in the centre of Bogotá, and she's a famous artist. Her apartment is lovely and light with modern furniture and there are lots of her pictures on the walls.

2 I go there every month. When I'm there, she usually cooks lunch for me and after lunch we sit on the balcony and chat about my life and hers. I always show her my latest photos and she shows me her new pictures.

3 I like it because it's a very beautiful and relaxing place. My aunt is really funny and there's always something interesting to talk about. I always feel good there.

Comment

V ROOMS AND FURNITURE

1 A Add the vowels to the furniture words.

1 _rmch_ _r 3 c_pb_ _rd 5 s_f_ 7 w_shb_s_n
2 b_d 4 sh_lv_s 6 w_rdr_b_ 8 t_l_v_s_ _n

B Think of a room in your flat/house. Write three objects that are in it.

It's got a TV, two armchairs and a sofa.

C Work in pairs and take turns. Student A: read out the objects. Student B: guess the room.

G THERE IS/THERE ARE AND PREPOSITIONS

2 A Read the sentences. Draw the things in the picture.

There's a newspaper on the chair and a shelf under the window. There's a flower on the shelf. There are two men on the left of the window.

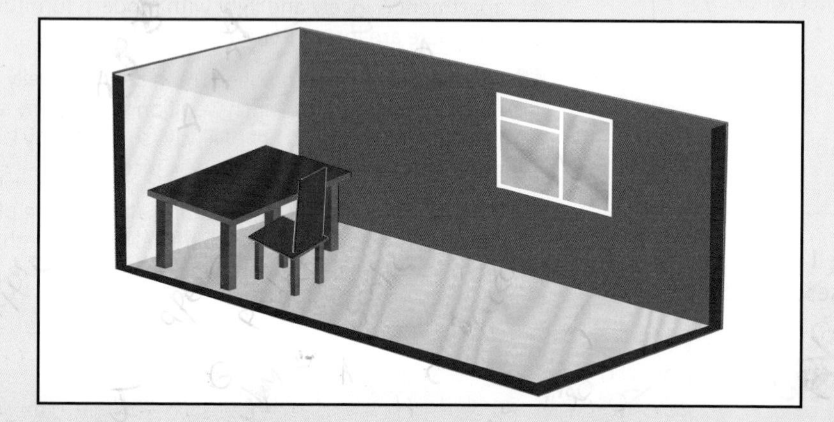

B Now add these things to your picture.

a woman	a bottle of water	a sandwich	keys

C Work in pairs and take turns. Ask and answer *yes/no* questions about your pictures.

A: Is there a sandwich on the table in your picture?
B: No, there isn't. It's on the shelf.

V PLACES IN TOWNS

3 Write the places in the word puzzle and find the secret message.
(Hint: What do you say after a day in town?)

1 buy a stamp at a
2 see a film at a
3 get help at a
4 shop for food at a
5 buy aspirin at a
6 see a play at a
7 Look at old things at a
8 Do exercise at a
9 look at paintings at an
10 borrow a book at a

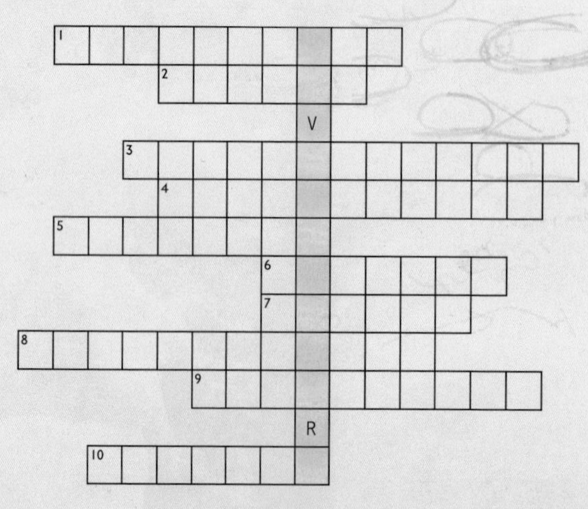

G CAN FOR POSSIBILITY

4 A Put the words in the correct order.

1 buy / SIM card / can / for / Where / mobile? / a / my / I
2 I / Where / sit? / can
3 I / can / 'beautiful' / in / How / Italian? / say
4 they / match? / football / can / Where / watch / the
5 Can / the / come / friend / my / to / lesson?
6 centre? / can / the / What / do / in / sports / we

B Write answers to the questions above.

1 At an electronics shop.

C Work in pairs and take turns. Student A: say the answer to one of the questions above. Student B: ask the question.

A: Yes, she can.
B: Can my friend come to the lesson?

F SHOPPING

5 A Correct the sentences below.

1 Have you got this shoes in size thirty-six?
2 They are too much small.
3 Have you got in them size thirty-four?
4 How much they are?
5 That's too very expensive.
6 I take them.
7 No, they're all right. Thanks anyway.
8 I'm not sure. I need think about it.

B Work in pairs. Choose four of the sentences above and write a conversation in a shop.

C Work in pairs. Role-play your conversation.

5 food

SPEAKING 5.1 Talk about your eating and drinking habits 5.2 Conduct a class food survey 5.3 Order a meal in a restaurant 5.4 Describe a special dish

LISTENING 5.1 Listen to a photographer talk about food 5.3 Listen to people ordering in a restaurant 5.4 Watch an extract from a cookery programme with a famous chef

READING 5.2 Read about eating and drinking habits

WRITING 5.2 Use paragraphs to write a short report about your class 5.4 Write an email with a recipe

BBC INTERVIEWS

What's your favourite dish?

G countable and uncountable nouns
P weak forms: *a, an, some, any*
V food and drink

VOCABULARY

FOOD AND DRINK

1 A Look at the people and their fridges. Work in pairs and discuss the questions.

1 What do you think are their ages, jobs and personalities?
2 Is your fridge at home similar to fridge A or B?

B Look at the words in the box. Write fridge (A) or (B) next to each item. Which things are *not* in the fridges?

cheese *B* chicken a banana an apple eggs fruit juice a pear peppers butter garlic milk potatoes salmon broccoli strawberries

C Write the words from the box in the correct word web below.

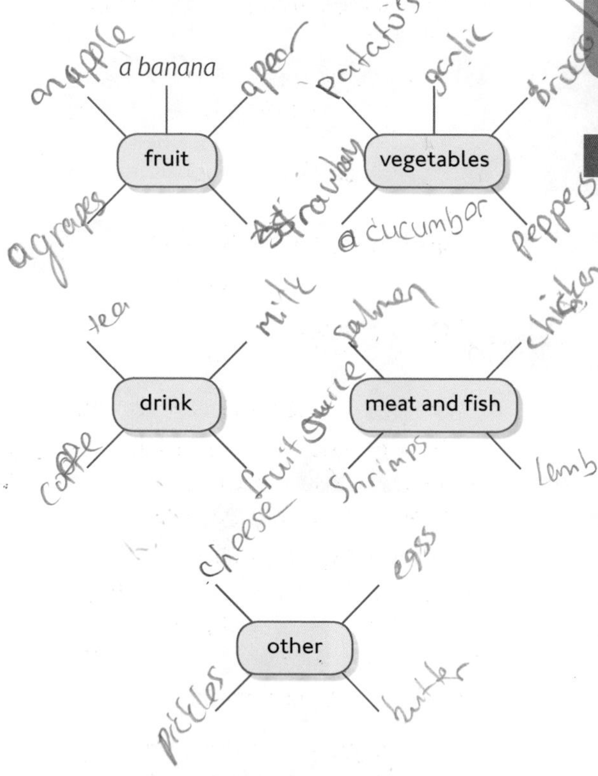

D Add words to complete the word webs. Use the photo bank on page 157 to help.

▷ page 157 PHOTOBANK

E Work in pairs and take turns. Look at the fridges. Student A: say a type of food or drink. Student B: say which fridge it's in.

A: *strawberries*
B: *fridge A*

You are what you eat ...

GRAMMAR

COUNTABLE AND UNCOUNTABLE NOUNS

2 A Write the words from Exercise 1B in the correct column below.

Words you can count		Words you can't count
Countable singular	Countable plural	Uncountable
a banana	*potatoes*	*cheese*

B ▶ 5.1 Listen and check. Then listen and repeat.

3 A Underline the correct alternative.

1 I love *cheese/cheeses*.
2 I really like *banana/bananas*.
3 *Egg/Eggs* are OK.
4 I don't like *garlic/garlics*.
5 I really don't like *milk/milks*.
6 I hate *vegetable/vegetables*.

B Change the food/drink words to make the sentences above true for you. Then work in pairs and compare your answers.

▷ page 136 LANGUAGEBANK

speakout TIP

When you write a noun in your notebook, write (C) countable or (U) uncountable, e.g. *a steak (C)*. Write five new words from the photo bank on page 157 in your notebook. Write (C) or (U) next to them.

... so are you the food in your fridge? Photographer André Banka asks this question and tries to get the answer in his latest photo project. 'I travel around the world and I usually stay with friends, not in hotels. I always take photos of my friends, and last year I started taking photos of their fridges, too. It's amazing what a fridge can tell you about a person.'

LISTENING

4 A Read the text above. Why does André take photos of people's fridges? Who are the people in his photo project?

B 5.2 Look at the people and their fridges. Write A, B or AB next to the phrases. Then listen to an interview with André and check your ideas. Who ...

1 tries/try to be healthy? *AB*
2 is/are serious?
3 is/are funny?
4 likes/like having visitors?
5 likes/like cooking?
6 eats/eat takeaway food?

C Listen again. What food items does he talk about for each fridge?

GRAMMAR

NOUNS WITH *A/AN, SOME, ANY*

5 A 5.3 **WEAK FORMS:** ***a, an, some, any*** Listen and underline the correct alternatives. Listen again and notice the pronunciation of *a, an* and *some*.

He's got *a/some* broccoli, *a/some* peppers and *an/some* apple.
Has he got *some/any* milk? He hasn't got *some/any* milk.

B Complete the table with *a/an, some* and *any*.

	Countable singular	Countable plural	Uncountable
We've got	___ pear.	___ grapes.	___ water.
We haven't got	___ banana.	___ oranges.	___ cheese.
Have we got	___ tomato?	___ carrots?	___ milk?

6 A Read about Zoe's meal. Would you like to eat it?

'[1] *Some* friends are coming for dinner and so my fridge is full. I've got [2] ___ prawns and fresh fish to grill and [3] ___ broccoli. There's [4] ___ lettuce to make a salad and [5] ___ tomatoes. I haven't got [6] ___ onions for the salad – I don't like them, but I've got [7] ___ cucumber. Now, have I got [8] ___ oil? Ah yes, here it is, and there's [9] ___ bottle of mineral water, but I haven't got [10] ___ juice or other drinks.'

B Complete the text in Exercise 6A with *a/an, some* and *any*.

C Draw a fridge in your notebook. In the fridge, write or draw two types of fruit, two vegetables and two drinks.

D Work in pairs. Ask questions and guess what's in your partner's fridge. The first person to guess four items wins.

A: *Have you got any milk?*
B: *Yes, I have. Are there any apples in your fridge?*
A: *No, there aren't. Have you got any oranges?*

page 136 **LANGUAGEBANK**

SPEAKING

7 A Complete sentences 1–8 about you.

1 For breakfast, I sometimes have ...
2 For lunch, I never have ...
3 In the evening, I usually drink ...
4 My favourite vegetable is ...
5 My favourite fruit is ...
6 I really hate (a food/drink) ...
7 My favourite snack is ...
8 Before I go to bed, I have ...

B Work in groups. Ask and answer questions. Find out if any students have got similar eating habits to you.

A: *What do you usually have for breakfast?*
B: *I always start with a coffee.*
A: *Me too. Black coffee.*
C: *Do you? I usually have ...*

G *how much/many*; quantifiers
P numbers
V containers

VOCABULARY

CONTAINERS

1 A Look at pictures A–J. What food or drink can you see?

B Match pictures A–J with the words in the box below.

a bowl a jar a bottle a bag a cup a tin/can a carton a packet a glass a mug

C Work in pairs. Say the name of each food or drink with its container. Then say one more food or drink that comes in the container.

A: a carton of milk
B: a carton of yoghurt

How much food does an average person eat in a lifetime? And how much do they drink?

The answer is A LOT!!!

Do you eat meat? Meat-eaters in Europe eat [1] *21* sheep, [2] ___ chickens and [3] ___ cows in their lifetime. Or do you prefer fish? Japanese people eat about **69** kilos a year; that's an amazing **4,830** kilos in a lifetime.

If you're a vegetarian, do you like beans? On average, Brazilians eat about [4] ___ kilos of beans in their lives. Beans are popular all around the world, from Latin America to Asia.

Why is weight a problem for so many people? The average American has about **4,500** kilos of sugar a year, often as part of food and drink. Soft drinks have an average of [5] ___ spoonfuls of sugar in a can or bottle. And how many cookies do Americans eat in their lifetime? Over [6] ___!

How much water, tea and coffee do people drink? An average person drinks about [7] ___ litres of water in their lifetime. People in the UK drink about [8] ___ cups of tea a year, and the top coffee-drinkers in the world are from Finland – they use **13** kilos of coffee beans a year. Maybe it isn't surprising that people use [9] ___ rolls of toilet paper a year! That's about [10] ___ in their lifetime.

READING

2 A 5.4 **NUMBERS** Work in pairs. How do you say the numbers in the box below? Listen and check. Then listen again and repeat.

4½ 7 21 61 980 1,200 4,010 4,300 35,000 60,000

B Read the text. Complete it with numbers from Exercise 2A.

C 5.5 Work in pairs and compare your answers. Then listen and check.

D Work in pairs and discuss the questions.

1 Which food in the article do you eat a lot? Which do you never eat?
2 What other food and drink do you eat or drink a lot of?

GRAMMAR

HOW MUCH/MANY; QUANTIFIERS

3 A Complete the sentences below. Then underline the correct alternatives to complete the rule.

1 ___ food does an average person eat in a lifetime?
2 ___ cookies does the average American eat?

RULES
1 Use *how much* with *countable/uncountable* nouns.
2 Use *how many* with *countable/uncountable* nouns.

B Match the words below with pictures A–D.

not many a lot/lots none quite a lot

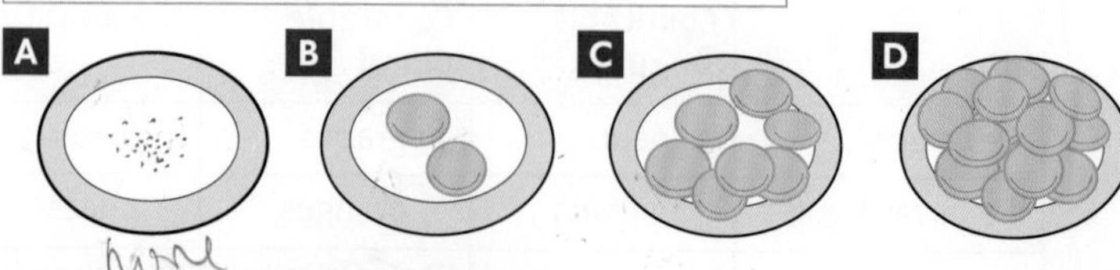

▷ page 136 LANGUAGEBANK

4 A Complete the questions.

1 How *many* times does a six-year-old child laugh every day?
2 How ______ times does a person laugh every day?
3 How ______ milk does a person drink in their lifetime?
4 How ______ words does a woman say in a day?
5 How ______ words does a man say in a day?
6 How ______ shampoo do people use in their lifetime?
7 How ______ friends does a person make in their lifetime?
8 How ______ hair does a person grow in their lifetime?

B Work in pairs. Student A: turn to page 163 and find the answers to questions 1, 3, 5 and 7. Student B: turn to page 164 and find the answers to questions 2, 4, 6 and 8.

C Work in pairs and take turns. Student A: ask one of your questions and say both possible answers. Student B: listen and choose the correct answer.

A: *How many times does a six-year-old child laugh every day? a) about three hundred times or b) about a hundred times?*
B: *I'm not sure. I think a hundred times!*

SPEAKING

5 A Work in groups. Ask and answer questions using the prompts below to complete the table. Use *a lot/lots, quite a lot, not much/many, none* and one extra piece of information in your answers.

In a week	You	Student 1	Student 2	Student 3
vegetables / eat?	*Quite a lot. I love peas.*	*Not many. Potatoes with dinner, that's all.*	*A lot! I love them!*	
water / drink?				
biscuits / eat?				
fruit / eat?				
coffee / drink?				
exercise / do?				

A: *How many vegetables do you eat in a week, Julio?*
B: *Not many. Potatoes with dinner, that's all.*
A: *How about you, Yumi?*
C: *A lot! I love them!*

B Discuss. Which students have a good diet/healthy lifestyle?

I think Yumi has a good diet because she eats a lot of vegetables.

WRITING

PARAGRAPHS

6 A Look at the text on page 50. Match a)–d) below with paragraphs 1–5.

a) drinks
b) introduction *1*
c) sweet food
d) meat-eaters
e) vegetarians

B Read the sentences below. Underline the correct alternatives.

A paragraph is a group of *words/sentences* about *one/two* main topic(s). It usually has *one sentence/two or more sentences.* When you finish one topic, start a new *sentence/paragraph.*

C Read the student report below. Work in pairs and discuss. Which photo is best for this report?

Healthy living

HOW HEALTHY ARE WE? Do we have a healthy lifestyle and a good diet? We asked the members of our class some questions, and this is the result. How much exercise do we do? It's interesting to find out that many people do sport or other exercise two or three times a week. So, maybe it isn't surprising that we drink on average 2.5 litres of water a day. How about our diet? Do we like sweet food? Well, lots of people love biscuits, and only two of us never eat them. It's not so good that all of us like chocolate and eat it every day. Maybe we're not as healthy as we think!

D Read the text again. How many paragraphs can you make? Draw a line between each one.

E Write a report about your group. Use your notes from Exercise 5A to help. Write three or four paragraphs.

5.3 ARE YOU READY TO ORDER?

F ordering in a restaurant
P polite intonation; linking
V restaurant words

VOCABULARY

RESTAURANT WORDS

1 A Work in pairs and discuss. Where do you go when you want to:

1 have a drink with a friend in the afternoon?
2 eat something fast before you go to the cinema?
3 have an evening meal in a good restaurant?

There's a very good café in … called …

B Match each word to its meaning.

1 a menu — a) you pay this at the end
2 a chef — b) he/she brings the food
3 a dish — c) food cooked in a special way
4 a bill — d) a list of food with prices
5 order — e) he/she cooks
6 a tip — f) ask for food
7 a waiter/waitress — g) extra money for service

FUNCTION

ORDERING IN A RESTAURANT

2 A Look at expressions a)–k). Where do you usually hear them? Write restaurant (R) or fast food restaurant (FF).

a) Would you like something to drink? *R*
b) Small, medium or large?
c) Can we have the bill, please?
d) Are you ready to order?
e) Is that eat in or take away?
f) Thanks. Have a nice day!
g) Tonight's special is …
h) Afternoon. What can I get you?
i) Large fries with that?
j) Good evening. A table for two?
k) Anything else?

B ▶ 5.6 Listen and tick the expressions you hear.

C Number the ticked expressions in order. Then listen again and check.

3 A ▶ 5.7 Listen and complete the sentences below.

1 Could ____ ____ an *orange juice*, please?
2 Can ____ ____ a ____ of mineral ____, please?
3 ____ like some ____, please.
4 The ____ for ____, please.

B Listen again and check your answers. What do the customers order?

▷ page 136 **LANGUAGEBANK**

4 A Complete the conversation with the words in the box.

like	can	for	any	'd	Could

A: Good evening. Would you something to drink?
B: Yes, we have two colas and some water, please?
A: Fine. Are you ready to order?
B: Yes. We like the fish and the chicken.
A: Would you like vegetables?
B: Yes, please.
A: We've got carrots, beans and spinach.
B: I have some carrots and some spinach?
C: The same me, please.

B Work in pairs and practise the conversation. Then change roles and practise the conversation again with your books closed.

5 A ▶ 5.8 Listen to the customers in a restaurant. Are they polite or not very polite? Write P or N.

1 *N* 3 ____ 5 ____ 7 ____
2 ____ 4 ____ 6 ____ 8 ____

B ▶ 5.9 **POLITE INTONATION** Look at the question. Listen to the polite intonation. Then listen and repeat.

Could I have an orange juice, please?

C Work in pairs. Student A: say the customer's sentences from Exercise 4A. Student B: say if Student A is polite or not polite.

SPEAKING

6 A Look at the menu. Which dishes would you like to try? What do you think is in today's special dishes?

MENU

Starter

Onion soup	5.50
Melon	4.50
Smoked salmon	6.00

Main course

Roast lamb with mint sauce	23.95
Thai chicken with noodles	17.95
Fish of the day with chips or rice	20.95
Served with seasonal vegetables	

Today's specials

Chef's Sunday special	18.95
Garden delight	22.95
Spring mix	21.95

Dessert

Apple pie with ice cream	5.90
Chocolate cake	5.90
Fresh fruit	5.90

All prices in euros. Service not included.

B Work in pairs. Student A: you are the customer. Look at the menu on this page and order your food. Ask the waiter about the specials. Student B: you are the waiter. Look at page 164.

B: Are you ready to order?

A: Can I ask about today's specials? What's the Garden delight?

C Work with a new partner and change roles. Student B: you are the customer. Look at page 163. Student A: you are the waiter. Look at page 161.

LEARN TO

UNDERSTAND FAST SPEECH

7 A 5.10 Listen to the conversation in a fast food restaurant. What does the man order? Circle the correct answer.

B 5.11 Listen and write the sentences you hear.

speakout TIP

When one word finishes with a consonant and the next word starts with a vowel, the two words join and sound like one word, e.g. *Good‿evening. How much‿**is‿it**?*

C LINKING Look at the example below. Then underline the key stressed words in the other four sentences you wrote. Draw lines to show the linking.

Afternoon. What can‿I get you?

D Listen again and check. Then listen and repeat.

E Work in pairs. Choose one long sentence from audio script 5.6 on page 172. Read it at the same time and try to finish the sentence faster than your partner.

5.4 BBC BEACH BARBECUE

DVD PREVIEW

1 A Work in pairs and discuss.

1 What types of food do you like, and from which countries? E.g. Italian, Greek, Thai …
2 Do you like cooking?
3 How often do you cook or eat outside? Do you like it?

B Look at the photo and read the text. Then answer the questions.

1 Who is Ainsley Harriott?
2 What type of cooking does he like?
3 Which place does he visit in the programme?
4 What does he cook?

Ainsley Harriott's Beach Barbecue

BBC

Ainsley Harriott is an English chef who loves cooking outside on a barbecue, or 'barbie'. He travels around the world to learn new dishes. He also meets and talks to the people who cook them. In this BBC programme, he visits the Greek island of Alonissos and cooks one of his favourite dishes, stuffed squid, on a barbecue by the sea.

DVD VIEW

2 A Work in pairs and look at the words in the box. Check the meaning and pronunciation of any words you don't know in a dictionary.

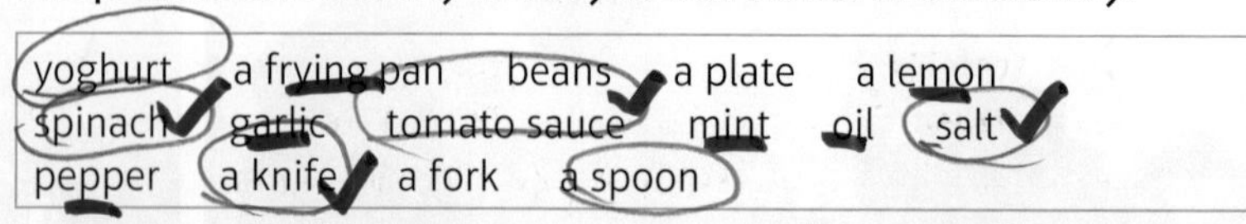

yoghurt
a frying pan
beans
a plate
a lemon
spinach
garlic
tomato sauce
mint
oil
salt
pepper
a knife
a fork
a spoon

B Write six items from the box in your notebook. Watch the DVD and tick the things on your list that you see. Are any of your things not in the DVD?

3 A Match the verbs 1–6 with pictures A–F.

1 grill *C*
2 stir
3 boil
4 fry
5 chop
6 sprinkle

B Work in pairs and discuss. Are the sentences below true (T) or false (F)? Watch the DVD again and check.

1 Ainsley fries some onion and garlic. *T*
2 He boils some rice.
3 He chops some mint.
4 He sprinkles the mint over the onion.
5 He adds some salt and pepper.
6 He stirs the tomato sauce.

C Look at the programme extracts below. Watch the DVD again and cross out the incorrect alternative.

1 These waters really are full of ~~lovely~~/*beautiful* seafood, just like this squid.
2 I'm going to do you a beautiful chargrilled squid stuffed with rice, *mint/garlic* and spinach.
3 I've got about *three/four* ounces* of cooked rice.
4 I've also got here some *good/nice* fresh mint.
5 And remember, you don't need to *cook/fry* this too long – five or six minutes.
6 And it tastes *good/nice* too.

*an ounce = 28 grams

D Work in pairs and discuss. Would you like to eat Ainsley's stuffed squid? Would you like to cook it? Do you know any other good things to have on a barbecue?

speakout a favourite dish

4 A Choose a favourite dish. Make notes about:

- the name of the dish
- the ingredients
- how you make it
- why you like it

B 5.12 Listen to a woman describe her favourite dish, American pancakes. Tick the items above she talks about. Would you like to try American pancakes?

C Listen again and tick the key phrases you hear.

KEYPHRASES

One of my favourite dishes is …
I like it/them because …
It's/They're easy to make.
You need [a/an/some/…]
Mix together the …
It's/They're really good with …
It's/They're [delicious/sweet/salty/very hot].

D Work in pairs. Tell your partner about your dish. Use the key phrases to help.

E Work with other students and tell them about your dish. Listen to the other students. Which dish would you like to try?

writeback describing a dish

5 A Read the email. Why does Pedro need a recipe? Would you like to try the dish?

To

Hi Pedro,

Congratulations! Your new girlfriend sounds great. Yes, I've got an idea for an easy recipe. I'm sure her parents will like it. People always love this dish and it's easy to make.

First, cook some pasta. Then you need a lot of different vegetables, for example some onions, peppers, aubergine and tomatoes. Cut them all up into small pieces (but not too small). Next, heat some oil in a big frying pan or wok, and put the vegetables in. I usually start with the onions and add the tomatoes last. But it's not so important, just fry everything and stir it together. After that, add salt and pepper, and then lots of chopped garlic, and soy sauce. Finally, add the pasta to the cooked vegetables, stir it all around and cook it some more. That's it! Good luck!

Or you can order a pizza!

Best wishes,

Sandra

B Look at the underlined linkers. Which ones can change places?

C Your friend needs an easy recipe for five people for dinner. Write an email with a recipe. Remember to use linkers.

V FOOD AND DRINK

1 A Read the clues below and complete the food words.

1 It's green, it's a fruit and it starts with 'a'. _an apple_
2 It's a drink and it starts with 'm'. ______
3 It's a vegetable and it starts with 'po'. ______
4 It's a fruit, it's yellow and it starts with 'b'. ______
5 They're sweet and they start with 'st'. ______
6 It's usually yellow, it's got six letters and it starts with 'ch'. ______

B Write four more sentences to test your partner.

It's a drink and it starts with …

C Work in pairs and take turns. Student A: read out your sentences. Student B: say the name of the food.

G COUNTABLE AND UNCOUNTABLE NOUNS WITH *A/AN, SOME, ANY*

2 A Look again at the two fridges on pages 48 and 49. Complete the sentences below so that they are true. Use *be* and *a/an*, *some* or *any*.

1 There _isn't any_ water in Vinnie's fridge.
2 There ______ tomatoes in Liz and Mike's fridge.
3 There ______ broccoli in Vinnie's fridge.
4 There ______ fruit juice in Liz and Mike's fridge.
5 There ______ peppers in Vinnie's fridge.
6 There ______ orange in Liz and Mike's fridge.

B Write four questions about the things in the fridges.

Is there any yoghurt in Liz and Mike's fridge?

______
______
______

C Work in pairs. Ask and answer your questions.

V CONTAINERS

3 A Find eleven words for containers.

B Work in pairs and take turns. Student A: start a phrase with a container. Student B: complete the phrase with the correct item.

A: A cup of …
B: A cup of coffee.

G *HOW MUCH/MANY*; QUANTIFIERS

4 A Write the questions in full.

1 How / water / drink every day?
How much water do you drink every day?
2 How / chocolate / eat / every week?
3 How / sisters / have got?
4 How / people / be / there in your family?
5 How / sugar / have / in your coffee?
6 How / tea / drink / every week?
7 How / rooms / be / there in your home?
8 How / salt / like / in your food?

B Answer the questions in Exercise 4A with numbers or phrases.

Four glasses, not much, three …

C Work in groups. Try to guess the question for each number or phrase.

A: Eight
B: How many rooms are there in your home?
A: Yes!

F ORDERING IN A RESTAURANT

5 A Change the sentences to make the customer and waiter polite.

W: Come on, order now!
C: Give me some pea soup!
W: Do you want a main course?
C: Yes, roast beef.
W: And vegetables?
C: I want peas and potatoes.
W: Do you want a drink?
C: Give me water.

B Work in pairs and practise the polite conversation.

6 A Work in pairs. Look at the menu for a new restaurant. Write a description of dishes 1–3.

menu

1 King's delight:

2 Winter warmer:

3 Light and tasty:

B Work in groups. Student A: you are the waiter. Say the names of the dishes. The other students: ask about the dishes and order food.

A: Good evening. Are you ready to order?
B: Nearly. Can I ask …

6 the past

SPEAKING **6.1** Describe your favourite childhood things **6.2** Talk about past events in your life **6.3** Talk about how your weekend was **6.4** Interview a special person

LISTENING **6.1** Hear interesting facts about famous people's lives **6.3** Listen to people talking about their weekends **6.4** Watch an extract from a documentary about a great leader

READING **6.2** Read about time twins

WRITING **6.2** Link sentences with *because* and *so*; Write your life story in 100 words **6.4** Write a profile about a special person

BBC INTERVIEWS

Did you go out last night?

6.1 IN THEIR PAST

G *was/were*
P weak forms: *was/were*
V dates and time phrases

A Oprah Winfrey

B Taylor Swift

C Quentin Tarantino

D Michelle Yeoh

LISTENING

1 A Work in pairs and discuss. What do you know about the famous people in photos A–F?

B Work in pairs and read the information about the people. For each person tick two pieces of true information and put a cross by the false information.

1 Lionel Messi, football player:
  a) He's from Spain.
  b) He was a very good student.
  c) He always plays football with his hair wet.

2 Oprah Winfrey, famous TV presenter and philanthropist*:
  a) She was very poor when she was a child.
  b) She was a millionaire at the age of twenty-three.
  c) She hates chewing gum.

3 Benedict Cumberbatch, actor:
  a) His hobbies at school were acting, sport and painting.
  b) He rides a motorbike around London.
  c) He was a French teacher before he was an actor.

4 Taylor Swift, singer and songwriter:
  a) Her childhood was on an apple tree farm.
  b) She was a songwriter at five years old.
  c) Her grandmother was an opera singer.

5 Michelle Yeoh, actress:
  a) She was a singer before she was an actress.
  b) She was in a James Bond film.
  c) She was the winner of the Miss Malaysia beauty contest in 1983.

6 Quentin Tarantino, director:
  a) He hates violence.
  b) He wants to stop making movies at age eighty.
  c) His mother was part Cherokee, part Irish.

*philanthropist = a rich person who gives a lot of money to help other people

C 6.1 **Listen and check your answers.**

D Work in pairs. Choose three of the people. Listen again and write down one extra fact about each one.

GRAMMAR

WAS/WERE

2 A Underline the verbs in the sentence below. Are the verbs in the present or the past? Are they singular or plural?

Oprah's parents were very poor, but at the age of thirty-two she was a millionaire.

B Complete the tables below.

Present		
Taylor Swift	is	a singer and songwriter.
Her songs	are	about her life.

Past		
Her grandmother	______	an opera singer.
Her first hobbies	______	horse riding and singing.

C Change the sentences below. Make a) negative and b) a question. Then complete the rules.

a) Yeoh's first films were American.
b) Lionel Messi was a good student.

RULES
Make the negative with *was/were* + ______
Make the question with ______ + subject

3 A 6.2 **Listen to the sentences. Are they in the past or present? Write past (P) or now (N).**

1 ______ 3 ______ 5 ______ 7 ______
2 ______ 4 ______ 6 ______ 8 ______

B 6.3 **Listen and write the four sentences you hear.**

C Listen again and underline the stresses in each sentence.

D WEAK FORMS: *was/were* Listen again and notice the weak forms of was /wəz/ and were /wə/ in the sentences. Practise saying the sentences.

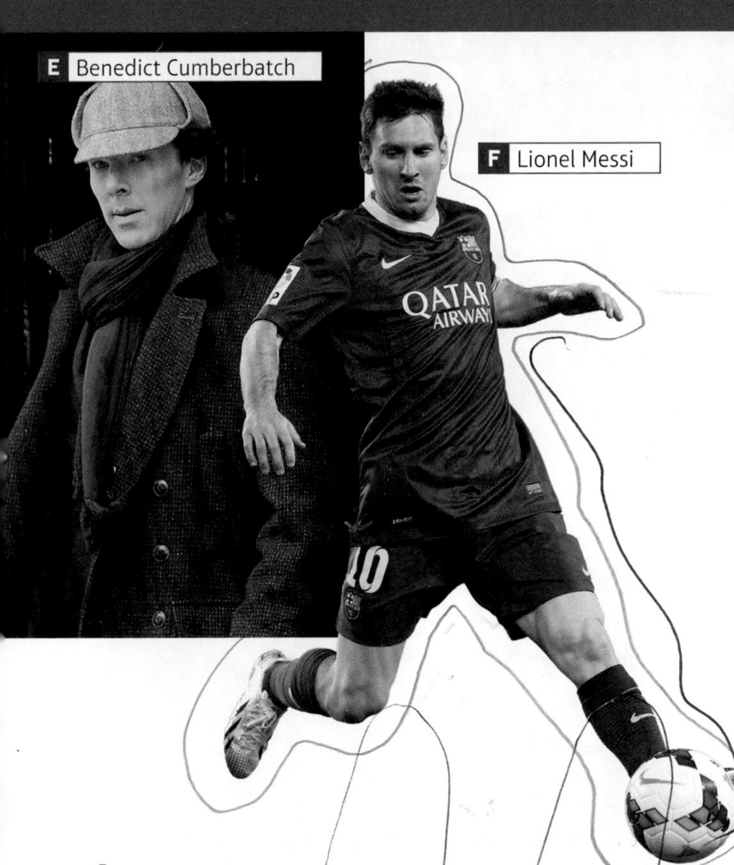

4 A Write the questions with prompts 1–8.

1 you / born in this country?
Were you born in this country?
2 you / born in the summer?
3 you / a very quiet child?
4 you / afraid of the dark when you were a child?
5 your first teacher / a man or a woman?
6 your parents / childhood friends?
7 your grandfather / born in another country?
8 your grandmother / a good cook?

B Work in groups. Ask and answer the questions above. How many answers were the same?

A: *Were you born in this country?*
B: *Yes, I was. And you?*
A: *Me too.*

▷ page 138 **LANGUAGEBANK**

SPEAKING

5 A What were your favourite things when you were a child? Think of examples for each of the items in the box.

people	music	activity or sport
TV programme	food	

B Work in pairs and compare your ideas.

A: *Who were your favourite people?*
B: *One of my favourite people was my uncle Luciano. He was really funny.*

C Work in pairs and each write six sentences about your favourite things above, three for each of you.

D Exchange sentences with another pair. Guess which student each sentence is about.

VOCABULARY

DATES AND TIME PHRASES

6 A ▶ 6.4 Listen and underline the years you hear.

1 1999 / 1990 3 1987 / 1997 5 1941 / 1951
2 2030 / 2003 4 2012 / 2021 6 1672 / 1772

B Work in pairs and take turns. Student A: say one of the years above. Student B: point to the year.

C ▶ 6.5 Take turns to say the months of the year. Then listen and check your pronunciation.

A: *January*
B: *February*

▷ page 158 **PHOTOBANK**

7 A Match the dates A–F with these special occasions.

A	B	C	D	E	F
OCT 31	JAN 1	MAR 8	DEC 25	JULY 4	FEB 14

1 Christmas Day ______
2 New Year's Day ______
3 Valentine's Day ______
4 Halloween ______
5 International Women's Day ______
6 Independence Day (USA) ______

B ▶ 6.6 Listen and check your answers.

C Write the numbers.

1st	*first*	4th	______	21st	______
2nd	______	5th	______	22nd	______
3rd	______	12th	______	30th	______

D Write three important dates from last year. Work with other students and tell each other about the dates. Do any students have similar dates?

8 A Complete the time phrases below with the words in the box.

~~yesterday~~	on	in	ago	last

1 *yesterday* morning, afternoon, evening
2 ______ night, Friday, weekend, week, month, year
3 ______ Saturday, Sunday, 12th June
4 ______ July, 1999, 2015
5 a week, ten days, ten minutes ______

B Choose five of the time phrases and write past sentences. Make them true for *you*.

I was at home last night.

C Work in pairs and take turns. Student A: say one of your past events, but don't say when it was. Student B: guess the time phrase.

A: *I was with some friends.*
B: *On Saturday?*
A: *Yes. That's right!*

- **G** past simple
- **P** past simple verbs: *-ed* endings
- **V** life story collocations

READING

1 A Look at the pictures and discuss. Why are the women time twins? What else can you say about their lives?

B Read about their lives and put the sentences in the correct order.

C 6.7 Listen and check your answers.

D Find three things that Samiya and Lidia have in common.

GRAMMAR

PAST SIMPLE

2 A Read the life stories again and circle the past form of these regular verbs: *study, finish, live, work, start, walk, move, hate, love, play, want.* Then complete the rule.

RULES	Make the past simple of regular verbs by adding ______ or ______ to the verb. With a verb ending consonant + *y*, change the *y* to ______ and add ______ .

B 6.8 **PAST SIMPLE VERBS: *-ed endings*** Listen to the pronunciation of the regular verbs and write them in the correct place in the table.

/t/	/d/	/ɪd/
finished		

C Write the past form of the irregular verbs below. Use the life stories to help.

1 go *went*
2 have ______
3 make ______
4 know ______
5 buy ______
6 take ______
7 become ______
8 think ______

D Read the sentences and complete the rules.

1 Samiya's parents didn't have a lot of money.
2 Did she go to university?

RULES	Make the negative by adding ______ before the infinitive. Make the question form by adding ______ + subject (*you/he/she*, etc.) + verb.

speakout TIP

A dictionary shows the past tense of a verb, e.g. *give (gave)*. In your notebook, always write (REG) for a regular verb or the past form for an irregular verb. Do this now with *ask, join, meet, give* and *stop*.

A Samiya was born in Nigeria on 18th August 1993, in a village near Lagos. *1*

B When she was fifteen she went to university and studied information technology. In her fourth year at university she met her future husband, Obi, and after they finished university they got married.

C Her parents didn't have a lot of money, and the family lived in a small house. Samiya's father worked as a taxi driver and her mother was a teacher.

D Their apps made a lot of money and with the money, Samiya bought her parents a new house.

E In her childhood, Samiya was shy, but her parents knew she was very intelligent; she was really good at maths and computer games.

F Samiya and Obi had some great ideas for apps and together they started a company. The company made apps for teaching children maths and English.

3 A Complete the sentences with the past form of the verbs in brackets.

1 She *started* university at the age of fifteen. (start) *S*
2 She ______ her life in the village (love)
3 She ______ to be the best player. (try)
4 Her apps ______ children learn English. (help)
5 Her mother ______ in a school. (work)
6 Her parents ______ to a new home. (move)
7 She ______ sport but not studying. (enjoy)
8 She ______ the man about the pictures. (ask)

B Which sentences are about Samiya (S) and which are about Lidia (L)?

A Lidia was born on 18th August 1993, in Poland in a large town near Gdansk. *1*

B One day she went to a park in Rome to play basketball, and a man walked up to her and took pictures of her.

C It was her big moment, but she didn't become a basketball star; the man was a fashion photographer, and Lidia became a professional model. With the money from her first year's work, she bought her parents a new house.

D When she was fifteen, her family moved to Italy.

E Lidia thought 'This is it, it's my big moment!'

F She was tall for her age and very beautiful, but she was shy. She hated school, but she loved sport and played basketball every day after school with a group of boys. She wanted to be an international basketball star.

4 A Complete the sentences with the past form of the verbs in brackets. Look at the irregular verbs on page 127 to help.

1 I ______________ a car. (not have)
2 I ______________ a lot of sport. (do)
3 I ______________ a lot of junk food. (eat)
4 I ______________ English a lot. (speak)
5 I ______________ to any concerts. (not go)
6 I ______________ a new mobile phone. (buy)
7 I ______________ a lot of apps. (use)
8 I ______________ a new job. (start)

B Make the sentences above true for you last year.

C Work in pairs and compare your sentences. Find three things in common.

5 A Think about a friend you don't see now. Complete the questions below.

1 Where and when ______? (you / meet)
2 Why ______ each other? (you / like)
3 ______ a lot of things together? (you / do)
4 How often ______ to each other? (you / speak)
5 When ______ him/her? (you / last / see)
6 What ______ then? (you / do)

B Work in pairs. Ask and answer the questions.

▷ page 138 **LANGUAGEBANK**

VOCABULARY

LIFE STORY COLLOCATIONS

6 A Complete the phrases with a verb from the box.

~~go~~ meet work get become start

1 *go* to school/to university
2 ______ a chef/a model
3 ______ married/a job
4 ______ your husband/your wife
5 ______ a new job/a company
6 ______ for Samsung/as a taxi driver

B Work in pairs and take turns. Student A: say the end of the phrase. Student B: say the verb.

A: *as a taxi driver* **B:** *work*

SPEAKING

7 A Think of three important events in your life. Write the event and the year.

Met Nina – 2014

B Work in pairs and talk about the important events in your lives.

A: *2014 was a great year.*
B: *Why?*
A: *I met my girlfriend, Nina.*

WRITING

BECAUSE AND *SO*

8 A Complete the sentences with *because* or *so*.

1 Lidia loved basketball, ______ she went to the park every day to play.
2 She became a model ______ she was beautiful.

B Complete the sentences about your life.

1 At school I liked ______, so I ______.
2 I started English lessons because ______.

C Write your life story in 100 words. Remember to use *and*, *but*, *because* and *so*.

6.3 WHAT DID YOU DO?

Ⓕ asking follow-up questions
Ⓟ linking: *did you*
Ⓥ activities

VOCABULARY

ACTIVITIES

1 Work in pairs and discuss. What's your favourite day of the week? Why? What do you do on that day?

A: *Why is Thursday your favourite day?*
B: *Because I don't work in the morning, so I have a yoga class and then I often meet a friend for lunch.*

2 A Work in pairs. How many activities can you remember with these verbs: *read, listen to, have, play, watch, do, go?* Check on page 18.

read newspapers

B Look at the word webs and cross out the phrase which does not go with the verb.

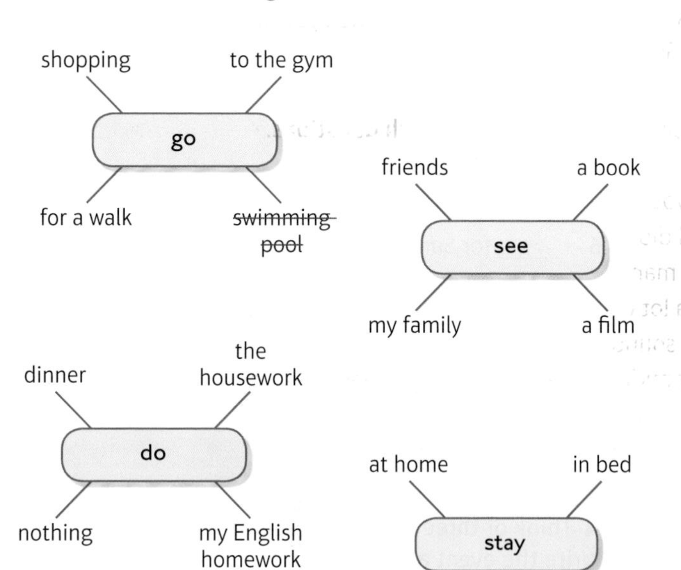

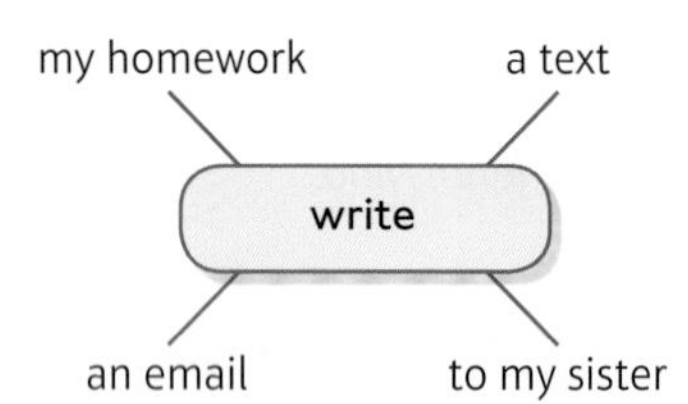

C Look at the word webs again. Tick which activities you sometimes do at the weekend. Put a cross for activities which you never do.

D Add another activity you often do to three of the word webs above.

E Work in pairs. Student A: use the verbs above and ask questions about last weekend. Student B: answer the questions. Find three things that you both did.

A: *Did you see your friends?*
B: *Yes, I did.*
A: *Me too. Did you go for a walk?*

FUNCTION

ASKING FOLLOW-UP QUESTIONS

3 A ▶ 6.9 Listen to the conversations. Which weekend is similar to your last weekend, Isabel's, Ahmed's or Jane's?

B Listen again and complete the table.

	Saturday	Sunday
Isabel		//////
Ahmed		
Jane		

C Look at the phrases. Write question (Q), answer (A), or show interest (I) next to each phrase.

1 Did you have a good weekend? *Q*
2 Not bad./It was OK./So-so.
3 Where did you go?
4 That sounds good/interesting/awful!
5 Why was that?
6 Nothing special/much.
7 That's great/a shame/terrible.
8 What did you do?
9 Who did you go with?
10 It was great/amazing/terrible!
11 How was your weekend?
12 Why? What happened?

D Listen again. Tick the phrases above you hear.

E Which questions above start a conversation? Which ones are follow-up questions?

4 ▶ 6.10 **LINKING: *did you*** Look at the pronunciation of *did you*. Listen and repeat.

did‿you /dɪdʒʊ/
1 /dɪdʒʊ/ have a good weekend?
2 What /dɪdʒʊ/ do?
3 Where /dɪdʒʊ/ go?
4 Who /dɪdʒʊ/ go with?

LEARN TO

EXTEND CONVERSATIONS

6 A Work in pairs. Look at the extract and discuss the questions.

1 How many pieces of information does Isabel give in her answers? Why?
2 How does Ahmed show interest?

Ahmed: What did you do?
Isabel: On Saturday I went for a walk. It was really good. Nice weather.
Ahmed: Yes, it was lovely. Where did you go?
Isabel: Down by the sea. It was really beautiful.
Ahmed: That sounds nice.

speakout TIP

To have a good conversation, ask follow-up questions after your first question. Show interest in the answers. When you answer, don't say only one thing. Give extra information.

5 A Work in pairs and use the prompts to role-play the conversation.

Student A
How / weekend?
Student B
It / so-so
Oh, why / that?
We / go / Dublin
Sound / good. / What / happen?
It / really wet
That / shame. / What / do?
We / go / museum / then we / listen to / Irish music / café
Sound / good. / Who / go with?
Two friends / mine

B Work in pairs and take turns. Ask and answer questions about your weekend. Use your own ideas and the photos to help.

▷ page 138 **LANGUAGEBANK**

B Complete the conversation with questions, extra information and phrases to show interest.

A: Did you go to Atsuko's party?
B: Yes, I did. It was ______!
A: How many ______?
B: Oh, a lot of people. They were all very ______.
A: That sounds ______! What time ______?
B: After midnight. I left at ______. When I got home, I ______.
A: Are you tired?
B: Not really. I ______, so I'm not very tired.

C Work in pairs and practise the conversation.

D Work in groups and take turns to role-play your conversation. Listen to the other pairs. Did everyone like Atsuko's party?

SPEAKING

7 A Imagine that you had a perfect/terrible weekend. Write answers to questions 1–4.

1 Where did you go?
2 Who did you go with?
3 What did you do?
4 Why was it perfect/terrible?

B Work in groups. Tell each other about your weekend. Remember to ask follow-up questions, show interest and give extra information. Who had the best or worst weekend?

A: How was your weekend?
B: Terrible. I had an awful weekend.
C: Really? Why?

DVD PREVIEW

1 A Work in pairs and read the information below about Nelson Mandela. What information is the most interesting/surprising?

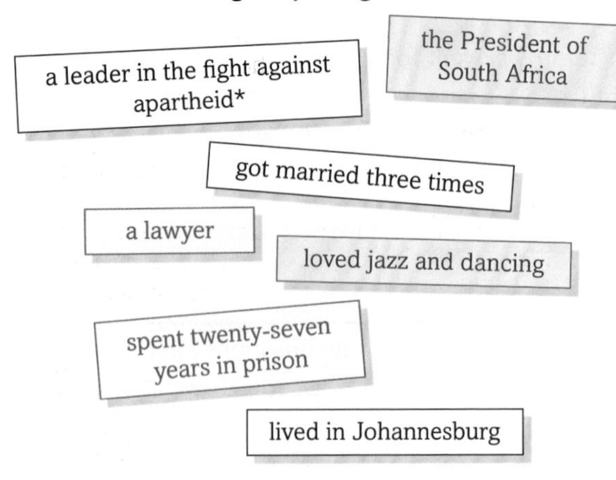

a leader in the fight against apartheid*
the President of South Africa
got married three times
a lawyer
loved jazz and dancing
spent twenty-seven years in prison
lived in Johannesburg

* apartheid /əˈpɑːtaɪd/ = the separation or segregation of whites and blacks

B Read the programme description and answer the questions.

1 Does the programme look at Mandela's public or private life?
2 How old was he when he died?

Nelson Mandela: The Fight For Freedom

BBC

This programme looks back at the life of Nelson Mandela: his birth in South Africa in 1918, his life as a young lawyer in Johannesburg, his fight against the apartheid system, his release after twenty-seven years in prison, his time as President of South Africa, and the years after he retired, when he travelled around the world meeting people and giving talks. Mandela died in 2013, the freedom fighter who became a man of peace.

DVD VIEW

2 A Look at the timeline of Mandela's life. What do you think was the best and worst time for him?

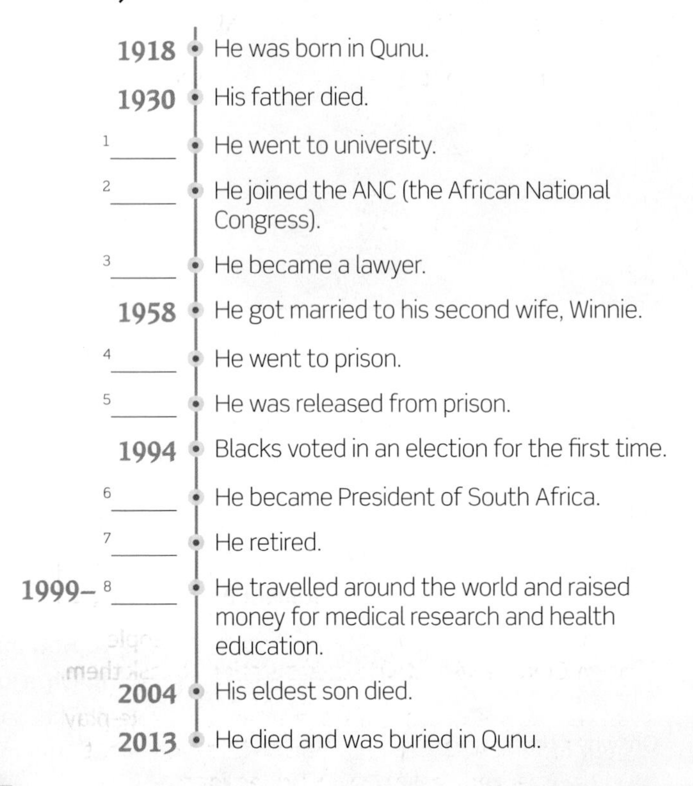

Year	Event
1918	He was born in Qunu.
1930	His father died.
1 ______	He went to university.
2 ______	He joined the ANC (the African National Congress).
3 ______	He became a lawyer.
1958	He got married to his second wife, Winnie.
4 ______	He went to prison.
5 ______	He was released from prison.
1994	Blacks voted in an election for the first time.
6 ______	He became President of South Africa.
7 ______	He retired.
1999– 8 ______	He travelled around the world and raised money for medical research and health education.
2004	His eldest son died.
2013	He died and was buried in Qunu.

B Close your book and watch the DVD. Then open your book and tick the events on the timeline that the video talks about.

C Watch again. Complete 1–8 on the timeline with the correct dates.

D Work in pairs and underline the correct alternative. What do the people say? Then watch the DVD again and check your answers.

'I wish to put it plainly, that the government has taken a firm decision to [1]*release/free* Mr Mandela unconditionally.' President de Klerk

'Take your guns, your knives and your pangas* and [2]*throw/put* them into the sea.' Mandela

'If I am your leader, you have to listen to me. And if you don't want to listen to me, then [3]*drop/don't have* me as a leader.' Mandela

'People can't believe it when you say, "Hey, I'm free! I'm free!" and you're [4]*walking/feeling* tall.' Desmond Tutu

'I, Nelson Rolihlahla Mandela, do hereby swear to be [5]*faithful/true* to the Republic of South Africa.' Mandela

*panga = a very large knife

E Work with other students. What was the best thing that Nelson Mandela did? Do you know any other great 'men or women of peace'?

speakout an interview

3 A Work in pairs. Think of a hero or someone you admire, e.g. a famous person, a friend or someone in your family. Tell each other about the person. Why is he/she important to you?

B 6.11 Listen to an interview with Fernanda Espinosa. What is one special thing about her?

C Listen again and tick the key phrases you hear.

KEYPHRASES

Interviewer:

Thank you for joining us today and welcome to the programme.

Can I ask you about [your childhood/mother/first wife/…]?

Where/When did you [decide to/first meet/…]?

That's very interesting.

What's your favourite [film/book/band/…]?

Are there any questions [from the audience/for …]?

Interviewee:

That's a good question.

Let me think about that.

D Work in pairs. Choose one of the special people from Exercise 3A and write five questions to ask them.

E Work in groups and take turns. One pair: role-play your interview. Other students: make notes about the answers and ask follow-up questions.

writeback a profile

4 A Read the profile about Fernanda Espinosa and number the paragraph topics in order.

a) A life-changing experience
b) Her early life *1*
c) Why I admire her
d) Her work

A special person: Fernanda

Fernanda Espinosa was born in San Pedro in Honduras in 1973. She was the fourth of eleven children. Her father was a teacher and her mother worked as a cleaning woman for rich people.

When Fernanda was at school, one of her friends lost his parents and moved to an orphanage because he had no other family members to live with. Fernanda visited her friend at the orphanage and felt very sorry for the children there. So she decided to work with orphans, to try to give them a good life.

Fernanda met her husband Emilio in 1997, and they got married in 2000. They opened an orphanage in 2006 near Quito, and they still work together. They started with ten children and now they have sixty-three children living in the orphanage.

Fernanda is a hero for me because she gives her life to helping children. She is an amazing woman and I admire her work very much.

B Write a profile of a special person from Exercise 3A. Write about the events in his/her life and say why you admire him/her.

G *WAS/WERE*

1 A Put the words in the correct order.

1 was / work / I / afternoon / at / yesterday
2 six / Where / o'clock / at / you / were?
3 evening / my / was / at / flat / I / Wednesday / friend's / on
4 at / were / shops / you / the / When?
5 half / you / Were / home / at / twelve / at / past?
6 morning / Where / you / Monday / were / on?

B Look at the table below. Where were you yesterday? Fill in the table.

⇦ Yesterday ⇨	
8.45	*At home*
12.30	
19.00	

C Work in pairs and take turns. Ask and answer questions about yesterday. Fill in the table when your partner says *yes*.

A: *Where were you at 8.45 yesterday?*
B: *I was at home.*
A: *Were you in bed?*
B: *Yes, I was./No, I wasn't.*

⇦ Yesterday ⇨	
8.45	
12.30	
19.00	

V DATES AND TIME PHRASES

2 Complete the time phrases so they mean the same as phrases 1–8.

Today is Monday 8th June 2015.

Vicky is twenty-three.

1 When she was twenty = three years *ago*
2 On Sunday afternoon = ______ afternoon
3 Last month = ______ May
4 5th June = ______ Friday
5 A week ago = ______ week
6 Yesterday = ______ 7th June
7 In January = five months ______
8 Last year = ______ 2014

3 A Write two things you can:

eat *beef* ______
read ______ ______
visit ______ ______
watch ______ ______
buy ______ ______
play ______ ______

B Work in pairs and take turns. Use the lists above to ask and answer questions.

A: *When did you last eat beef?*
B: *Last month./A week ago.*

G PAST SIMPLE

4 A Make the sentences true for you. Use the positive and negative form of the verbs.

1 I ______ lunch yesterday. (miss)
2 I ______ some friends at the weekend. (meet)
3 I ______ English yesterday evening. (study)
4 I ______ very well last night. (sleep)
5 I ______ breakfast for myself this morning. (make)
6 I ______ to this lesson by car. (come)

B Work in pairs and compare your answers. Add an extra piece of information.

I didn't miss lunch yesterday. I had a sandwich in the park.

5 A Look at the sentences and write questions to ask your partner.

1 He/She was born in a hospital.
2 He/She grew up in a city.
3 He/She usually walked to school when he/she was ten.
4 He/She went abroad every summer when he/she was a child.
5 He/She played a lot of sports at school.

B Work in pairs and take turns to ask and answer the questions.

V LIFE STORY COLLOCATIONS

6 A Add the missing letters to complete the sentences.

1 The best place to me_ _ a husband or wife is **at work**.
2 It's best to g_ _ married before **twenty-five**.
3 You can't st_ _ _ a new career after age **thirty**.
4 It's not good to wo_ _ as **a doctor** in my country.
5 When I was young, I wanted to be_ _ _ _ **a teacher**.

B Tick the sentences you agree with. For the sentences that you disagree with, change the words in bold to make them true for you.

C Work in pairs and compare your answers.

F ASKING FOLLOW-UP QUESTIONS

7 A Put the question words in the correct place. One question is correct.

1 What was your weekend?
2 Where did you do at the weekend?
3 Who happened?
4 Why was that?
5 What did you go?
6 How did you go with?

B Work in pairs. Choose four of the questions and write a conversation.

C Role-play your conversation.

7 holidays

SPEAKING 7.1 Talk about how you like to travel 7.2 Plan and talk about a long journey 7.3 Give directions in the street 7.4 Describe part of a town/city you know

LISTENING 7.1 Listen to people talk about how they like to travel 7.3 Understand directions 7.4 Watch an extract from a travel show about Hong Kong

READING 7.2 Read an article about a bike tour across Asia

WRITING 7.2 Check and correct information about a holiday 7.4 Write a short travel article about a town/city

BBC INTERVIEWS

How was your last holiday?

7.1 TRAVEL PARTNERS

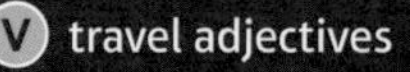

G comparatives
P word stress; sentence stress
V travel adjectives

A

B

C

D

VOCABULARY

TRAVEL ADJECTIVES

1 A Work in pairs. Do you enjoy travelling? Do you ever go abroad? What places/things can you see in the photos? Make a list of adjectives to describe them.

Market: hot, busy …

B Match the adjectives in column A with their opposites in column B.

A	B
hot	noisy
fast	empty
crowded	boring
expensive	cheap
comfortable	cold
interesting	uncomfortable
quiet	slow

C 7.1 **WORD STRESS** Listen and underline the stressed syllable in each adjective. Then listen again and repeat.

crowded

D Work in pairs and take turns. Student A: choose one of the photos A–D. Describe it using four adjectives from Exercise 1B. Student B: guess the photo.

SPEAKING

2 A Do the travel quiz below. Circle your answers.

B Work in pairs and compare your answers. Are you good travel partners? Why/Why not?

TRAVEL QUIZ

Going on holiday this year? Do the quiz and find your perfect travel partner!

1 **I like travelling …**
a) by plane **b)** by train **c)** by car

2 **I like staying in …**
a) a hotel **b)** a self-catering apartment **c)** a tent

3 **I prefer …**
a) relaxing on a beach **b)** doing something sporty
c) going sightseeing

4 **I like going on holiday …**
a) in spring **b)** in summer **c)** in winter

5 **When I'm on holiday I like eating …**
a) local dishes **b)** the food I usually eat **c)** fast food

6 **In the evenings I like …**
a) going for a walk **b)** going to a restaurant
c) going to a nightclub

7 **My perfect holiday is …**
a) a weekend **b)** a week **c)** a month

LISTENING

3 A 7.2 **Listen to two people doing the quiz. Answer the questions.**

1 How many of their answers are the same?
2 Are they good travel partners?

B Listen again. Write man (M) and woman (W) next to the answers in the quiz in Exercise 2A.

C Work in pairs and discuss. Is the man or the woman a good travel partner for *you*? Why/Why not?

GRAMMAR

COMPARATIVES

4 A Look at audio script 7.2 on page 172 and complete the sentences.

1 Planes are fast______ ______ trains.
2 Summer's hot______ ______ spring.
3 A hotel's ______ expensive ______ an apartment.

B 7.3 **SENTENCE STRESS Underline the stressed words in the sentences above. Listen and check. Notice the pronunciation of *than* /ðən/. Then listen again and repeat.**

C Complete the table.

	Adjective	Comparative	Rule
short adjectives	fast	fast__*er*__	Use adjective + - ______
long adjectives	comfortable	______ comfortable	Use ______ + adjective
irregular adjectives	good/bad	better/worse	

page 140 **LANGUAGEBANK**

5 A Write comparative sentences. Use the adjectives in brackets.

1 shoes, trainers (comfortable) for travelling
Trainers are more comfortable than shoes for travelling.
2 autumn, spring (romantic)
3 travelling by car, travelling by bus (bad) on a hot day
4 cafés, restaurants (cheap) in my city
5 an e-book, a book (good) on holiday
6 museums, art galleries (interesting)
7 city, beach (nice) for a day out
8 a cheap hotel, a good hotel (easy to find)

B Work in pairs and compare your answers.

6 A Choose two places you know, e.g. cities, cafés, nightclubs. Which one do you like more? Write two sentences about each place using comparatives.

I like Krakow more than Warsaw because it's smaller and cheaper.

B Talk to other students and tell each other about your places. Which place would you like to visit?

A: *I like Krakow more than Warsaw.*
B: *Why?*
A: *Because it's smaller and more beautiful.*

SPEAKING

7 A Write notes about a good or bad holiday *you* went on. Think about the questions below and use the photos to help.

- Where and when did you go?
- Who did you go with?
- Where did you stay? Was it good?
- What did you do? Did you enjoy it?
- Where did you eat? Did you like the food?
- Was it hot?
- Did you like it more than your town/city? Why/Why not?

B Work in pairs. Ask and answer the questions above. What's similar about your holidays?

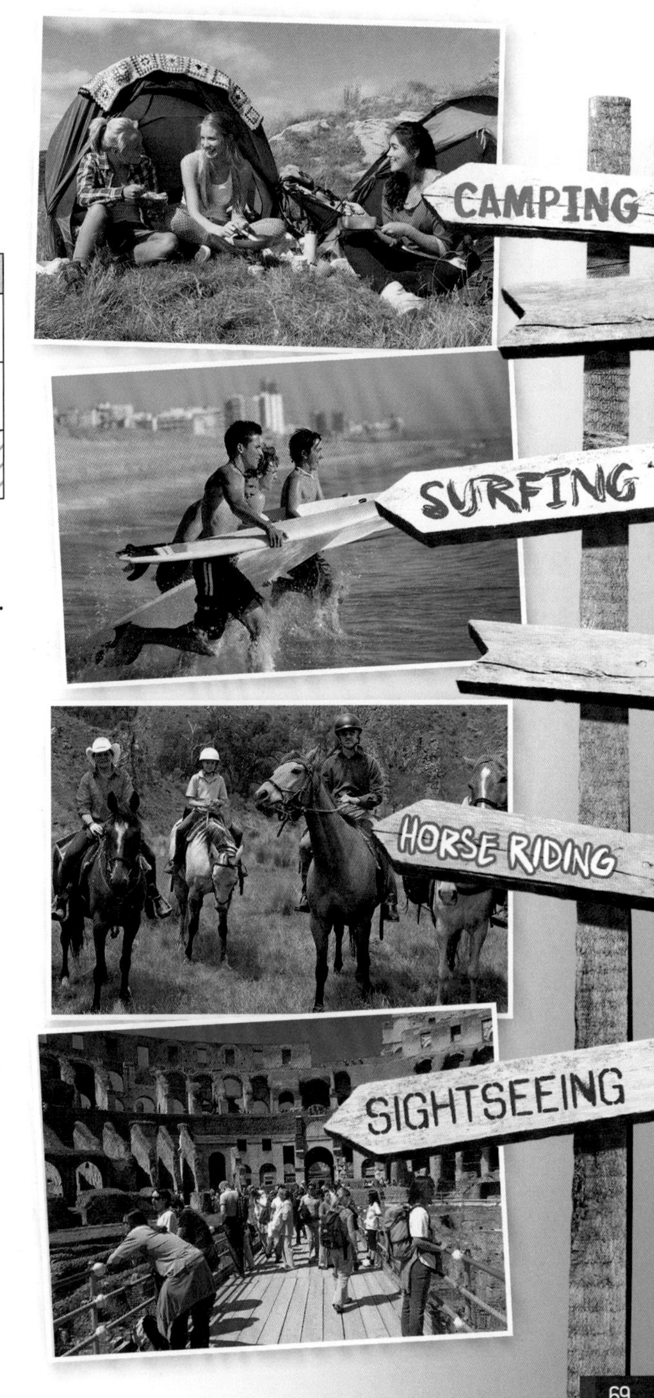

7.2 THE LONGEST BIKE RIDE

G superlatives
P weak form: *the*
V places

VOCABULARY

PLACES

1 A Work in pairs. Look at photos A–E. Which of the things in the box can you see?

a mountain a hill a river a lake a forest a village a market a famous building a desert

B Work in pairs. Look at the words in the box in Exercise 1A and write an example for each word. Use your country if possible.

A mountain: Monte Cervino (Italy)

The Silk Route Bike Tour: is it the greatest journey in the world? The company calls it 'the longest, hardest, highest, hottest, coldest bicycle tour in the world'. In eighteen weeks you travel over 12,000 kilometres through seven different countries and have the most exciting ride of your life.

'A thousand years ago people went by camel and did about twenty-five kilometres a day,' says Nate Cavalieri, one of the Silk Route Tour staff. 'But on a bike you do twenty-five kilometres in an hour.' And along the way you see some of the most beautiful places in the world.

From Shanghai, you go across Asia, through Iran and arrive in Istanbul, Turkey, at the end. You travel across the deserts of China and cycle the Pamir Highway to over 4,600 metres, across the 'Roof of the World' in the mountains of Tajikistan. On the way there are villages, markets and ancient buildings.

At night, you stay in ancient roadside hotels or in camps. A chef cooks dinner for about half of the 133 days; on other days cyclists can eat in local restaurants or shop in local markets for their food.

One cyclist blogged, 'The best thing was the friendliness of the people.' And the worst things? 'The snow and the cold in the Pamirs.'

So is it the greatest journey in the world? Cyclist and blogger Miles MacDonald thinks so. 'The Silk Route is a true expedition. It is long and difficult, but it's such an amazing experience that you arrive in Istanbul a completely changed person.'

Istanbul

READING

2 A Read the introduction to the article about the Silk Route Tour and answer the questions.

1 What is the Silk Route Tour?
2 How many countries does it travel through?

B Work in pairs. What else would you like to know about the Silk Route Tour? Write three questions using the words in the box to help.

countries sleep people food bikes price

Which countries does it visit?

3 A Read the article. Did you find the answers to your questions?

B Read the article again. Are sentences 1–6 true (T) or false (F)?

1 The Silk Route Tour travels through seven countries in eighty weeks.
2 A bicycle is faster than a camel.
3 The tour starts in Istanbul and ends in Shanghai.
4 Cyclists stay in hotels and camps.
5 They take turns cooking dinner every evening.
6 One cyclist thought the snow and the hills were the best things.

C Would you like to go on the Silk Route Tour? Why/Why not?

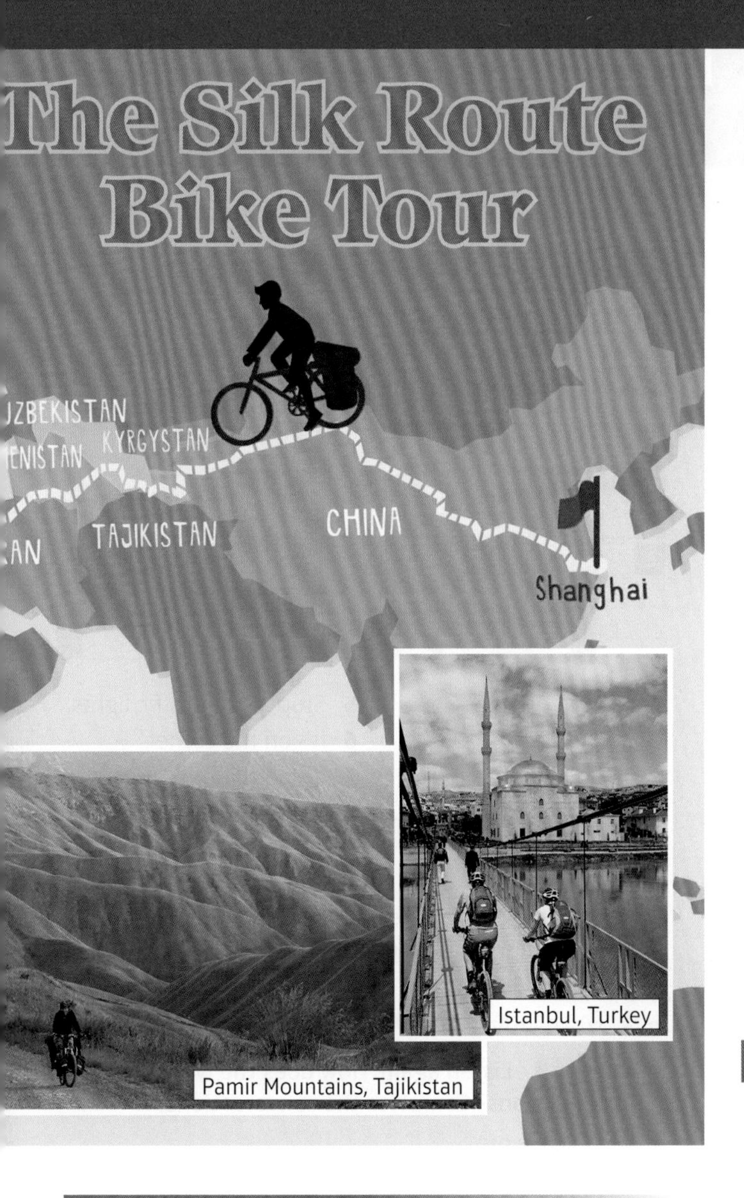

Istanbul, Turkey

Pamir Mountains, Tajikistan

GRAMMAR

SUPERLATIVES

4 A Complete the sentences with words from the article above.

1 Is it the _______ journey in the world?
2 You see some of the _______ _______ places in the world.
3 The _______ thing was the friendliness of the people.

B Underline other examples of superlatives in the introduction. Then complete the table below.

	Adjective	Superlative	Rule
short adjectives	great	*the greatest*	Use _______ + adjective + - _______
longer adjectives	exciting	_______	Use _______ + _______ + adjective
irregular adjectives	good bad	_______ _______	

C 7.4 **WEAK FORM: *the*** Listen to the pronunciation of *the* in the sentences in Exercise 4A. Then listen and repeat.

▷ page 140 **LANGUAGEBANK**

5 A Make questions about the Silk Route Tour.

1 What / cold / place you visited?
What was the coldest place you visited?
2 What / hot / place?
3 What / friendly / place?
4 What / far / distance you travelled in one day?
5 What / beautiful / building you saw?
6 What / amazing / experience of the journey?

B Match answers a)–f) with questions 1–6.

a) 'It was Turpan, China.'
'For me, the Gobi Desert: fifty degrees centigrade!'
b) 'The Blue Mosque. I took 100 photos.'
'The Bibi-Khanym Mosque.'
c) 'Meeting locals everywhere.'
'Arriving in Istanbul.'
d) 'About 150 kilometres, in western China.'
'I don't remember … at least 100 kilometres.'
e) 'The mountains in Kyrgyzstan.'
'The desert at night. There was snow!'
f) 'Iran; the people there were so kind.'
'Everywhere, really.'

C 7.5 Listen to a conversation with a Silk Route Tour cyclist. Underline the answers he gives in a)–f).

SPEAKING

6 A Work with other students. Plan a long journey to another country. Choose five places to visit: the most exciting, the most beautiful, the highest, etc.

First we go to … , then we visit the oldest/most famous … in …

B Tell the class about your journey. Ask and answer questions about each journey.

A: Where do you sleep at night?
B: In small hotels.

C Discuss. Which journey is the most interesting?

WRITING

CHECKING AND CORRECTING

7 A Read the student's homework below. Find and correct ten mistakes with:

• spelling • past simple • singular/plural
• comparatives/superlatives

On Saturday we went by bus across the ~~dessert~~ desert. We meet a lot of peoples. The peoples in the villages was friendlyer than in the city. At night we staid in a camp. It was not very comftable, but it was more cheaper than the hotels. We buyed all our food in markets.

B Write four sentences about your last holiday.

7.3 CAN YOU TELL ME THE WAY?

F giving directions
P sentence stress: correcting
V places

VOCABULARY

PLACES

1 A Work in pairs and look at the photos and the information. Why is Liverpool famous? What can a tourist do there?

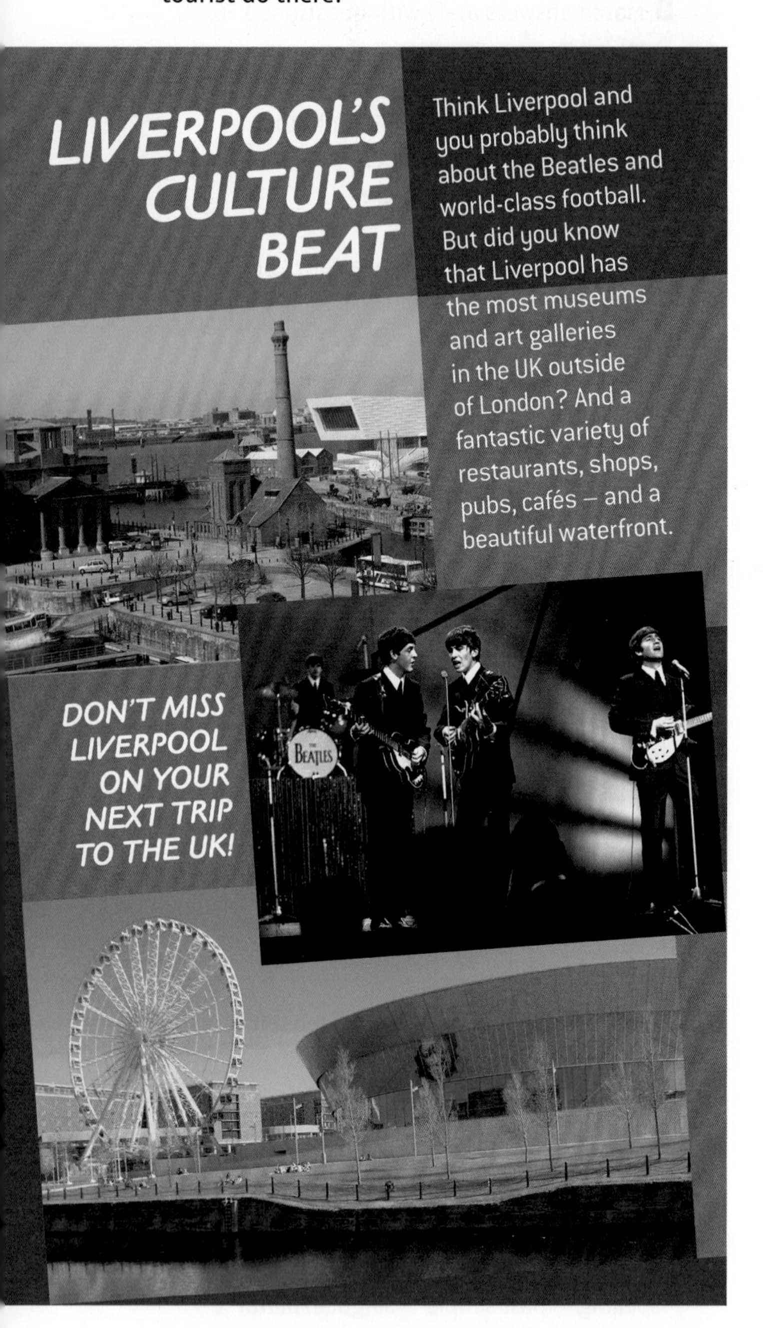

LIVERPOOL'S CULTURE BEAT
Think Liverpool and you probably think about the Beatles and world-class football. But did you know that Liverpool has the most museums and art galleries in the UK outside of London? And a fantastic variety of restaurants, shops, pubs, cafés – and a beautiful waterfront.
DON'T MISS LIVERPOOL ON YOUR NEXT TRIP TO THE UK!

B Look at the map of Liverpool on page 73. In the box below tick the places you can find on the map.

a road/street	a park	a square	traffic lights
a corner	a pedestrian street	a car park	
a crossroads			

C Work in pairs. Cover this page and take turns. Student A: point at one of the places above on the map. Student B: say the place.

FUNCTION

GIVING DIRECTIONS

2 A Match directions 1–8 with diagrams A–H.

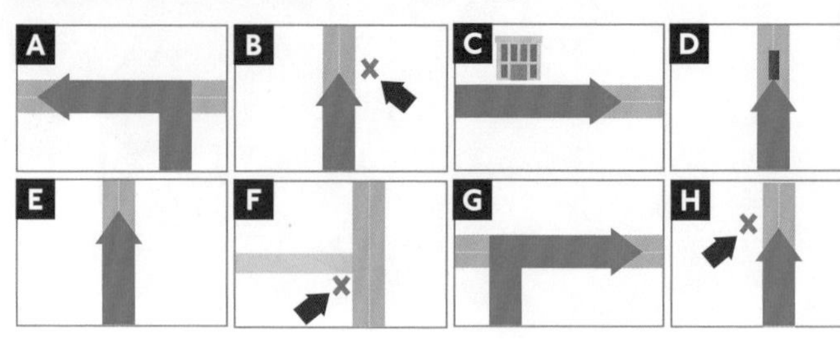

1 Turn right. *G*
2 Turn left.
3 Go straight on.
4 Go past the cinema.
5 Stop at the traffic lights.
6 It's on the corner.
7 It's on the right.
8 It's on the left.

B 7.6 Listen and check. Then listen and repeat.

3 A 7.7 Look at the map and find 'Start here'. Listen to a woman asking for directions. Write the letter (A–M) for:

1 The Beatles Story Museum
2 The cinema

B 7.8 Listen again. How does the woman ask for directions? Complete the conversations.

W: Excuse me.
M: Yes.
W: [1]______ you [2]______ me [3]______ ______ ______ the Beatles Story?
M: Yeah. You go straight on here.
W: Excuse me. [4]______ ______ a cinema [5]______ here?
M: Erm. Let me think. Yes, there's a cinema in Liverpool One.

C Listen again and underline the stressed words in the woman's sentences. Then listen and repeat.

D 7.9 Number the directions to Liverpool One in order. Then listen again and check.

a) the cinema is on the left
b) go past the big car park
c) go straight on here *1*
d) go straight on at the traffic lights
e) you can't miss it
f) turn right at the traffic lights
g) there's a pedestrian street

▷ page 140 LANGUAGEBANK

4 Work in pairs. Student A: look at page 165. Student B: look at page 168.

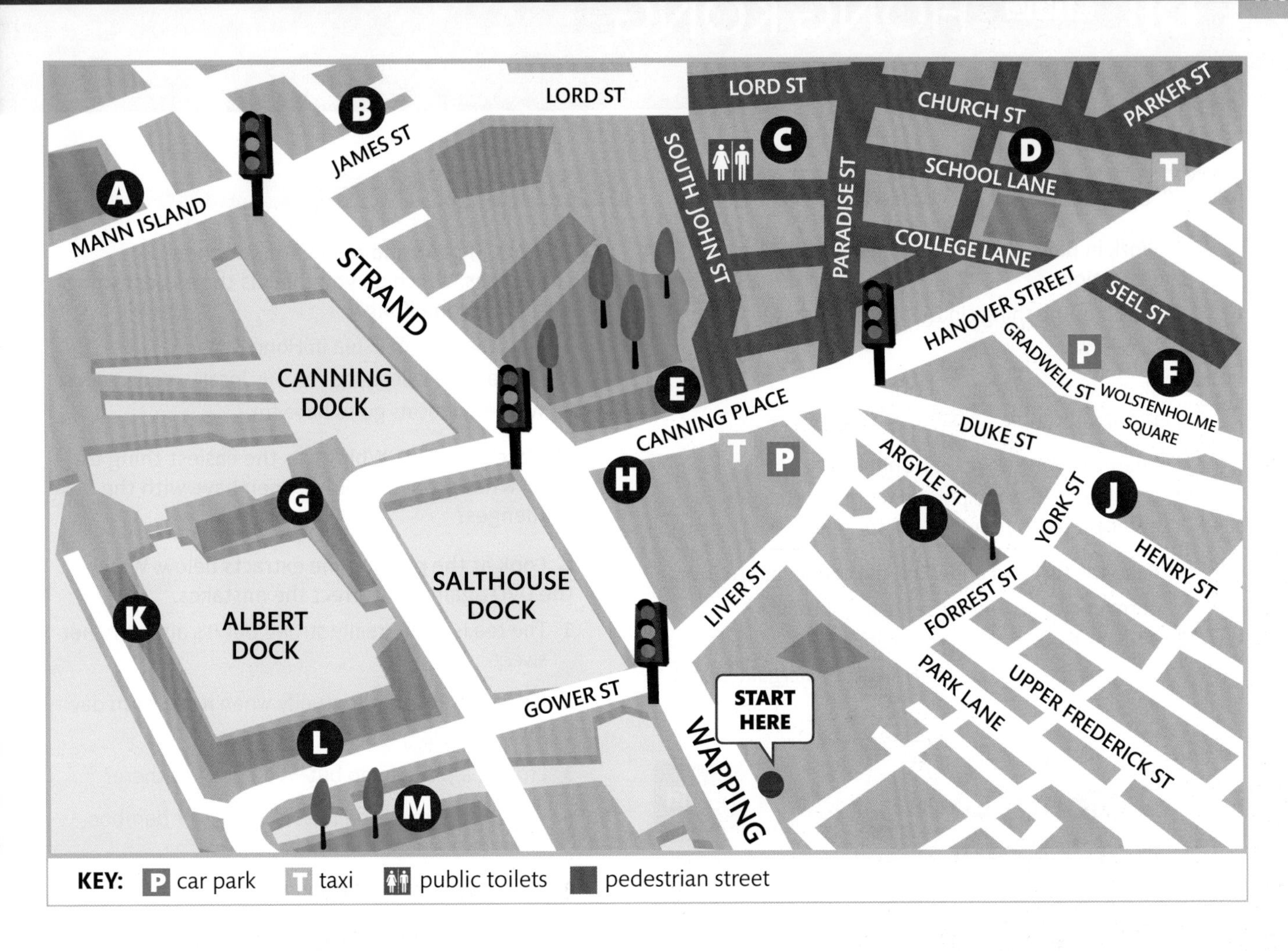

LEARN TO

CHECK AND CORRECT DIRECTIONS

5 A Read the extracts. How does the woman check the directions? Underline the phrases she uses.

M: You go straight on here, and can you see those traffic lights?
W: Yes.
M: Well, turn left at the traffic lights.
W: Turn left?
M: Yes … and the Beatles Story is on your right …
W: Thanks. So, it's left at the traffic lights and then past some water and then it's on the right, at Alba … ?
M: Albert Dock.
W: Albert Dock. Right, thanks.

M: And then you can see Liverpool One in front of you. You can't miss it. It's really big.
W: Can I just check the first part? So straight on here, then turn left at the traffic lights.
M: No, turn right.
W: Turn right and go straight on.
M: Yes.

B 7.10 **SENTENCE STRESS: correcting** Look at the conversation extracts below. Listen and underline the stressed words in B's answers.

1 **A:** Turn left.
B: No, turn right.
2 **A:** So it's in Wood Road.
B: No, it's in Wood Street.
3 **A:** So it's in College Lane.
B: No, it's in School Lane.
4 **A:** So it's past the traffic lights.
B: No, past the park.

C Listen again and repeat B's answers.

speakout TIP

When you want to correct a mistake, you can use stress. Remember to say the correct word higher, LOUDER and l o n g e r.
Is it fifty-two High Street? *No, it's **thirty**-two.*

D Work in pairs and take turns. Student A: look at page 167. Student B: look at page 163.

SPEAKING

6 Work in pairs. Student A: choose a starting point on the map and give directions to one of the places (A–M). Student B: listen and follow the directions. Check you understand everything.

HONG KONG

DVD PREVIEW

1 A Work in pairs. Look at the page and answer the questions.

1 Which of the things in the box can you see on the page?

a skyscraper karaoke a tram a shopping centre a bamboo steamer

2 What can you see/do in Hong Kong?
3 Which activities are popular in Hong Kong a) for tourists b) for locals c) for both?

B Read the text and underline the correct alternative.

1 Carmen is a *new/business/travel* journalist.
2 She has *two/three/four* questions.
3 She gets information from *local people/guidebooks and tourists.*

Going Local: Hong Kong

In *Going Local*, BBC journalists go to cities around the world and try to see the city through the eyes of a local person. In this programme, travel journalist Carmen Roberts is in Hong Kong. She has three questions or challenges* and she travels around the city to find the answers. There are two rules: no guidebooks and no tourists – so Carmen can only ask local people for help. Join Carmen as she leaves the skyscrapers, shopping centres and tourist places and tries to get to the heart of Hong Kong.

*a challenge = a difficult but exciting activity or task

DVD VIEW

2 A Work in pairs and read Carmen's three challenges. Which do you think is the easiest thing to find in Hong Kong?

1 Find the best milk tea in Hong Kong.
2 Find a shop where you can buy locally made goods.
3 Where do locals go to have fun?

B Watch the DVD. Which was the easiest thing to find? What problems did Carmen have with the challenges?

C Look at the programme extracts below. Watch the DVD again and correct the mistakes.

1 The tea is really, really strong but it's also very ~~hot~~. *sweet*
2 It's quite refreshing actually when it's a warm day here in Hong Kong.
3 I found a place to go but when do I get there?
4 Look at the rows and rows and rows of bamboo baskets, as far as the eye can look.
5 How long does it take you to finish one?
6 What do you do for friends?
7 There's a place like right next door actually called Blue MR or something.
8 Pick a song that you can definitely hear, a classic.

3 Work in pairs and answer the questions.

1 For you, what is the most interesting thing to do or to see in Hong Kong?
2 Can you think of two other challenges to give Carmen?
3 Do you think Hong Kong is a good place to visit? Why/Why not?

speakout a city challenge

4 A Work in pairs and read the questions. Tick one question you would like to answer for a town/city you know.

1 Where do locals go to have fun?
2 Where is there a walk that tourists don't know about?
3 Where can you find great street food?
4 Where can you see something tourists never see?
5 Where can you take the best photo in the town/city?

B Answer the questions below about your challenge. Write notes not full sentences.

- Where is it?
- What can you find or see there?
- When is the best time to go there?
- Why do you like it?

C 7.11 Listen to a man talk about a place in his city. Which challenge in Exercise 4A does he speak about?

D Listen again. Which questions in Exercise 4B does he answer?

E Listen again and tick the key phrases you hear.

KEY PHRASES

It's in the [north/south/west/east] of London.
It's [near/next to …]
There are lots of …
It's got lots of …
You can [find/see/eat/…]
It's [the best place to/one of the best places to] …
Most tourists don't know about it.
Tourists [don't usually/often] go there.
It's really [interesting/delicious/fun/quiet/beautiful/…]

5 A Work in groups. Student A: answer the question you chose in Exercise 4A. Use the key phrases to help. Other students: ask some questions about the place.

B Which place or experience was the most interesting for you?

writeback a travel article

6 A Work in pairs and read the article. Which question in Exercise 4A does it answer? Which of the three places would you most like to visit?

My London

London is the capital of the UK. It's in the south-east of England on the River Thames. Tourists love its famous sites: Buckingham Palace, Big Ben, the wonderful art galleries and museums. But where do you go to escape the tourists? Here are three ideas:

1 **Little Venice** – This is a beautiful area in the north of London with water all around. It's a good place to sit, have a coffee and watch people on their houseboats.

2 **Sir John Soane's Museum** – John Soane was an architect and an art collector and in his house (the museum) there are many strange and amazing objects. Morning is the best time to go there – it's nice and quiet then.

3 **Temple Gardens** – These are some of my favourite gardens in London. They're in the centre of London near the River Thames in an area for lawyers and law companies. They're perfect for a walk or a picnic lunch especially in summer.

B Read the article again. For each place, which questions does the writer answer?

Where is it?
What can you see or do there?
When is a good time to visit?

C Write a website article about two or three places in your town/city which are away from the tourist centres. Use the ideas and phrases from Exercise 4 and the article above to help. Write 100–150 words.

V TRAVEL ADJECTIVES

1 A Complete the travel adjectives.

1 f_st
2 c_ld
3 sl_w
4 cr_wd_d
5 ch_ _p
6 _mpty
7 b_r_ng
8 c_mf_rt_bl_
9 n_ _sy
10 _nt_r_st_ng
11 h_t
12 q_ _ _t
13 _xp_ns_v_
14 _nc_mf_rt_bl_

B Work in pairs. Which adjectives in 1A describe …

… the building you are in now?
… your last weekend?
… your last holiday?
… your favourite café or restaurant?
… your favourite type of car?

G COMPARATIVES

2 A Look at the two ways of travelling from Moscow to Beijing. Write six sentences comparing them. Use adjectives from Exercise 1A.

China Airlines flight: €1,130, Business class, seven hours twenty minutes, two meals, two movies

Trans-Siberian Railway: €590 second class, seven days, four beds per compartment, restaurant on train

The train is cheaper than the plane.

B Work in pairs and discuss. Which way of travelling from Moscow to Beijing is better: the train or the plane? Why?

V PLACES

3 Work in pairs. Look at the words in the box below and find one place:

1 where you can swim.
2 with a lot of trees.
3 where people live.
4 where you can buy things.
5 that's hot in the day and cold at night.
6 that is high.
7 that tourists often visit.
8 that usually has a name.

a mountain a village a desert a lake a hill a market a river a forest a famous building

G SUPERLATIVES

4 A Complete the quiz with superlatives of the adjectives in brackets.

City quiz

1 *The friendliest* (friendly) city in the world is:
a) Rio de Janeiro **b)** Cairo **c)** Kuala Lumpur

2 The world's ____________ (big) city is:
a) Seoul **b)** Mexico City **c)** Tokyo

3 ____________ (good) place to live is:
a) Zurich **b)** Vancouver **c)** Melbourne

4 ____________ (safe) city in the world is:
a) Vienna **b)** Singapore **c)** Dublin

5 ____________ (beautiful) city is:
a) Cape Town **b)** Sydney **c)** Prague

6 ____________ (popular) tourist destination in the world is:
a) Spain **b)** the USA **c)** France

7 ____________ (fast)-growing cities in the world are in:
a) China **b)** Africa **c)** India

8 ____________ (busy) shopping street in the world is in:
a) London **b)** Hong Kong **c)** Shanghai

Key 1 a 2 c 3 b 4 a 5 a 6 c 7 b 8 a

B Work in pairs and do the quiz. Then check your answers in the key.

F GIVING DIRECTIONS

5 A Put the words in order. Start with the underlined words.

1 there / restaurant / here / Is / a / near?
2 corner / turn / Go / left / straight / at / on / the / and
3 bank / turn / Go / the / and / right / past
4 left / on / It's / the
5 the / at / Stop / crossroads
6 way / you / to / tell / the / Can / me / supermarket? / the
7 the / The / station / on / right / police / is
8 it / miss / can't / You

B Work in pairs and take turns. Student A: think of a place near where you are now. Give directions. Student B: guess the place.

A: Go out of the main entrance and turn left …

HAVING A GREAT TIME p78

WHAT A DIFFERENCE! p80

WHAT DO YOU RECOMMEND? p82

CHANGING TRENDS p84

SPEAKING **8.1** Talk about what people are doing **8.2** Describe people's appearance **8.3** Ask for and give recommendations **8.4** Talk about a survey on trends

LISTENING **8.2** Listen to people talk about actors **8.4** Watch an extract from a BBC programme about changing shopping trends

READING **8.1** Read research about language people use on social networking sites

WRITING **8.1** Improve your use of pronouns; Write comments on a photo **8.4** Write a summary of a survey

BBC INTERVIEWS

What was the last film you saw?

8.1 HAVING A GREAT TIME

G present continuous
P weak forms: prepositions and articles
V verbs + prepositions

1 Researchers from Penn University looked at over fifteen million Facebook messages, and tried to answer some questions: Do men and women use different words in their messages? How is the language of a younger and older person different? They found some surprising things.

2 The researchers studied messages from over 75,000 people. They looked at the language in the messages and also the most popular topics for messages.

3 They found some big differences between men and women. Women use more adjectives and phrases for feelings, for example: 'excited', 'wonderful', 'love you' and <3, the emoticon for a heart. They often talk about family and friends.

4 Men talk about sport, computers, game consoles and videos (Xbox and YouTube are popular). They also often use swear words. It's interesting that men use 'my wife' and 'my girlfriend' more than women. Women often put 'amazing' in front of 'husband' or 'boyfriend'.

5 And what about age? It isn't surprising that thirteen- to eighteen-year-old kids talk about school a lot ('school', 'homework', 'English') but people from twenty-three to twenty-nine speak about work ('at work', 'new job', 'office'). Older people are more interested in family and friends and their favourite words are 'son', 'daughter', 'my kids' and 'friends'.

6 So, let's see how the research works for us. Look at these messages from two friends. What can you say about the writers?

"Wonderful birthday! Katya brought me breakfast in bed this morning and now Yuri is cooking dinner (tomato pasta). I'm lucky to have such a lovely family."

"I'm having a great time here in Brazil with my girlfriend. We're relaxing by the swimming pool AND Brazil won the football last night! Life is perfect. Thinking about you all in the office! See you next week."

READING

1 **Work in pairs and discuss. Which alternative is true for you?**

1 I take photos with *my camera/my mobile/my camera and mobile.*
2 My favourite subjects are *people/places.*
3 I put my photos *online/in a book.*
4 I write comments on the photos in *English/my language.*

2 A **Read the introduction to the article (paragraph 1) and choose the best title.**

Your age, your personality
Women talk more than men
Your words, your identity

B **Work in pairs. Match the people in A to the language in B.**

A People	B Words people use
1 women	a) 'daughter'
2 men	b) 'at work'
3 teenagers	c) 'homework'
4 people in their 20s	d) '<3' (= ♥)
5 people from 30 to 65	e) 'YouTube'

C **Read paragraphs 2–5 and check your ideas.**

D **Read paragraph 6 and answer the writer's question. Check your answer on page 168.**

E **Work with other students. Do you agree with the research? Is it true for you or your friends?**

GRAMMAR

PRESENT CONTINUOUS

3 A **Complete the table. Use examples from the messages.**

Yuri	______ <u>cooking</u>	dinner.
I	______ ______	a great time.
We	______ ______	by the swimming pool.

B **Underline the correct alternative to complete the rule.**

RULES
Use the present continuous to talk about your life *every day/at this moment.*
Make the present continuous with subject + ______ + verb + - ______.

C 8.1 **Complete the questions with *'s* or *are*. Then listen and check.**

1 What ______ you thinking about?
2 What ______ he doing?

D **Listen again and underline the stressed words. Then listen and repeat.**

▷ page 142 LANGUAGEBANK

VOCABULARY

VERBS + PREPOSITIONS

5 A Complete the sentences. Check in the reading.

They also looked ______ the language.
Men often talk ______ sport.

B Underline the correct alternative.

1 think *about/on* a problem
2 listen *with/to* the radio
3 take a photo *of/about* a friend
4 wait *to/for* a train
5 read *on/about* a film star
6 chat *with/from* a friend
7 talk *for/on* the phone
8 ask *about/to* pronunciation

C 8.2 **WEAK FORMS: prepositions and articles** **Listen and check. Notice the weak sound of the prepositions and articles. Then listen and repeat.**

D Work in pairs and take turns. Student A: say a verb from Exercises 5A and 5B. Student B: say the whole verb phrase. Then add other possible nouns.

A: *think*
B: *think about a problem, think about a person*

4 A Match photos A–C with comments 1–3.

1 Great party! The kids *are dancing* in the garden and we ______ the beautiful spring day. I ______ with Laura's mum and we ______ another piece of cake.
2 Don't come to Rome in summer! We ______ for the museum to open. My husband ______ pictures of the buildings and the crowd. I ______ very bored.
3 We ______ to Sarah and Jeff – they ______ a new CD at the studio. I <3 Sarah's voice! She ______ and Jeff ______ guitar, and they sound great!

B Complete the comments above with verbs from the box.

~~dance~~ chat eat enjoy feel listen make play sing take wait

C Work in pairs. Student A: choose a person from one of the photos. Student B: ask *yes/no* questions in the present continuous and guess who it is.

A: *It's a man.*
B: *OK. Is he standing in a queue?*
A: *No, he isn't.*

D Work in pairs and take turns. Write the names of three people you know. What are they doing now?

My friend Julia lives in Sydney. I think she's getting up now.

SPEAKING

6 Work in pairs. Student A: look at page 165. Student B: look at page 168.

WRITING

PRONOUNS

7 A Match this comment with one of the comments in Exercise 4A.

I saw them at a club last week. They were great – and her voice IS amazing!

B Read the comment above again. Write the people's names under the pronouns *them, they* and *her*.

C Read more comments below. Use pronouns to replace the underlined phrases.

Where did you take the photo of ~~Sarah and Jeff~~ *them*?

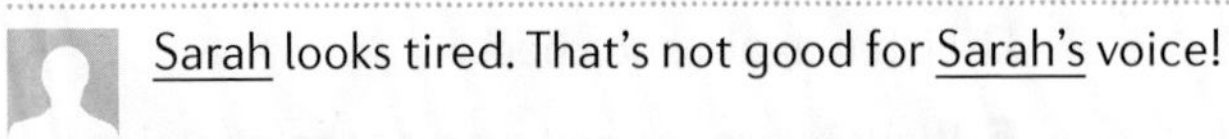
Sarah looks tired. That's not good for Sarah's voice!

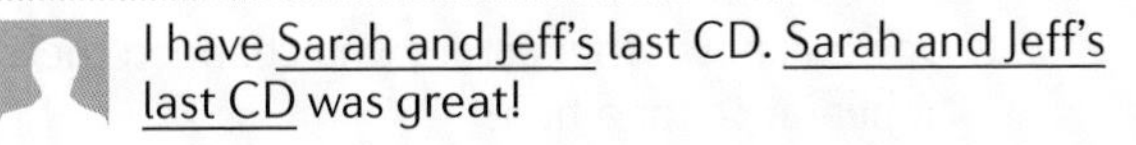
I have Sarah and Jeff's last CD. Sarah and Jeff's last CD was great!

D Write a comment to go with a photo. Write two or three sentences and use pronouns.

E Swap your message with other students. Write a new comment about their photos.

8.2 WHAT A DIFFERENCE!

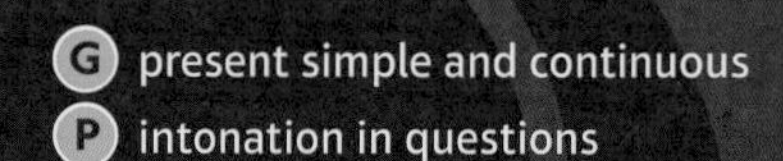

A Christian Bale, *American Hustle*

B Christian Bale, *Batman Begins*

LISTENING

1 A Look at the photos. Do you know the actors or the films? For which films did they lose weight? For which films did they put on weight?

B 8.3 Listen to the conversation and number the photos in the order the people talk about them.

C Work in pairs and discuss. What do the speakers say about these things?

D Listen again and check.

E Work in groups and discuss the questions.

1 Do you know other actors who changed their appearance for a film?
2 What are good and bad things about losing and putting on weight for a job?
3 Would you like to do it?

VOCABULARY

APPEARANCE

2 A Work in pairs. Look at the photos and answer the questions. Write the letter (A–E).

1 Who is:
a) very thin? *E*
b) slim?
c) a little overweight?
d) in his/her thirties?
e) wearing make-up?
f) wearing black?

2 Who has got:
a) long blonde hair?
b) short brown hair?
c) a beard?
d) a moustache?
e) glasses?

B 8.4 Listen to a man describing two of the photos. Which two is he talking about?

C Listen again and write the questions. Use the prompts to help.

1 Is / man / or / woman?
2 What / she / look like?

page 159 **PHOTOBANK**

D 8.5 **INTONATION IN QUESTIONS** Listen again. Which question goes down? Which question goes up then down?

E Work in pairs and take turns. Look at the jobs vocabulary on page 153. Student A: choose one of the people and describe him or her. Student B: ask questions and guess the person.

C Renée Zellweger, Bridget Jones's Diary
D Renée Zellweger, Leatherheads
E Christian Bale, The Machinist

GRAMMAR

PRESENT SIMPLE AND CONTINUOUS

3 A Look at the sentences and underline the verbs. Which tenses are they?

1 She's wearing make-up.
2 He changes his appearance for every film.

B Underline the correct alternative to complete the rules.

RULES	1 Use the *present simple/present continuous* for something we're doing now or around now. 2 Use the *present simple/present continuous* for something we do every day or usually.

C Complete the table with the verb *wear*.

What	______	you	usually ______	to work/ school?
What	______	you	______	now?

I	usually ______	a suit.
Now, I	______	jeans and a sweater.

4 A Look at the cartoons and discuss. What are the problems?

B Underline the correct alternatives below.

In an office, men usually [1]*wear/are wearing* dark suits, ties and shoes, but now Sam [2]*wears/'s wearing* jeans, a T-shirt and trainers. He [3]*doesn't wear/isn't wearing* a tie. Another problem is that today he [4]*wears/'s wearing* sunglasses and most businessmen [5]*don't wear/aren't wearing* sunglasses at work.

C Complete the information about the second cartoon.

Walkers [1]______ (not) usually [2]______ a suit; they usually [3]______ trousers and walking jackets. Today, Jenny [4]______ boots, but her boyfriend [5]______ sandals – dangerous on a country walk. Another problem is that he [6]______ (not) a backpack now, he [7]______ a suitcase!

▷ page 142 LANGUAGEBANK

SPEAKING

5 Work in pairs. Sit back-to-back. Student A: say six things you're wearing – four true and two false. Student B: say which things are true and which are false.

A: *I'm wearing a grey shirt.*
B: *True!*

6 A Work in pairs and discuss. What clothes do you usually/never wear for:

- a walk in the country?
- dinner at a friend's house?
- a job interview?
- meeting friends in a bar or club?
- a party?
- an exercise class?

B Work with a new partner. Student A: say the clothes you usually/never wear for the situations above. Student B: guess the situation.

A: *I usually wear jeans and a top. I never wear shorts.*
B: *A walk in the country?*

F recommending
P word stress; linking
V types of film

SPEAKING

1 A Complete the questionnaire below.

MOVIEWATCH

1 What was the last film you saw?
2 What's your favourite film?
3 Who is your favourite film actor?
4 Who is your favourite film actress?
5 Do you like watching films:
a) at home/at the cinema?
b) on TV/on your computer?
c) on your own/with someone?
d) only once/more than once?

B Work in pairs and compare your answers.

A
From the director of Pretty Woman comes a day in the life of love.
JESSICA ALBA KATHY BATES JESSICA BIEL BRADLEY COOPER
ERIC DANE PATRICK DEMPSEY HECTOR ELIZONDO
JAMIE FOXX JENNIFER GARNER TOPHER GRACE ANNE HATHAWAY
ASHTON KUTCHER QUEEN LATIFAH TAYLOR LAUTNER GEORGE LOPEZ
SHIRLEY MACLAINE EMMA ROBERTS JULIA ROBERTS TAYLOR SWIFT
VALENTINE'S DAY
2.12.10

B
DON'T
LET
GO
SANDRA BULLOCK
GEORGE CLOONEY
GRAVITY

C FIGHT DREAM HOPE LOVE
HUGH JACKMAN
RUSSELL CROWE
ANNE HATHAWAY
AMANDA SEYFRIED
HELENA BONHAM CARTER
Les Misérables
THE KING'S SPEECH

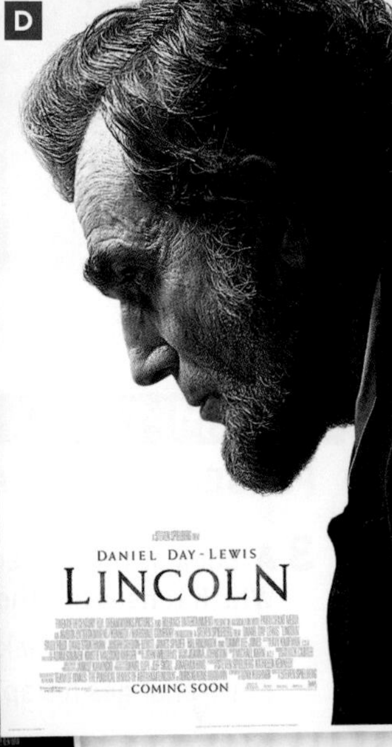

VOCABULARY

TYPES OF FILM

2 A Match the posters in pictures A–H with the types of film in the box.

~~a romantic film~~ *A* a horror film a drama a comedy an animated film a musical an action film a sci-fi film

B Complete the sentences with the types of film.

1 People fall in love in *a romantic film*.
2 There's a lot of singing and dancing in ______.
3 I laugh a lot when I watch ______.
4 ______ is usually about space travel or aliens.
5 ______ can be too scary for me.
6 There are usually a lot of guns and car chases in ______.
7 I often cry when I watch ______.
8 My four-year-old son's favourite film is ______.

C WORD STRESS Work in pairs. Find four types of film in Exercise 2A with the stress pattern Ooo. What are the stress patterns of the other types of film?

O o o
horror film

D 8.6 Listen and check.

E Work in pairs and discuss. Do you like the same films? Why/Why not? What kind of films don't you like? Why?

A: *What kind of films do you like?*
B: *I like musicals.*
A: *Oh, really? Why?*

"vastly entertaining and very funny"
"wonderful and vibrant"
"fresh and funny, joyful and life-affirming"
"a joy to behold"
★★★★★
Silver Bear 58
a mike leigh film
sally hawkins eddie marsan alexis zegerman
happy-go-lucky

ON IN THE AMAZO
G
Rio 2
APRIL 11

H
"SENSATIONAL!"
TRIBECA
LET
THE RIGHT ONE
IN
A FILM BY TOMAS ALFREDSON

FUNCTION

RECOMMENDING

3 A ▶ 8.7 Listen to two conversations. Which films from the posters do the people talk about?

B Listen again. In which conversation does someone talk about these topics? Write 1 or 2.

1. action films *1*
2. comedies
3. dramas
4. romantic films
5. horror films
6. sci-fi films
7. the acting
8. the photography

4 A Put the words in the correct order.

1. you / can / film / good / recommend / a?
2. like / of / kind / what / films / you / do?
3. *Gravity* / about / how?
4. don't / sci-fi / I / like / really / films.
5. know / you / *Happy-Go-Lucky* / do?
6. about / it / what's?
7. it / who's / in?
8. you'd / it / like / think / I.

B ▶ 8.8 Listen and check. Then listen and repeat.

C Look at the sentences in Exercise 4A. Who is asking for a recommendation? Write A. Who is giving a recommendation? Write G.

▷ page 142 **LANGUAGEBANK**

5 Work in pairs and take turns. Look again at the film posters A–H. Student A: ask your partner to recommend a film. Student B: recommend a film.

A: *I've got a long train journey this weekend. Can you recommend a good film?*
B: *Let me think. What kind of films do you like?*

LEARN TO

LINK WORDS TO SPEAK FASTER

6 A Read the flowchart and complete 1–6 with two words in each gap.

B ▶ 8.9 Listen and check your answers.

Student A
Can [1] __________ a good action film?
Student B
Let me think. [2] __________ *Unstoppable*? Do you [3] __________?
No, I don't think so. What's [4] __________?
Well it's about two guys on a train. And the train is travelling fast into a city and it can't stop.
Sounds good. Who's [5] __________?
Denzel Washington and Chris Pine.
Oh, I like Denzel Washington.
I enjoyed it a lot. I think you'd [6] __________. It's very exciting.

speakout TIP

Word linking can help your speaking sound more natural. Remember you can link the consonant at the end of one word and the vowel at the beginning of the next word, e.g. *I enjoye**d** **it** **a** lot.*

C LINKING Look at sentences 1–6 in Exercise 6A and draw the links between words.

D ▶ 8.10 Listen and repeat the sentences.

E Work in pairs and write ten key words to help you remember the conversation. Then close your books and practise the conversation.

7 A Work as a class and make a list of eight films. Write the titles in English or in your language.

B Work in pairs. Student A: choose one of the films and answer Student B's questions. Student B: ask questions from Exercise 6A. Guess the name of the film.

SPEAKING

8 Work with a new partner. Recommend one of your favourite films or a film you saw recently.

A: *One of my favourite films is …/Last week I saw …*
B: *What's it about?*

DVD PREVIEW

1 Underline the best alternative for you. Then work in pairs and discuss.

1 I prefer shopping *in small shops/in big shopping malls/online.*

2 The most important thing for me in shopping is *price/convenience/enjoyment.*

3 My shopping habits are *very/not very/a little* different from five to ten years ago.

2 Read the programme information and answer the questions.

1 What different types of shopping does the programme look at?

2 What kind of shop is the programme mostly about?

Robert Peston Goes Shopping

It's hard to believe that once upon a time everyone did their shopping in small shops. The small shop was once an important part of our lifestyle, a place to meet and talk. But things are very different today compared to fifty years ago, and life for small shops has been difficult. In this BBC programme, we look at different trends in shopping over the years, from shopping malls to hypermarkets and of course online shopping. We find out how small shops are trying to stay alive.

DVD VIEW

3 A Work in pairs. Write down one positive and one negative thing about (a) shopping in small shops and (b) shopping on the internet.

B Watch the programme. Does it mention any of your ideas?

C Which words and phrases does the programme use to talk about small shops and which about internet shopping? Write small shop (S) or internet (I) next to each one. Then watch the programme again and check your answers.

easy cold
like car showrooms
not just a place to shop
the fashion human

D Underline the correct alternative. Then watch the programme again and check.

1 It was the place where people met to *talk/chat* and find out the latest *news/information.*

2 Internet shopping became the *fashion/trend*, the way everyone wanted to shop.

3 Big shops and small shops are now more like car showrooms. Shoppers go there to look at, *feel/touch* and try on products.

4 They have to *offer/give* something that people can't get anywhere *else/at all.*

5 A lot of people don't want to sit at home and shop. They want the *feeling/lifestyle* that small shops can give.

4 Work in pairs and discuss. Does the programme make you feel more positive or negative about shopping in small shops? Do you think it's important for shopping to have a 'human side'?

speakout a survey on trends

5 A Work in pairs and choose two topics from the list to discuss. What's different about these things now compared to 5–10 years ago? Which things are changing the most?

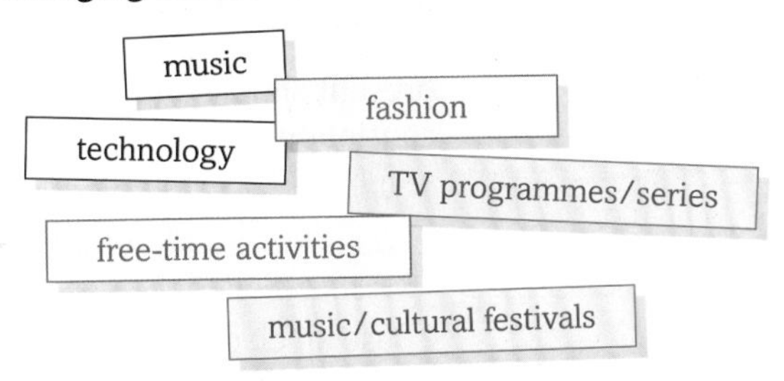

B 8.11 Listen to a man answer questions about festivals. What does he say about changes in price, security, fashion and technology? Make notes.

C Read the key phrases below. Then listen again and tick the ones you hear.

KEYPHRASES

Can I ask you a few questions?
What kind of [festivals] do you like?
[It's/They're] very popular at the moment.
How [are they/is it] different [now/from before/…]?
[Security/prices/…] is/are much [better/more expensive/cheaper/…] than before.
People like it because …
It depends on [the festival].
Years ago you couldn't always [get information on the internet].

6 A Work in pairs and choose one topic from Exercise 5A. Write 3–5 questions to ask other students about how this topic is different now from before.

B Talk to other students and ask your questions. Make notes on their answers.

C Tell the class three things that you found out in your survey.

writeback a summary of a survey

7 A Read this summary of the results of a class survey. Tick the opinions which are the same as the man's. Put an X by the ones that are different.

We asked everybody in our class about festival changes and trends. This is a summary of our results.

Everybody said they go to festivals. Most people go to rock music festivals, some go to folk music festivals, but only one of us goes to literature festivals.

We asked everyone about the changes in festivals. Here are the answers:

- **Price** – Everyone said festivals are more expensive than before.
- **Security** – Some people said there's no change. The rest of the group said there's much more security now than five years ago.
- **Fashion** – Some people didn't have an opinion about fashion at festivals. A few people said people wore more interesting and colourful clothes in the past.
- **Technology** – Two students said the biggest changes were in technology, but most of the group said there's no change. People found information and bought tickets on the internet five years ago, the same as now.

B Read the summary again. Underline phrases for talking about the whole group, and circle phrases for talking about part of the group.

C Write a summary of your survey results from Exercise 6B.

D Read other students' summaries. How is your opinion on a topic different from the whole group's?

G PRESENT CONTINUOUS

1 A Complete the sentences. Use the present continuous of the verbs in brackets.

1 It ______. (rain)
2 A plane ______ over the building. (fly)
3 Someone ______ and reading. (sit)
4 Students ______. (talk)
5 Someone ______ on his/her computer. (work)
6 People ______ past the building. (drive)
7 Children ______. (play)
8 Someone ______ a phone call. (make)

B Work in pairs. Which of the things above are happening outside your classroom at the moment?

V VERBS + PREPOSITIONS

2 A Write the missing preposition.

1 look ______ a painting
2 talk ______ a TV programme
3 take a photo ______ a friend
4 wait ______ a bus or train for a long time
5 think ______ food
6 read ______ a film
7 chat ______ an old friend
8 listen ______ music
9 talk ______ the phone in English
10 ask ______ grammar

B Work in pairs and take turns. When did you last do these things?

A: *When did you last look at a painting?*
B: *Last month. I went to the National Gallery and I looked at some paintings by Monet. What about you?*
A: *I never look at paintings!*

V APPEARANCE

3 A Complete the appearance words.

1 brown, blond, bla_ _ or re_ hair
2 sh_ _ _ hair or lo_ _ hair
3 a mou_ _ _ _ _ _ or a bea_ _
4 gl_ _ _es
5 wearing ma_ _-up
6 brown or blue ey_ _
7 very th_ _ or a little ove_ _ _ _ _ _ _
8 in his or her twent_ _ _ or thirt_ _ _

B Work in pairs. Use the prompts below to make questions.

Is he or she ... ?
Has he or she got ... ?

C Work with other students and take turns. One student: look at the photos on pages 58 and 59. Choose one and close your book. Other students: Ask *yes/no* questions and guess which photo the student chose.

4 A What are the clothes? Add the vowels.

1 trainers
2 j_ _ns
3 T-sh_rt
4 sh_ _s
5 tr_ _s_rs
6 j_ck_t
7 s_cks
8 sk_rt
9 t_p

B Work in pairs. Student A: say an item of clothing. Student B: say the name of a person in the class who is wearing it.

G PRESENT SIMPLE AND PRESENT CONTINUOUS

5 A Write questions about students in your class. Use the present simple and present continuous.

1 wear glasses (*usually/today*)
Does Mia usually wear glasses? Is she wearing them today?
2 use an electronic dictionary (*usually/now*)
3 chew gum (*often/at the moment*)
4 speak English (*always in class/now*)
5 wear black (*often/today*)

B Work in pairs and take turns. Ask and answer the questions.

F RECOMMENDING

6 A Write the missing words to complete the conversation. One word is missing from each line.

A: I haven't got anything to read. Can *you* recommend a good book?
B: How this book? *Doors of Stone*. It's sci-fi.
A: I don't really sci-fi.
B: What kind books do you like?
A: I travel books and romantic stories.
B: About *Life of Pi* by Yann Martel?
A: What it about?
B: It about a boy and a tiger on a boat.
A: That interesting.
B: I think you like it.

B Ask other students for book recommendations. Which of the books would you like to read?

9 transport

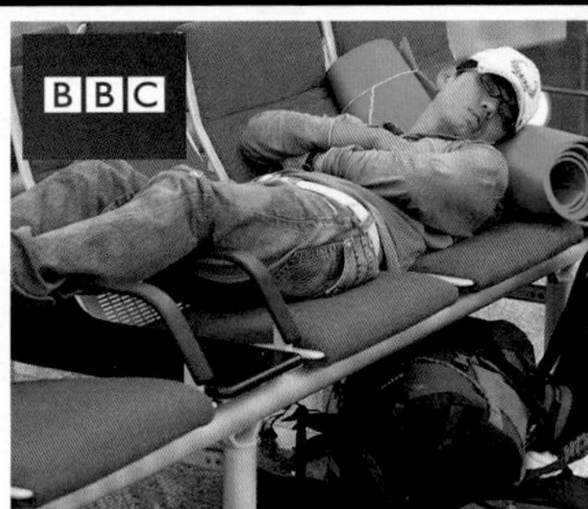

SPEAKING **9.1** Talk about transport in different cities **9.2** Talk about types of transport **9.3** Apologise for being late **9.4** Deal with problems when flying

LISTENING **9.2** Listen to a man talk about travelling for free **9.3** Listen to a woman talk about her problems getting to work **9.4** Watch an extract from a documentary about a day at Heathrow airport

READING **9.1** Read an article about Mexico City's EcoBici

WRITING **9.3** Write a story using linkers **9.4** Write a website entry about your experience at an airport

BBC INTERVIEWS

How do you get to work?

9.1 CITYBIKES

G can/can't, have to/don't have to
P word stress; weak sound /ə/
V adjectives

SPEAKING

1 Work in pairs and discuss.

1 Is there a lot of traffic where you live?
2 When is the worst time to travel?
3 Do you prefer to travel around your town/city by car, by public transport, by bike or on foot? Why?

VOCABULARY

ADJECTIVES

2 A Circle three adjectives to complete the sentence:

Cycling in the city is ...

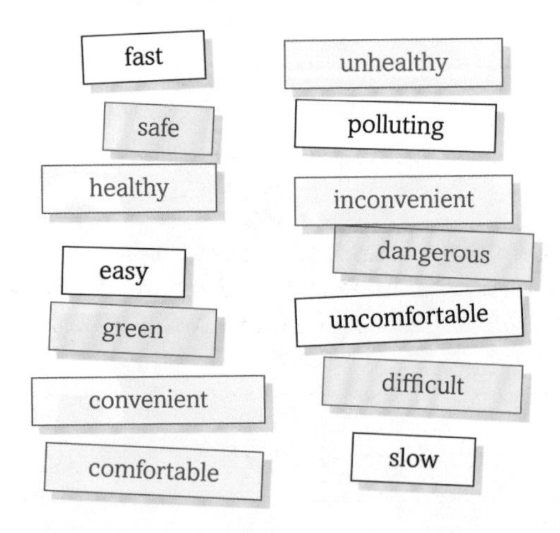

B Match each adjective with its opposite.

fast – slow

C 9.1 Listen and check.

D WORD STRESS Listen again and underline the stressed syllable.

speakout TIP

Look in your dictionary to find the pronunciation of new words. *Longman WordWise Dictionary* shows the word stress with a ' before the main stress, e.g. /'dɪfɪkəlt/ *difficult*. Find *dangerous* in your dictionary. How does it show stress?

E Work in pairs. Student A: you like cycling in the city. Student B: you like driving. Discuss which is better and why.

A: *Driving is faster.*
B: *It depends. In the mornings cycling is often faster because of the traffic jams!*

MEXICO'S BIKE REVOLUTION

It's a quiet Sunday morning on the city's Avenida Reforma. On weekdays there are tens of thousands of cars here, but today there's not one car. In 2007, Mexico City closed its main road to cars on Sundays. That was the first big step towards becoming a bike-friendly city, and three years later, in 2010, it started a new bike sharing system, the 'EcoBici'.

Now, with over 4,000 bikes, 276 cycle stations, and 87,000 users, Mexico City has one of the most successful bike share systems in the Americas. Cyclists can take a bike from one cycle station and leave it at any other station in the city between the hours of 6.00a.m. and 00.30a.m. Users have to be over sixteen and pay 300 pesos by credit or debit card for a year's use. They don't have to pay anything for the first forty-five minutes of each journey.

Forty-nine-year-old businessman Mateo Reyes likes the scheme. 'I only use my car when I'm too tired to cycle, but I go by bike when the traffic is bad. And the traffic is almost always bad.' But he thinks it will take some time before cyclists and drivers learn to be happy sharing Mexico City's roads.

READING

3 A Look at the photo of EcoBici, the bike share system in Mexico City. Write four questions with *how much*, *how many*, *who* and *where*.

1 How much _does it cost_?
2 How many ________?
3 Who ________?
4 Where ________?

B Read the article. Did you find the answers to your four questions?

C Are the sentences true (T) or false (F)? Change the false sentences so that they are true.

1 The Avenida Reforma has no cars on Sunday afternoons.
2 You always take and leave the bicycle in the same place.
3 You can't get an EcoBici bike at 2a.m.
4 It costs nothing for one hour's cycling.
5 Mateo Reyes always uses a bike.
6 Rafael thinks driving a taxi is more difficult now.

D Work in pairs and discuss. Is this kind of bike system a good idea for your town/city? Why/Why not?

Not everyone likes the EcoBicis. 'There are more and more cyclists on the road, and that's not so good,' says Rafael, a taxi driver. 'We have to be extra-careful now. They ride in the middle of the traffic, they go too fast. It's dangerous for everyone.'

GRAMMAR

CAN/CAN'T, HAVE TO/DON'T HAVE TO

4 A Underline the correct alternative. Then check your answers in the article.

1 You *can/can't* leave the bike at any cycle station in the city.
2 A fifteen-year-old kid *can/can't* use the bikes.
3 Users *have to/don't have to* pay by debit or credit card.
4 Users *have to/don't have to* pay for the first forty-five minutes.

B Match sentences 1–4 above with meanings a)–d).

a) It's necessary. **c)** It's OK.
b) It's not necessary. **d)** It's not OK.

C Complete the table below.

Adults	*can*	use	the bikes.
Children	______	______	the bikes.
Users	*have* ______	give	their credit card details.
You	______ have to	______	for the first forty-five minutes.

D 9.2 **WEAK SOUND /ə/ Listen to sentences 1–4. Circle the correct pronunciation. When do we use the weak sound /ə/?**

1 /kən/ /kæn/ 3 /hæftu:/ /hæftə/
2 /kənt/ /kɑ:nt/ 4 /dəʊnthæftu:/ /dəʊnthæftə/

E Listen again and check. Then listen and repeat.

5 A Complete the sentences with *can/can't, have to/don't have to*.

1 You ______ go by car, bus or taxi to get to the airport.
2 You ______ drive on the left in the UK.
3 You ______ drive in the town centre, so come by bus. You ______ usually find a free seat on the bus.
4 You ______ be seventeen or over to drive in Spain.
5 You ______ use your mobile when you drive. It's dangerous!
6 You ______ wear a seatbelt in your car – the driver and all the passengers.
7 You ______ wear a helmet on bikes, but it's safer if you wear one.
8 You ______ park here for free between eleven and three. Other times you ______ pay.

B Work in pairs. Which sentences are true for your town/city?

▷ page 144 **LANGUAGEBANK**

SPEAKING

6 A Work in groups. Student A: look at page 164. Student B: look at page 162. Student C: look at page 167. Complete the table below with information about each city's tourist card.

	The Amsterdam card	The Madrid card	The Prague card
Price			
Transport			
Entry to museums, etc.			
Other			

B Work in groups. Ask and answer questions to complete the information about the other cities. Which city has got the best tourist card system?

I think Prague has got the best system because it's the cheapest.

C Work in pairs. Talk about travelling in two or three towns/cities you know. Which one has got the best transport system?

A: *How is the transport system in your city?*
B: *Well, you can buy a travel card for the metro and buses, but sometimes it's faster to walk!*
A: *Why's that?*

9.2 FREE RIDE

- **G** articles: *a/an*, *the*, no article
- **P** weak forms: *a*, *an*, *the*
- **V** transport collocations

VOCABULARY

TRANSPORT COLLOCATIONS

1 A Work in pairs. Cover the word webs below and look at the photos. What types of transport can you see?

B Write a list of eight more types of transport. Then check in the photo bank.

▷ page 160 **PHOTOBANK**

2 A Look at the word webs below and cross out the type of transport that does not go with the verb. Then add a correct type of transport to each word web.

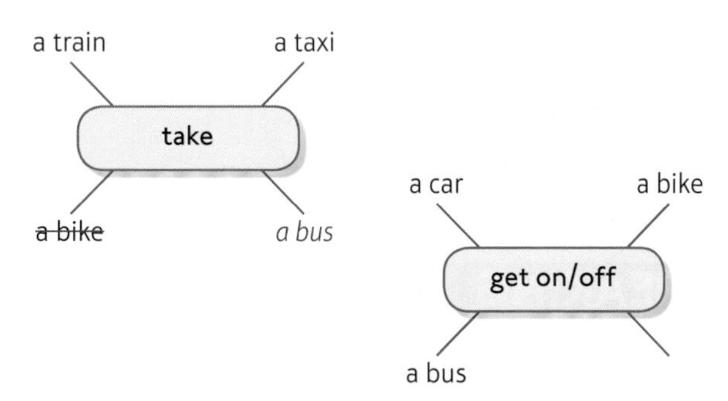

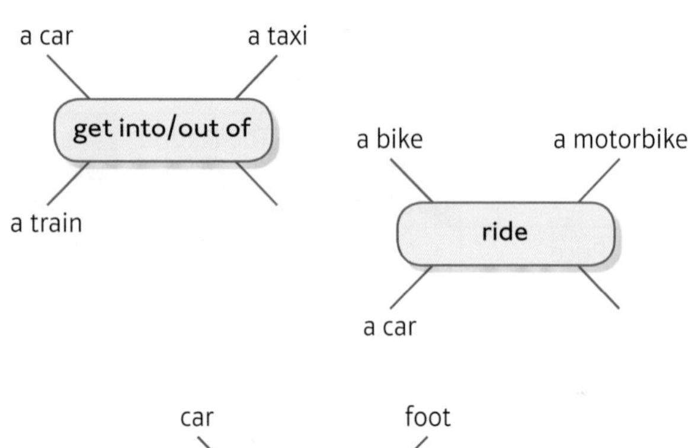

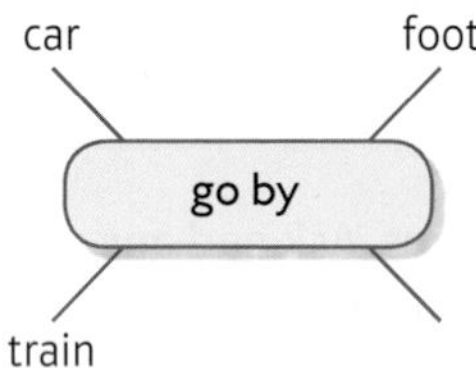

B Work in pairs and take turns. Student A: say a type of transport. Student B: say the verbs that can go with it.

A: bike
B: go by bike, get on a bike, ride a bike …

C Work in pairs and discuss.

1. How do you usually get to work/school?
2. What's your favourite type of transport? Why?
3. Which types of transport don't you like using? Why not?

D Choose one of the questions and ask other students. How many gave the same answer as you?

LISTENING

3 A Work in pairs and discuss.

1. How many different ways can you travel by road in your country?
2. Which is the most expensive, travelling by road, by rail or by water?
3. Is it possible to travel for free?

B ▶ 9.3 Listen to the conversation and answer the questions.

1. Which types of transport do the people talk about?
2. How did the man travel for free?

C Listen again. Write one good thing and one bad thing about each way of travelling for free.

D Work in pairs and discuss. Which of the two ways of travelling would you like to try? Why?

GRAMMAR

ARTICLES: *A/AN, THE,* NO ARTICLE

4 A 9.4 **Listen to an extract from the conversation and complete the text with *a/an, the,* - (no article).**

But they needed their car in [1]_____ Los Angeles. So they went by [2]_____ plane, and I drove their car to Los Angeles, to their hotel in [3]_____ city centre. I had [4]_____ week to get there. I stopped in [5]_____ Grand Canyon on [6]_____ way. It was [7]_____ best journey ever – I love driving and I love [8]_____ cars.

B Find examples for rules a)–g) from the text above.

RULES

a) Usually use *a/an* before countable singular nouns:
I've got a car. 4

b) Usually use no article before plural nouns:
I don't like buses. __

c) Usually use no article before cities and countries:
Madrid is in Spain. __

d) Use no article in some phrases:
by bus, on foot, at work, on holiday __

e) Usually use *the* before nouns when there's only one:
the moon, the Eiffel Tower __

f) Use *the* in some phrases:
in the morning, on the right, on the metro __

g) Use *the* in superlatives:
the most beautiful, the worst __

C 9.5 **WEAK FORMS: *a, an, the*** **We usually pronounce *a* /ə/, *an* /ən/ and *the* /ðə/ in phrases/ sentences. Listen and write the four sentences you hear. Then listen again and repeat.**

1 ______
2 ______
3 ______
4 ______

5 A Work in pairs and complete the sentences. Use *a/an, the* or - (no article).

1 I like travelling by __-__ train and I love going by _____ car.
2 Last year I was on _____ holiday in _____ US.
3 There was _____ family in _____ New York.
4 I had _____ week, so I stopped in a few _____ places.
5 I have _____ friends there.
6 Is that _____ longest journey?
7 It's _____ city in _____ Kenya.
8 In _____ evenings I loved watching _____ sun go down.

B Check your answers in audio script 9.3 on page 174.

6 A Look at questions 1–5. Choose one of the endings and write a short answer.

1 How do you get *to school/to work/home?*
By car.
2 What are three things *you like/you don't like/you liked when you were a child?*
3 What's a famous city in *India/China/Africa?*
4 When do you *check your emails/do your homework/relax?*
5 What's the name of *the President of the USA/the student next to you/the teacher?*

B Work in pairs and take turns. Student A: read your answers to the questions above. Student B: close your book and guess the question.

A: *By car.*
B: *How do you get to school?*
A: *No.*
B: *How do you get to work?*
A: *Yes!*

speakout TIP

When you write a noun in your notebook, put it in a short phrase. This shows how to use the word with the articles *a/an, the* or no article. For example: *in the city centre, he's a doctor, I like cats.*

▷ page 144 **LANGUAGEBANK**

SPEAKING

7 A Read the information about transport in different places. Circle the ones that are the same in your country. Tick the ones you think are good ideas.

Believe it or not!

1 In Cuba all government cars, vans and lorries have to pick up hitchhikers.
2 There is no speed limit on autobahns (motorways) in Germany.
3 In Milan, Italy, you have to pay to drive in the city centre.
4 In Zermatt, Switzerland, you can't drive a petrol car, only electric.
5 You can't sleep in your car in some cities in the USA.
6 On some airlines you can use your mobile phone on the flight.
7 In Japan, there are women-only carriages on some trains.
8 In Bangladesh passengers often travel on the outside of the trains.

B Work in groups and discuss your ideas.

A: *This is interesting about Cuba. I think it's a good idea.*
B: *Yeah, some places don't have cheap transport.*
C: *In my country you can't hitchhike. It's illegal.*
B: *Do you hitchhike?*
A: *Yes, but not very often. When I was eighteen I …*

9.3)) SORRY I'M LATE

F apologising
P intonation in apologies
V excuses

VOCABULARY

EXCUSES

1 A Work in pairs and discuss. Are you often late for work, school or meetings? Why/Why not?

B Work in pairs and match 1–5 with a)–e) below.

1 I lost	**a)** broke down.
2 I missed	**b)** the alarm clock.
3 My car	**c)** the train.
4 The traffic	**d)** my keys.
5 I didn't hear	**e)** was bad.

C Look at the collocations above and write five more excuses with the words in the box.

the bus   my ticket   was terrible   my phone   didn't start

FUNCTION

APOLOGISING

2 A Look at these reasons for being late. Which one is the best reason? Which one is the worst?

Amazing excuses

We asked managers around the country what reasons their workers give for being late. Here are some of our favourites.

1 I'm very sorry I'm late. I thought today was Sunday, so I stayed in bed.
2 Sorry to be late. There was a long queue at the coffee shop. I brought you one – here.
3 I'm terribly sorry I'm late. My train hit a cow.
4 I'm really sorry I'm late. My son took my car keys to school, so I took the bus to his school to get them.
5 I'm so sorry I missed the meeting. I feel awful about it. I drove to my old office by mistake.
6 I'm afraid I didn't hear my alarm clock because I had ear plugs in.

B Look at reasons 1–6 again. Underline seven expressions for saying sorry and how you feel.

C ▶ 9.6 **INTONATION IN APOLOGIES** Listen and check. Does the voice sound high or low? Then listen and repeat.

D Look at the responses below. Is the manager happy (✓) or unhappy (✗) about the situation?

1 I don't believe you.
2 It's half past nine!
3 Don't worry about it.
4 That's OK. No problem.
5 Don't let it happen again.

▷ page 144 **LANGUAGEBANK**

3 A Work in pairs. Complete the conversation between a student and a teacher.

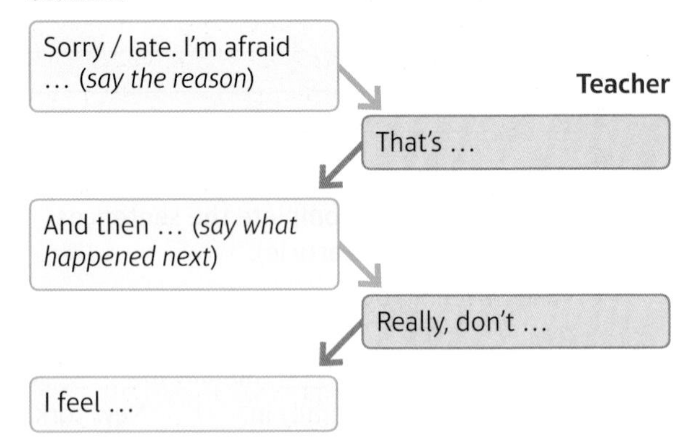
Student
Sorry / late. I'm afraid … (say the reason)
Teacher
That's …
And then … (say what happened next)
Really, don't …
I feel …

B Work in pairs and have another conversation. Apologise for being late and give a reason. Choose one of the pairs below.

a student – a teacher
a friend – a friend
a worker – a boss
a child – a parent
a husband – a wife

C Listen to other students' conversations. Guess their roles.

LEARN TO

TELL A LONG STORY

4 A **Look at the online diary extracts below. Why was the woman late each day?**

Monday: ____________________

Tuesday: ____________________

Wednesday: ____________________

Monday

The train left fifteen minutes late. But that wasn't the problem – it simply didn't go very fast. We really knew there was a problem when a man on a bike went faster than us! I was an hour late for work. The boss wasn't happy … but she doesn't take the train.

Tuesday

OK, I didn't hear my alarm so I woke up late and missed my train. I got the next one, but then the train stopped in the middle of nowhere … for twenty minutes! The guard said there was a signal problem and then the air-conditioning stopped working! Imagine, no air-conditioning in the middle of summer! I was two and a half hours late for work and really hot and sweaty. My boss was very unhappy.

Wednesday

Service: 0 points. Originality: 10 points. We stopped again, for no reason, but then there was a reason – not the signals, not the engine but a cow on the line! Poor thing, we didn't stop in time. This time, I was two hours late for work and my boss didn't believe me …

B 9.7 **Listen to the woman talk to a colleague. Which two days does she talk about?**

C **Listen again. Which two things are different from the online diary above?**

5 A **Look at the linkers in the box and circle them in the listening extract below.**

~~first of all~~ and but so finally because then after that

First of all I got up late because I didn't hear my alarm, so I only woke up at eight thirty. I ran to the train station – usually I walk – but I missed the train by two minutes! Then I waited for the next train, the nine fifteen, and everything was fine until we just stopped – just *stopped* – in the middle of nowhere. The guard said that there was a signal problem. After that, the air-conditioning stopped working. It was like an oven – at least a thousand degrees! Finally, after forty minutes, we started moving … very, very slowly.

B **Work in pairs and discuss.**

1 Which linkers do you use for the beginning and end of the story?
2 Which two linkers mean next in the story?

SPEAKING

6 A **EITHER: Imagine you are late for an important event, e.g. a wedding, a date with a boy/girlfriend, a job interview. OR: Think of a real situation when you were late. Make notes about five things that happened. Use these questions to help.**

- When was it?
- Where were you?
- What happened?
- What did you do?
- What happened finally?

B **Work in pairs and take turns. Student A: tell your story. Student B: show interest and ask follow-up questions.**

A: *This happened last year. I was on the way to Latvia and my plane was late.*

C **Write your story using your notes from Exercise 6A. Remember to use linkers.**

This happened last week. I was in …

DVD PREVIEW

1 Work in pairs and discuss. What are the good and bad things about airports and flying?

2 A Put the actions below in the correct order.

a) check in *1*
b) the plane takes off
c) go through security
d) wait in the departure lounge
e) get on the plane
f) go to the departure gate
g) do some tax-free shopping
h) go through passport control

B 9.8 Listen and check. Then listen and repeat.

C Work in pairs and take turns. Student A: say one of the actions in Exercise 2A. Student B: say the next action.

A: You check in and then you … ?
B: Go through security and then you … ?

3 Read the programme information and underline the correct alternative.

1 There's a *computer/weather* problem.
2 The programme is about the activities of *airline workers/passengers.*

Airport

BBC

Airport is a TV series about day-to-day life at one of the busiest international airports in the world, London Heathrow. In tonight's programme, there's a computer problem in air traffic control and flights are delayed for hours or cancelled. Hundreds of passengers have to wait in the crowded terminal, so the programme looks at how people are feeling and how they spend their time waiting.

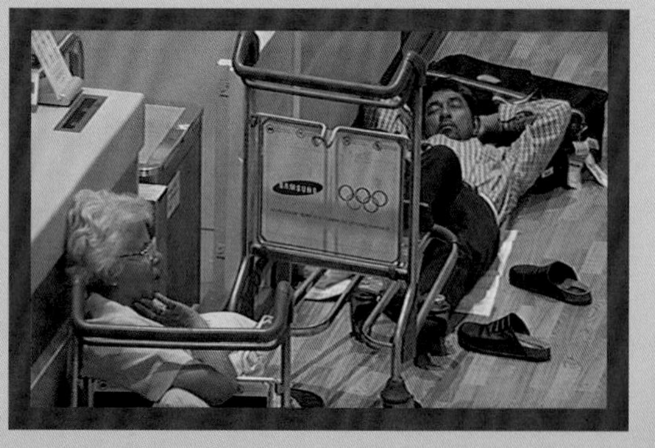

DVD VIEW

4 A Work in pairs and discuss. Which things 1–8 below do you do when you have to wait a long time at an airport? Which do you never do? What other things do you do?

1 stand in a queue
2 make phone calls
3 watch a film
4 have a snack
5 go outside
6 argue with airline workers
7 play a board game
8 sleep on the floor

B Watch the DVD. Tick the activities above you see.

C Watch again and match the person with the activity/activities.

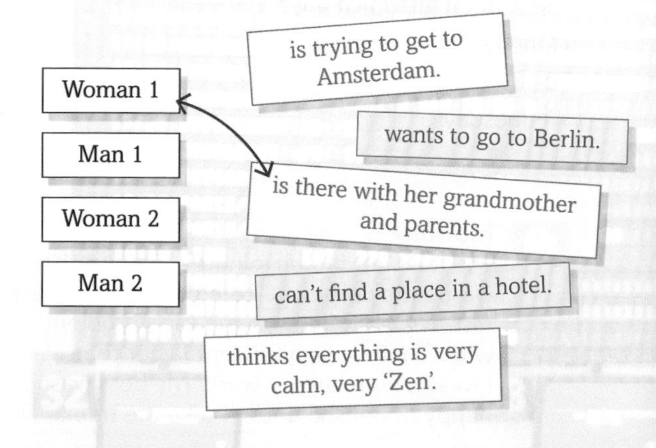

speakout deal with a problem

5 A **Work in pairs. Read problems 1–6 below and discuss. What are two solutions for each problem?**

At the airport:

1 Your baggage is too heavy, but you don't want to pay the €200 fee.
2 Your flight is delayed by twenty-four hours, and there's no place to sleep in the airport.
3 You arrive and go to get your luggage. Another passenger is walking out with your bag.

On the plane:

4 There's a screaming child in the seat behind you.
5 You ordered a vegetarian meal, but when your food arrives, it's chicken curry.
6 You can't sleep because a) you're cold and b) there's too much light.

B 9.9 **Listen to the conversation. Which problem does the passenger have? What solution does the person give?**

C **Listen again and tick the key phrases you hear.**

KEY PHRASES

There's a small problem here.
But it's very important that [I arrive on time].
You don't understand.
I see/understand, but …
Let me explain one more time.
It's your job to [bring me a meal].
Can I speak to the person in charge, please?

D **Work in pairs. Choose a problem from 5A and role-play the situation. Use the key phrases to help.**

writeback a website entry

6 A **Read the website about problems when flying. Which thing do you dislike the most?**

What do you hate about flying?

I hate it when …

… kids run around and scream. Why don't their parents ______ them?

… I'm in the middle seat, and the people on my right and left have a conversation. Why don't they ______ together?

… people stand up before the plane stops at the gate. Why don't they ______ in their seats?

B **Work in pairs and complete the questions in the text.**

C **Work in pairs and write three more things for the website list. Use these topics to help you with ideas.**

noise
kids
food/drink
electronics
luggage
couples
music/movies
smells

D **Add a question to each of your three ideas.**

E **Read the other students' lists and make a class list together.**

Ⓥ ADJECTIVES

1 A What are the adjectives? Add the vowels. Then match them with their opposites.

1 sl_w	comfortable
2 p_ll_t_ng	easy
3 d_ng_r_ _s	fast
4 d_ff_c_lt	green
5 _nh_ _lthy	healthy
6 c_nv_n_ _nt	inconvenient
7 _nc_mf_rt_bl_	safe

B Work in pairs. Which adjectives from Exercise 1A could you use to talk about 1–5?

1 A supermarket and a small local shop
2 Watching a film at home or at a cinema
3 A train and a car
4 Mineral water and tap water
5 Texting and phoning

C Work in pairs and discuss the topics above. Which of the two things do you like better?

A: *I like going to small shops because they're more convenient.*
B: *Really? I think a supermarket is more convenient because …*

Ⓖ CAN/CAN'T, HAVE TO/DON'T HAVE TO

2 A Complete the rules with the correct alternatives.

In a library …
1 you *can't/don't have to* talk on your mobile phone.
2 you *can't/don't have to* pay for a book before you take it out.

On a plane …
3 you *can/have to* wear a seatbelt when the plane takes off.
4 you *can't/don't have to* smoke.

At home …
5 you *can/have to* relax.
6 you *can't/don't have to* pay to eat.

B Choose three of the places below and write two sentences for each place. Use *can/can't, have to/don't have to.*

a restaurant
______
______

a classroom
______
______

a beach
______
______

a cinema
______
______

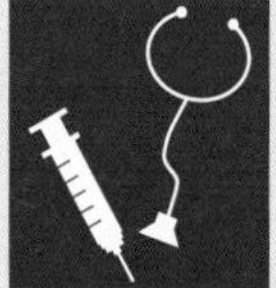

a hospital
______
______

a friend's house
______
______

C Work in pairs and take turns. Student A: read out your sentences. Student B: guess the place.

Ⓥ TRANSPORT COLLOCATIONS

3 A Write three types of transport that:

1 you can ride *a bike, …*
2 you can take
3 you can get on and off
4 you can get into and out of
5 you can go by

B Work in groups. One student: write down a phrase from Exercise 3A that you did yesterday. Tell the other students where you travelled from and to. Other students: ask questions and guess the type of transport.

A: *From my flat to my office.*
B: *Did you get into a taxi?*
C: *Did you get off a train?*

Ⓖ ARTICLES: *A/AN, THE,* NO ARTICLE

4 A Complete the sentences with *a/an, the* or no article (-).

1 Most of us have to use ______ alarm clock to wake up in ______ morning.
2 Two of us didn't have ______ breakfast this morning.
3 Three of us live in ______ town centre/city centre.
4 All of us think ______ bikes are better than ______ cars for travelling in the town/city centre.
5 One of us has got ______ motorbike.
6 Half of us took ______ taxi home last weekend.
7 None of us goes ______ home by train.

B Work in pairs. Write the questions and ask other students.

A: *Do you have to use an alarm clock to wake up in the morning?*
B: *Yes, I do. I have to use two because I can't wake up!*

C Was the information in Exercise 4A true or false?

Ⓕ APOLOGISING

5 A Write out the conversations.

Monday
A: I / sorry / I / late. I / not / hear / alarm clock.
B: That / OK. No problem.

Tuesday
A: I / terribly / sorry / late. I / miss / train / and / next train / be / late.
B: Not / worry / it.

Wednesday
A: I / so / sorry / late. I / lose / car keys / and then / car / not / start.
B: Not / let / happen / again!

B Work in pairs. Write two key words for each line of the conversations. Then close your book and practise the conversations.

10 plans

SPEAKING 10.1 Talk about your future plans/wishes 10.2 Make predictions about situations 10.3 Make and respond to suggestions for a day out 10.4 Describe unusual weather

LISTENING 10.1 Listen to a radio interview with lottery winners 10.4 Watch an extract from a documentary about the wettest place in Europe

READING 10.2 Read an article about nature's dangers

WRITING 10.2 Improve your use of linkers and write a short story 10.4 Write a message forum notice about your city

BBC INTERVIEWS

What are your plans for the future?

G *be going to; would like to*
P weak forms: *going to, would*
V plans

LISTENING

1 A Work in pairs and discuss. Is there a lottery in your country? Do you think it's a good idea? Do you ever play the lottery?

B Look at the photos below and read the newspaper extract. What's surprising about the story?

A gardener in Perth, Australia, thought he was the unluckiest person in town when he found a tree on top of his car after a storm. Then he saw a small coloured piece of paper under some leaves. 'I don't know why I picked it up.'

But he's happy he did, because today Martin and his wife are ten million dollars richer. The piece of paper was a winning Lotto ticket, and the couple found out yesterday they can keep the money. 'We're thrilled, of course, but we're not going to change our life very much,' said Martin's wife, Jean. 'He enjoys his work as a gardener, and I love my job at the sandwich shop.' 'But we do have some plans,' said Martin.

C Work in pairs and discuss. How do you think the couple plan to spend their money?

D ▶ 10.1 Listen to a radio interview and check your ideas. Tick the couple's plans.

- stop working
- give money to someone
- have a party
- move home
- start a family
- have a holiday
- learn to fly
- buy a new computer
- buy a new car

E Discuss. What do you think of Martin and Jean's plans? Is winning the lottery always a good thing? Why/Why not?

GRAMMAR

BE GOING TO; WOULD LIKE TO

2 A Look at the sentences. Then underline the correct alternative to complete the rules below.

1 We're going to have a party.
2 I'd like to learn to fly.

RULES	
	1 Use *be going to* when you *have/don't have* a definite plan. **2** Use *would like to* when you want to do something or when you *have/don't have* a definite plan.

B Look at audio script 10.1 on page 175 and complete the table with the correct forms of *be going to* and *would like to*.

I' ___ We' ___ He' ___	going ___	stay look for buy	in my job. a house. a new car.

I' ___ We' ___	like ___	go to Greece. move.

What	___	you	going ___	do?
	___		like ___	

C ▶ 10.2 **WEAK FORMS:** ***going to, would*** Listen and check your answers.

D Circle the correct pronunciation of *going to* and *would*. Then listen again and repeat.

1 going to /tuː/ or /tə/?
2 would /wʊd/ or /wuːld/?

▷ page 146 **LANGUAGEBANK**

3 A Write the sentences in full. Use *be going to* for plans (P) or *would like to* when you *want* to do something (W).

1 I / move into a big flat / city centre. (W)
I'd like to move into a big flat in the city centre.
2 I / drive / sports car. (W)
3 I / have / holiday / in the Caribbean. (P)
4 I / not / give / any presents / my family and friends. (P)
5 I / move / to another country. (W)
6 I / buy / a boat. (P)
7 I / start / my own business. (W)
8 I / not keep / all the money for myself. (P)

B Imagine you won the lottery yesterday. What are your plans? Change the sentences so that they are true for you.

C Work in pairs and compare your answers. Find three things the same.

VOCABULARY

PLANS

4 A Complete the collocations with verbs from the box.

~~have~~ go for get move start do go learn stay take

1 _have_ a holiday, a barbecue, a party
2 ______ married, some new jeans, a job
3 ______ some work, a course, something different
4 ______ shopping, clubbing, jogging
5 ______ in, with friends, in a hotel
6 ______ Spanish, to drive, to swim
7 ______ a walk, a meal, a drink
8 ______ a new job, a family, a new business
9 ______ to another country, home, into a flat
10 ______ a break, time off, photos

B Work in pairs. Student A: say the verb. Student B: say the phrases that go with the verb.

C Look at the collocations in Exercise 4A again. Add a new phrase to each verb.

speakout TIP

When you study, make lists of words that go together. Cover all the verbs and try to remember them. Then cover the other words and try to remember the full phrases.

SPEAKING

5 A Complete the table about what you are going to do/would like to do in the future.

	You	Student 1	Student 2	Student 3
this weekend	*shopping*			
next month				
next year				
in five years				

B Work in groups. Ask and answer questions about your plans/wishes for the future. Make notes in the table.

A: *Rafael, what are you going to do this weekend?*
B: *Well, I'm going to watch the Manchester United–Liverpool football match …*

C Tell the class about someone in your group. Can they guess who it is?

A: *This weekend, he's going to watch a football match and next month he's going to do a photography course. He'd like to go to the USA next year. In five years he'd like to start a new business.*
C: *Is it Rafael?*

G will, might (not), won't
P contractions
V phrases with get

VOCABULARY

PHRASES WITH *GET*

1 A Work in pairs and look at the photos. How can each situation be dangerous or scary?

B Complete the phrases with *get* in the sentences with the words in the box.

~~hot~~ wet hungry thirsty lost sunburnt warm stung tired cold

1 When I go to the gym in summer I get *hot*.
2 I didn't drink anything all day so I got ______.
3 I stayed up too late and I got really ______.
4 I forgot my umbrella yesterday and I got ______.
5 I'm really cold. Can I sit by the fire? I need to get ______.
6 I didn't eat breakfast so I'm getting ______.
7 I didn't have a map or my mobile and I got ______.
8 I put my hand on a bee and I got ______.
9 There's no central heating and I often get ______.
10 I stayed out in the sun and I got ______.

C Write a situation using *so* and one of the *get* phrases.

I was out in Istanbul. I didn't have my satnav or a map so I got lost.

D Work in groups and take turns. Close your books. Student A: read your sentence but stop after *so*. Other students: guess the *get* phrase.

speakout TIP

The verb *get* has different meanings in English. It can mean 'become' (*get hungry*), 'arrive' (*get home*), 'obtain' or 'buy' (*get a new car*).

Which meaning does *get* have in these phrases: *get to work, get angry, get a new motorbike, get sick, get some chocolate, get there?*

READING

2 A Work in pairs and discuss the questions in the text. Write two answers to each question.

Mother Nature's dark side
Nature is beautiful but it can also be dangerous. Are you ready for nature's little surprises? See how you do with these questions:
1 You are out walking, high up on a hill. There are a few trees and an open field below. Your car is five minutes away. Your mobile is in your pocket. A storm starts and there is lightning. What do you do?
2 You are at home and there is an earthquake. What do you do? And what do you do if you're in a car?
3 You are in a garden and you put your hand on a bee. You get stung on your arm. There are other bees nearby. What do you do?
4 You are out walking in a forest and you get lost. It's getting dark and there's no signal on your mobile. What do you do?

B Work in pairs. Student A: read the texts on page 168. Student B: read the texts on page 161. Were your ideas correct?

C Close your books and tell your partner about your text. Who is the best survivor?

D Work in pairs and discuss. Which three things from the box are connected to each situation? Read your texts again and say what the connection is.

a car a credit card some wood a shelter a mirror a mobile a pillow an ice pack an umbrella soap

GRAMMAR

WILL, MIGHT (NOT), WON'T

3 A Read the sentences from the texts and put *might, will ('ll)* and *won't* in the correct place on the line. Then complete the rules.

1 You'll be safe inside your car.
2 A mobile often won't work because there's no signal.
3 A building might fall on you.

a ______ b ______ c ______

I'm sure (negative) ←→ Maybe ←→ I'm sure

RULES	In speaking, *'ll* = ______ , *won't* = ______. After *will, might* and *won't* use ______.

B ▶ 10.3 **CONTRACTIONS** Listen to sentences 1–3 above. Then listen again and repeat.

C ▶ 10.4 Listen and number the pairs of sentences in the order you hear them. Then listen again and repeat.

1 **a)** You'll get too hot. __
b) You get too hot. __
2 **a)** We'll get cold. __
b) We get cold. __
3 **a)** They'll get tired. __
b They get tired. __
4 **a)** I'll get hungry. __
b) I get hungry. __

D Complete the sentences about the situations in the texts with *'ll, won't* or *might*. Then work in pairs and check your answers.

1 Don't stand under a tree because the lightning *might* hit the tree, or you!
2 Don't touch anything metal in your car and I'm sure the lightning ______ hurt you.
3 Get away from the bees because you ______ get stung again.
4 Don't pinch the bee-sting because the sting ______ get worse, that's for sure.
5 Don't leave your home in an earthquake. A building ______ fall on you outside.
6 Stay away from mirrors because they ______ break and cut you.
7 Build a fire so you ______ get cold.
8 Make a plan. You ______ feel better, that's sure.

▷ page 146 **LANGUAGEBANK**

SPEAKING

4 A Work in pairs. Look at the cartoon below and discuss. What are three problems the people might have?

B Work in pairs. Choose three objects from the box below that might help the people in the cartoon. Give reasons for your choice.

~~chocolate~~ a radio a box of matches a mobile phone sun cream a knife a bottle of water playing cards

I think chocolate is useful because they might get hungry.

C Think of three other objects that might be useful.

D Work with another pair and compare your objects. Decide which five objects will help the people in the cartoon the most.

WRITING

TOO, ALSO, AS WELL

5 A Look at the sentences. What is the position of *too, also* and *as well* in these sentences?

1 Stay away from windows and mirrors, and bookshelves **too**.
2 You can put an ice pack on your arm and **also** take some painkillers
3 Build a simple shelter and make a fire so you can get warm and feel safer **as well.**

B Put *too, also* and *as well* into the story. Use each word/phrase once.

Lost in the jungle

We left the jeep and walked all morning, and we walked for five hours in the afternoon too. We had a short break for lunch. We stopped for a rest in the afternoon. In the evening, Sam taught us how to kill a snake and how to cook it. I didn't like the look of it, but I ate some and Sam ate some.

C Finish the story with your own ideas. Use *too, also* and *as well.* Write four or five sentences.

F making suggestions
P intonation: sounding positive
V art and culture

VOCABULARY

ART AND CULTURE

1 A Work in pairs and look at the items in the box. Which items can you see in the pictures?

a film a painting a concert a play *3* a drawing a photograph a statue an exhibition a dance performance

B Work in pairs and look at the items in the box above. Which …

1 always have music?
2 don't move?
3 always have movement?

C Look at the word webs below and cross out the word which does not go with the verb. Why? Complete the word webs with words from the box above.

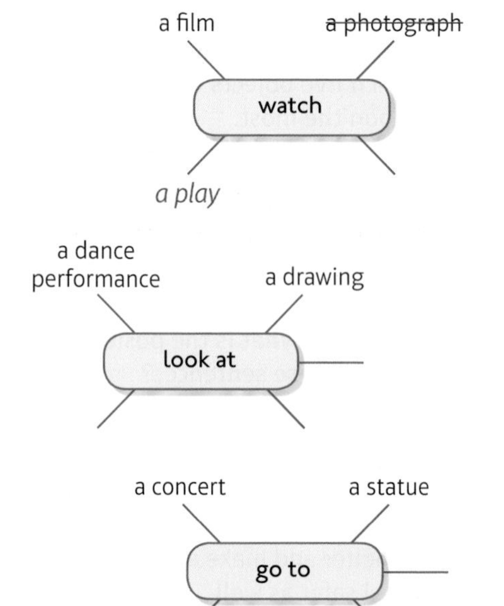

D Work in pairs. Cover the word webs and take turns answering the question 'What can you …'
… watch?
… look at?
… go to?

E Work in pairs. Take turns asking and answering. Ask follow-up questions.

1 Do you like … ?
2 When did you last … ?

A: *Do you like looking at photographs?*
B: *Yes, I do.*
A: *Really? What kind?*
B: *Oh, old black and white ones.*
A: *When did you last … ?*

AlternativeCity

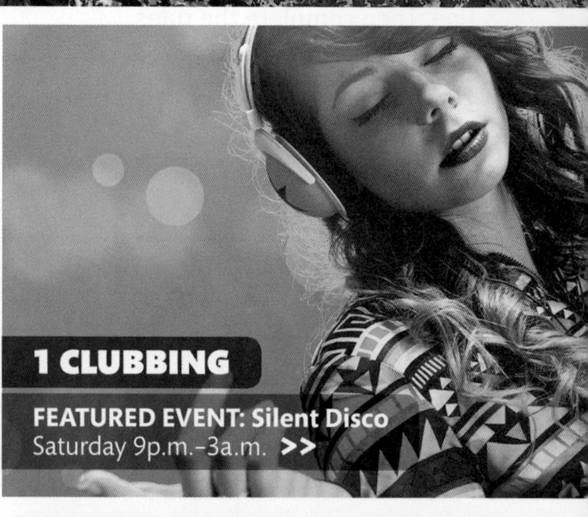

1 CLUBBING
FEATURED EVENT: Silent Disco
Saturday 9p.m.–3a.m. >>

2 FILM
FEATURED EVENT: Blind Date Cinema
Friday/Saturday 7.30p.m. >>

FUNCTION

MAKING SUGGESTIONS

2 A Work in pairs and look at the website. Why is it called AlternativeCity?

B Look at the website again and complete the table.

Event	What is it?	What do you think you do at the event?	Does it look interesting?
1			
2			
3			
4			

C ▶ 10.5 Listen to the conversation. Which events do the people decide to go to?

D Work in pairs. Were your ideas in Exercise 2B correct? Tick the correct ideas and change the incorrect ones. Then listen again and check.

E Work in pairs. Would you like to go to any of the events? Why/Why not?

For people who want to do something DIFFERENT in London

What do you want to do?

3 THEATRE
FEATURED EVENT: Improv Playback Theatre
Saturday 7p.m. >>

4 ART
FEATURED EVENT: Museum Meditation
Saturday and Sunday afternoons 3–4p.m. >>

3 A Look at the sentences. Underline four phrases for making suggestions.

1 Let's do something different.
2 How about going to the theatre?
3 Why don't we go to the museum?
4 Shall we go to the theatre in the evening?

B 10.6 Complete the suggestions below. Then listen and check.

1 How _______ _______ to an exhibition?
2 Shall _______ _______ to a concert?
3 Why _______ _______ _______ shopping?
4 _______ _______ to the park.

C INTONATION: sounding positive Listen to the sentences again. Does the speaker sound positive? Does his/her voice start high or low?

D Listen again and repeat.

E Work in pairs. Student A: make a suggestion. Use ideas from Exercises 3A and B or your own ideas. Student B: say *OK* if your partner sounds positive or *No, thanks* if he/she doesn't.

LEARN TO

RESPOND TO SUGGESTIONS

4 A 10.7 Listen to the extracts from the conversation. Match 1–5 with the responses a)–g) below.

1 something new
2 silent disco
3 blind date cinema
4 playback theatre
5 museum meditation

a) Brilliant!
b) I don't feel like doing that.
c) That's a good idea.
d) That sounds interesting.
e) It's not for me.
f) I'd like to go.
g) That doesn't sound very good.

B Look at phrases a)–g) above. Are they positive (+) or negative (-)?

C Work in pairs. Student A: choose three weekend activities and make suggestions. Student B: respond to the suggestions. When you respond negatively, give a reason.

A: Why don't we go for a walk in the park?
B: Mmm. I don't really feel like doing that. It's too cold!

page 146 LANGUAGEBANK

SPEAKING

5 A Make a note of three activities you would like to do next week. Write a place and a time next to each activity.

B Work in pairs and take turns to suggest activities from Exercise 5A. Use the flowchart to help you. Add your partner's information to your notes.

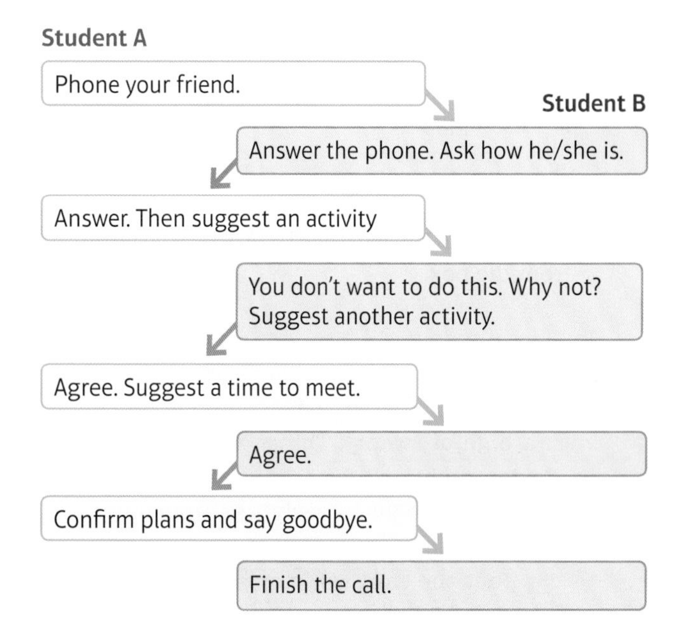

Student A
Phone your friend.
Student B
Answer the phone. Ask how he/she is.
Answer. Then suggest an activity
You don't want to do this. Why not? Suggest another activity.
Agree. Suggest a time to meet.
Agree.
Confirm plans and say goodbye.
Finish the call.

C Phone two more students and suggest activities. Add their information to your notes.

D Work in groups. Tell the other students about your plans. Who's got the most similar plans to yours?

I'm going to play tennis with Alfonso and then I'm going to …

BBC WILD WEATHER

DVD PREVIEW

1 A Match sentences 1–6 with pictures A–F.

1 It's stormy.	**4** It's sunny.
2 It's windy.	**5** It's cloudy.
3 It's snowing.	**6** It's raining.

B Work in pairs and take turns. Student A: point to a photo and ask about the weather. Student B: reply.

A: *What's the weather like?*
B: *It's raining.*

2 A Look at the adjectives in the box and find three pairs of opposites.

~~hot~~ warm wet cool cold dry

B Complete the weather forecast with the words from the box.

In Dublin today, it'll be [1] *hot* and sunny with temperatures up to twenty-five degrees Celsius. Tomorrow will be cloudy but [2]______, with a high of twenty. Things will change on Friday night: it'll be a [3]______ night with rain from midnight to early next morning. The temperature will fall to ten so it'll feel [4]______, but the rain will stop so we'll have a [5]______ day all Saturday. Sunday will be windy and cloudy ... and very [6]______, so make sure you wear your winter coat!

C 10.8 **Listen and check your answers.**

DVD VIEW

3 A Read the programme information. Which of these places do you think the presenter visits for each of the four programmes: a) Florida, USA, b) Greenland, c) Bergen, Norway, d) the jungle of Belize?

Wild Weather

In *Wild Weather* the intrepid adventurer, Donal MacIntyre, looks for the wildest weather in the world. He travels to different places and finds answers to the questions: Where does the weather come from? How does it work? There are four programmes: Hot, Wet, Wind and Cold. Follow his journey as he finds and experiences dramatic moments of amazing weather.

B Watch the DVD and answer the questions.

1 Which programme is it: *Hot*, *Wet*, *Wind* or *Cold*?
2 Would you like to live in Bergen?

C Watch the DVD again. Underline the correct alternative.

1 In Bergen it rains *one/two/three* out of three days.
2 There are *two/three/four* types of umbrellas.
3 They sell Bergen rain to tourists in *bottles/cups/cans*.
4 In one year, *105/125/225* tonnes of rain fall on a family house.
5 The longest period of rain in Bergen was in *1990/1992/1995*.
6 It rained for *73/83/93* days.

D Work in pairs and discuss the questions.

1 Do you like the weather in your town or city?
2 What weather do you like and dislike the most?
3 What's your favourite season? Why?

speakout a weather report

4 A Work alone. Think of a place and time when you experienced an interesting or unusual type of weather. Use the questions below to make notes about it.

1 When was it? What season/time of year?
2 Where were you?
3 Why were you there?
4 What was the weather like? Did it change?
5 How did you feel? How did other people feel?

B 10.9 Listen to a woman talk about her time in Italy and her experience of the sirocco wind. Write her answers to the questions in Exercise 4A.

C Look at the key phrases below. Listen again and tick the ones you hear.

KEYPHRASES

This happened about [five years ago].
But then one day the weather [changed/started to rain/got hotter/ ...].
Everything/Everywhere was [different/white/dry/ ...].
It lasted [a long time/three or four days/ ...].
It was difficult to [breathe/sleep/do anything].
To tell you the truth, I really [hated/loved] it.
Everyone got very [tired/angry/ill/ ...].
I was [glad/sorry] when it was over.

5 A Work in pairs. Use your notes from Exercise 4A and the key phrases to describe your experiences. Check that your partner answers all the questions in Exercise 4A.

B Work with other students and take turns. Student A: tell the other students about your experience. Other students: listen and ask follow-up questions. Who had the most unusual experience?

writeback a message forum

6 A Read the message and part of a reply from a travel website. When are the best months to travel? Why?

Message forum 02-Feb-16 12.26p.m.

Posted by: Maria, Spain:
My friend and I are going to visit Scotland next year for two weeks. We want to hire a car and drive round. When is the best time to go? What about clothes? Can you recommend any good places to visit? We like cities but also we'd like to see the countryside.

Message forum [03-Feb-16

Posted by: Doug, Scotland:
The best time to visit is May or September because the weather is usually OK – but in Scotland, the weather changes all the time. Be prepared for everything from hot sunshine to really bad rain. Also, the traffic is quieter in May and September and it's easier to get hotels and B&Bs. Bring a warm sweater and a raincoat and a hat as well because there's an old saying: 'If you can't see the mountains, it's raining. If you can see them, it's going to rain in five minutes.' And places to visit? Well, you have to visit Edinburgh and ...

B Write a reply to the same question about your city. Use some of these phrases to help you. Use 80–120 words.

Be prepared for ...
The best time to visit is ... because ...
Bring ... because ...
Also ...
You have to visit ...

G BE GOING TO; WOULD LIKE TO

1 A Look at the list. Write sentences using *be going to* and *would like to*.

1 *I'd like to have dinner with Gemma, but I can't – she's busy.*

2 *I'm going to Oxford. I've got my bus ticket.*

Weekend wish list

1 dinner with Gemma ✗ she's busy!
2 go to Oxford ✓ (got bus ticket)
3 go to the U2 concert ✗ not got tickets!
4 meet Andy for drink ✓ (he said OK)
5 Watch Gone with the Wind on DVD ✓ (borrowed it from Cindy)
6 sleep all day ✗ not got time!

B Make your own 'Weekend wish list'. Then look at the list and tick the things that are possible. Write reasons for the things that aren't possible.

C Work in pairs. Tell your partner about your plans for the weekend.

V PLANS

2 A Complete the questions with the correct verbs.

1 On your next holiday, do you want to:
- go to the beach or d_ something different?
- st_ _ in a hotel or with friends?

2 You have a free Saturday. Do you want to:
- g_ shopping or g_ _ _ _ a walk?
- in the evening, st_ _ in and do nothing, or h_ _ _ a party and then g_ clubbing?

3 Time for some big changes. Do you want to:
- g_ _ married or go travelling?
- m_ _ _ to an English-speaking country or stay in your country?
- st_ _ _ a business or t_ _ _ a long break from work?

B Work in pairs and take turns. Ask and answer the questions.

V PHRASES WITH GET

3 A Put the letters in order to find the words that go with *get*. The first letter of each word is underlined.

1 dclo
2 bunturns
3 gutns
4 hrityts
5 hto
6 irtde
7 otls
8 rmwa
9 tew
10 ughrny

B A man was lost at sea for five days. Read the information and make sentences with *get*.

1 He ate all the food on the first day.
He got hungry.
2 He didn't sleep very much.
3 He sat in the bottom of the raft.
4 He didn't have a jacket or a hat.
5 He drank seawater.
6 He went swimming.

C Work in pairs and discuss. What were his three worst mistakes and problems?

I think number one was his worst mistake. I think he got very hungry.

G WILL, MIGHT, WON'T

4 A You and ten friends are going to spend the weekend in a hotel on a high mountain. Read the information.

- It's a beautiful, quiet place.
- It always rains at this time of year.
- Walking in the mountains is beautiful, but very dangerous.
- There are ten beds.
- The hotel has a very good kitchen. Their restaurant can serve meals for twenty-five people maximum.
- Not all the students like 'mountain life'!

B Complete the sentences with *might, might not, 'll* or *won't*.

1 It ______ rain.
2 We ______ get bored.
3 It ______ be very peaceful.
4 Someone ______ get hurt.
5 The food ______ be very good.
6 There ______ be enough food.
7 Some people ______ like it but I'm sure I ______ like it.
8 There ______ be enough beds for all of us.

C Work in pairs and compare your answers.

D Discuss. Would you like to go on this kind of weekend break? Why/Why not?

F MAKING SUGGESTIONS

5 A Correct the sentences.

1 Why we don't have a party in the school garden?
2 Let's to have 90s music.
3 How about start at seven o'clock?
4 That sound good.
5 Shall make some pizza?
6 I don't feel like do that.
7 That's good idea.
8 I like to bring some drinks.

B Work in groups. Make suggestions for a class party. Think about the place, food, music, etc.

C Tell the other groups about your party. Which one would you like to go to?

We're going to have a barbecue in the park. We're going to bring some chicken and …

11 health

I DON'T FEEL WELL p108

ONE THING AT A TIME p110

HELP! p112

FAT OR SUGAR? p114

SPEAKING 11.1 Talk about what to do when you don't feel well 11.2 Talk about ways of reducing stress 11.3 Offer to help someone 11.4 Talk about diets

LISTENING 11.1 Listen to a radio programme about colds and flu 11.3 Listen to situations where people offer to help 11.4 Watch an extract from a documentary about fat and sugar

READING 11.2 Read an article about multi-tasking

WRITING 11.2 Make your stories more interesting with adverbs 11.4 Write some advice for a health forum

BBC INTERVIEWS

Do you have a healthy lifestyle?

G *should/shouldn't*
P weak form: *should*
V the body; health

VOCABULARY

THE BODY; HEALTH

1 A Look at photos A–E. How many parts of the body can you see and name? List any other words you know.

▷ page 159 **PHOTOBANK**

B Work in pairs and take turns.
Student A: say a part of the body.
Student B: point to it in photos A–E.

2 A Which health problems can you see in photos A–E?

1 I've got a headache.*
2 I have stomachache.
3 My leg hurts.
4 I've got a cold.
5 I have a temperature.
6 I've got a cough.
7 I have a sore throat.
8 I've got a runny nose.

*I've got a headache = I have a headache.

B ▶ 11.1 **SENTENCE STRESS** Listen and mark the stressed syllables (1 or 2) in each sentence. Then listen again and repeat.

speakout TIP

Many words in English have a very different pronunciation from their spelling. You can underline problem letters and write the sound underneath,

e.g. *cough* /f/ *headache* /k/

In your notebook, do the same for *thumb* and *stomachache.*

C Work in pairs and complete the sentences using the words in the box. You can use each word only once.

arm back tired ear finger better

1 I've got/I have _______ache/ _______ache.
2 My _______/_______ hurts.
3 I feel _______/_______.

D Work in pairs and take turns.
Student A: choose a problem from Exercise 2A or 2C and mime it.
Student B: guess what's wrong.

LISTENING

3 A Work in pairs and discuss.

1 What do you do when you have a cold? Do you go to work or school? Do you stay at home and rest or do you go to the doctor and take medicine?
2 What's the difference between a cold and flu?

B Look at the health problems in Exercises 2A and 2C and write them in the correct place in the table.

Flu	A cold	Both
a headache		

C ▶ 11.2 Listen to a radio programme and check your answers.

D Work in pairs. What did the doctor say? Underline the correct alternative. Then listen again and check.

1 Flu starts *suddenly/slowly*. You *can/can't* work.
2 A cold starts *suddenly/slowly*. You *can/can't* work.
3 After a cold you feel better after *two or three days/a week*.
4 After flu you often feel *fine/tired* after three weeks.

E Work in pairs and discuss. How often do you get a cold or flu? What information in the radio programme was new for you?

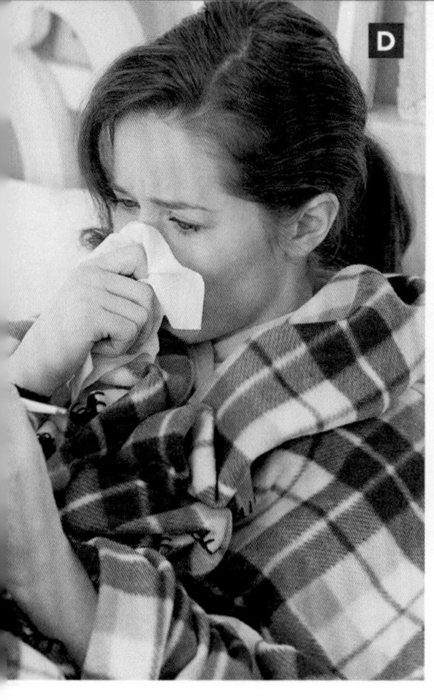

GRAMMAR

SHOULD/SHOULDN'T

4 A Look at the sentences and underline the correct alternative to complete the rules.

1 You should drink lots of water.
2 You shouldn't take antibiotics.

RULES	1 Use *should* for something that is *necessary/ a good idea.* 2 Use *shouldn't* for something that is *not necessary/a bad idea.*

B Complete the table.

You	should	______	to bed.
	______	go back to work	too soon.

C 11.3 Listen and check.

D WEAK FORM: *should* **Work in pairs and answer the questions. Then listen again and repeat.**

1 Is the pronunciation of *should* /ʃʊd/ or /ʃu:ld/?
2 Is *should* usually stressed or not stressed?

▷ page 148 LANGUAGEBANK

5 A Look at problems 1–4 and advice a)–h). For each problem, write two pieces of advice, one with *should* and one with *shouldn't*.

1 I'm tired.
You should get more sleep.
You shouldn't go to bed so late.
2 I'm hungry.
3 It's raining and I have to go.
4 I feel ill.

a) be here in the lesson
b) eat something
c) ~~get more sleep~~
d) go home
e) go out now
f) ~~go to bed so late~~
g) take an umbrella
h) miss breakfast

B Work in pairs and take turns. Cover the advice a)–h) above. Student A: say one of the problems. Student B: give advice with *should/shouldn't*.

SPEAKING

6 A Work in pairs and answer the questions.

1 In situations a)–f), do you usually go to a pharmacy, a doctor, a dentist or a hospital?
a) You ate some fish last night. This morning you've got terrible stomachache.
b) You broke a glass and cut your thumb badly.
c) You woke up this morning with earache.
d) Your eyes are really red and tired.
e) You've got terrible toothache.
f) You stayed out in the sun too long this morning and you got very sunburnt.

2 Discuss. Can you remember a time when you had any of these problems? Where were you? What did you do?

B Look at the phrases below. In a pharmacy, which phrases does the customer say and which ones does the pharmacist say? Write C or P.

Take these tablets three times a day. P
I've got (a) terrible …
Put this cream on your …
Put these drops in your …
Could I have some plasters?
Have you got anything for …
You should …
You shouldn't …
Can you recommend anything?
When did it start?

C Work in pairs. You are on holiday in another country. Choose a problem from Exercise 6A and role-play the situation.

D Work in groups and take turns. One pair: role-play your conversation. Other students: Do you agree with the advice?

11.2 ONE THING AT A TIME

G adverbs of manner
P sentence stress: adverbs
V communication

I had lunch with a friend yesterday. In one hour, she answered three text messages, had two short phone conversations, checked her email, ordered her food, ate it and paid for it. And in that one hour, she and I didn't stop talking for more than a few seconds.

My friend is a typical multi-tasker, and maybe you are too. Multi-tasking – doing two or more tasks at the same time – is normal for many people. But it's not good for you.

READING

1 A Work in pairs. Look at the photo and answer the questions.

1 What does a multi-tasker do?
2 Are you a multi-tasker?
3 How many different tasks can you do at one time?

B Read the introduction to the article. How many different tasks did the writer's friend do?

C Work in pairs. Write three ways that multi-tasking is bad for you. Then read part two of the text. How many of your ideas are the same?

What happens when you multi-task?

1 You think you work quickly, but in fact you work slowly. Multi-taskers do less work in an eight-hour day than non-multi-taskers.

2 Your memory gets worse. You forget names and numbers. You can't remember normal things easily, for example your bank PIN number.

3 You eat very fast, and you eat too much. You don't think about your food when you're eating.

4 You have problems with friends and loved ones. You don't listen to them carefully, and they feel this.

5 You do some tasks badly. You make mistakes because you are doing two things at the same time.

6 Finally – and this is the big one – your stress levels go up, and that's the biggest problem.

D Read the last part of the text. Work in pairs and discuss. Do you think the writer's plan is a good idea?

What can you do about it?

It's very easy: Do one thing at a time. When you eat, eat. When you read, read. And when you talk to a friend, only talk – and listen.

Remember my friend? Next week we're going to meet in the park, turn off our phones, have no food or drink, and just talk and listen. That's my plan – SHE doesn't know it yet. I'll let you know what happens.

VOCABULARY

COMMUNICATION

2 A Look at the word webs below and cross out the verb which does not go with the noun. Then look in the text and find one more word for each word web.

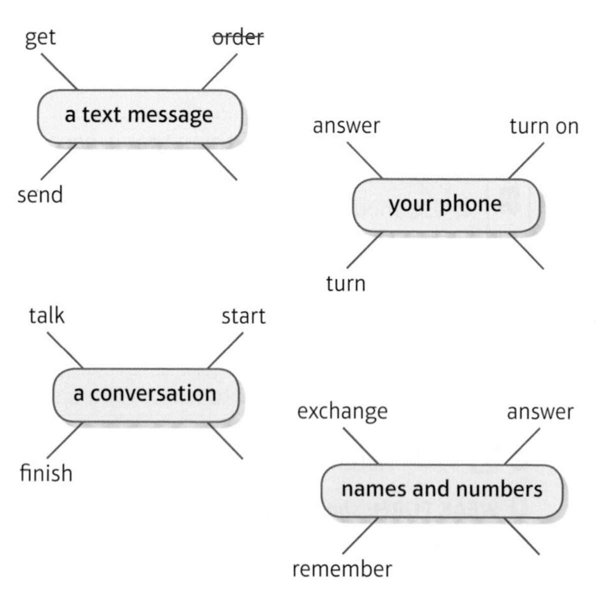

B Work in pairs and cover the word webs. Student A: say a phrase from Exercise 2A. Student B: say another phrase with the same noun.

A: *send a text message*
B: *get a text message*
A: *answer a text message*

C Work alone. Choose a verb from Exercise 2A to complete the questions.

1 How often do you _______ texts?
2 Do you always _______ a text straightaway?
3 Do you _______ your phone at night?
4 Is it easy for you to _______ a conversation in English?
5 Do you ever _______ someone's name?
6 Is it difficult for you to _______ phone numbers?

D Work in pairs and take turns. Ask and answer the questions.

GRAMMAR

ADVERBS

3 A Look at the sentence and the rule. Underline the correct alternatives to complete them.

You think you work *quick/quickly*, but in fact you work *slow/slowly*.

RULES	
	1 Use adverbs of manner to say *how/when* we do something. 2 Adverbs usually come *before/after* a verb phrase.

B Complete the table. Use the reading text in Exercise 1C to help.

Adjective	Adverb
slow	*slowly*
quick	
fast	
bad	
careful	
easy	

C Work in pairs. How do you make a regular adverb? Which adverb is irregular?

D 11.4 SENTENCE STRESS: adverbs Listen to the sentence in Exercise 3A. Notice how the stress is on the adverbs. Listen and repeat.

page 148 **LANGUAGEBANK**

4 A Complete the sentences and make them true for you. Use the correct form (adjective or adverb) of one of the words in brackets.

1 I like it when the teacher speaks *slowly*. (*quick/slow*)
2 It's ______ for me to remember new words in English. (*easy/hard*)
3 I think I speak English ______. (*good/bad*)
4 I've got a ______ memory. (*good/bad*)
5 When I have lunch or dinner, I usually eat ______. (*fast/slow*)
6 I think I usually eat ______. (*healthy/unhealthy*)
7 I can't study when it's ______. (*quiet/noisy*)
8 I usually get to work/school ______. (*late/early*)

B Work in pairs and compare your sentences. How many are the same?

SPEAKING

5 Work in pairs. Student A: look at page 164. Student B: look at page 161.

WRITING

ADVERBS IN STORIES

6 A Look at pictures A–D. What do you think happened? Put them in the correct order. Use the prompts 1–4 to help.

1 Saturday / Ken / get up / have breakfast / get on / bike.
2 he / ride / down the road / not / look / ahead. / cat / run / in front / him.
3 he / fall off / bike / break /arm.
4 evening / he / sit / home / with / broken arm.

B Use the prompts to write the story. Remember to use linkers.

1 On Saturday, Ken got up, had breakfast and …

C Change the adjectives in the box below into adverbs. Then add three of them to your story in Exercise 6A.

quick careful careless dangerous early fast late sad slow

On Saturday, Ken got up late, had breakfast quickly …

D Write the next part of the story with three more adverbs. Start with 'Six weeks later, on Saturday morning, Ken got up … '.

E Work in pairs and exchange your stories.

11.3 HELP!

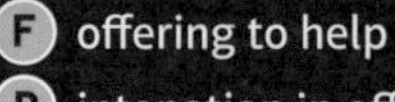
offering to help
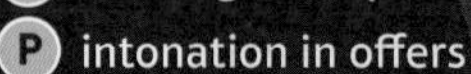
intonation in offers
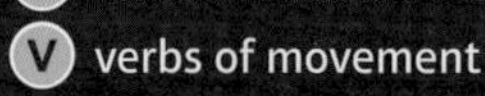
verbs of movement

VOCABULARY

VERBS OF MOVEMENT

1 A Look at the situations below. Which problems can you see in the photos?

1 You're sitting on a bus. You're feeling very tired and you have a long journey. You see a woman. She's **standing** and she's **carrying** a baby.

2 You are walking along a road. You see a young man. He's **pushing** his car.

3 You're in a busy city. You're in a hurry because you have an important meeting and you're late. A person in front of you **drops** his pen.

4 You see a woman of about twenty. She's carrying a heavy suitcase down some steps and she's in trouble because she can't **lift** it.

5 You see a person with a bad leg. He drops some magazines and papers and can't **pick** them **up** easily.

6 You see a man by the road. He is **lying** on the ground and he isn't moving.

7 You see a blind person. He's trying to **cross** the road but the traffic is busy.

B Work in pairs and discuss. In each situation, do you help? What can you say and do?

FUNCTION

OFFERING TO HELP

2 Read the article and guess the missing city name.

> **The most helpful city**
>
> When someone sees a person in trouble, do they stop and help or just 'walk on by'? Researchers from the USA decided to answer the question 'Which is the most helpful city in the world?'. They went to twenty-three capital cities and did three experiments to find out:
>
> **a)** A person is walking along the street and drops his/her pen.
> **b)** A person with a broken leg drops some papers.
> **c)** A blind person is trying to cross the road.
>
> They found that people in Spanish-speaking cities were usually the most helpful. Madrid, San Salvador and Mexico City each scored highly. People in these cities gave help with a smile and seemed happy to give their time. People in New York came near the bottom: they were often too busy or were in a hurry. They also said they sometimes didn't offer help because it was dangerous or because people got angry with them. And the most helpful city in the world? ____________, in Brazil.

3 A 11.5 Listen and match conversations 1–3 with situations a)–c) in the text.

B Listen again and complete sentences 1–4 below.

1 _______ me help.
2 _______ do it.
3 _______ I help you?
4 _______ I carry your bag?

C 11.6 Listen to two speakers. Tick the offer that sounds more polite.

1 A _______ B _______
2 A _______ B _______
3 A _______ B _______
4 A _______ B _______

D 11.7 **INTONATION IN OFFERS** Listen to the offers and repeat. Notice that they all start high.

D

E

4 A Match problems 1–5 with offers a)–e).

1 I can't open the window.
2 I'm hungry.
3 I can't reach the dictionary.
4 I can't lift this bag.
5 It's cold in here.

a) I'll get it for you.
b) Let me carry it.
c) I'll make you a sandwich.
d) Shall I close the window?
e) Let me try … Ooh, it's stuck.

B Work in pairs and take turns. Student A: say a problem. Student B: cover Exercise 4A. Listen to the problem and offer to help.

A: I can't open the window.
B: Let me try … Ooh, it's stuck.

C 11.8 Listen to the situations. What's happening?

D Work in pairs. Listen again and offer to help.

1 (glass breaking) Here, let me help. What a mess!

▷ page 148 **LANGUAGEBANK**

LEARN TO
THANK SOMEONE

5 A Look at audio script 11.5 on page 175 and complete the sentences.

Conversation 1
M: Here, let me help. What a mess!
W: Thank [1]_______. It's my leg. It's difficult …
M: Oh, don't move. I'll do it.
W: Thanks [2]_______.
M: No [3]_______.

Conversation 2
W: Er … Excuse me?
M: Yeah.
W: You dropped this.
M: Oh. Thanks [4]_______.
W: That's [5]_______.

Conversation 3
W: Shall I carry your bag?
M: No, no, it's fine, thanks.
W: Here you are.
M: Thanks [6]_______. That's [7]_______.
W: You're [8]_______.

B Underline five ways of thanking someone. Circle three ways to reply when someone thanks you.

6 A Look at the flowchart and put the conversation below it in the correct order.

Ask about the problem. → Say the problem. → Offer to help. → Accept the offer. → Reply.

1 **A:** That's OK.
2 **B:** Thanks a lot.
3 **A:** Sit down. I'll get you some water.
4 **A:** Are you OK?
5 **B:** No, I don't feel well.

B Use the flowchart and role-play the conversation. Student A: look at page 168. Student B: look at page 166.

SPEAKING

7 Work in pairs. Choose a situation from Exercise 1A or your own idea. Act out the situation and have a conversation of at least thirty seconds.

8 Work with other students. Can you remember a time when you helped someone or when someone else helped you? What happened? How did you feel?

BBC FAT OR SUGAR?

DVD PREVIEW

1 Work in pairs and discuss.

1 Which types of food in the photos do you eat a lot of? Which types of food do you rarely eat?

2 Look at photos A–F. Which are high in fat (F) and which are high in sugar/carbohydrates (S)?

2 Read the programme information and answer the questions.

1 Which types of food in the photos above can Chris eat? Which can Xand eat?

2 Who do you think wins the bike race?

3 Do the 'doughnut test'. Which doughnut do you think most people choose?

Horizon: Sugar Versus Fat

BBC

It's one of the big questions of our time: Which is worse for you, fat or sugar? Twin brothers (and doctors) Chris and Xand Van Tulleken go on a special diet to try to answer the question. For one month, Chris eats only high-sugar food and no fat and Xand eats only high-fat foods and no sugar. They do a number of experiments. For example, in a bike race up a hill, which one of them is the fastest? Finally, the twins do the 'doughnut test'. They ask people in New York and London to choose their favourite type of doughnut.

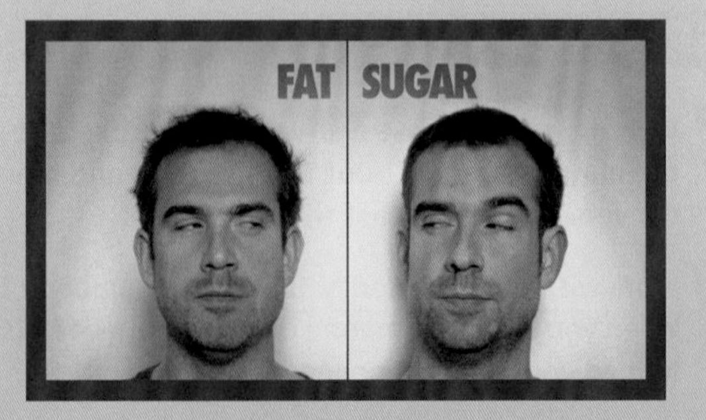

DVD VIEW

3 A Watch the DVD and check your answers to the questions in Exercise 2.

B Work in pairs and match these sentence halves from the video.

1 Which is worse for us: _d_

2 Is sugar really public enemy number one __

3 … you can have mayonnaise, __

4 I want you to remember the doughnut you chose, __

5 And it's thick, it's luxurious, it's rich, it's creamy, __

6 And there's something really special about this doughnut: __

7 It's the same 50–50 mix __

a) and it's really boring.

b) and we're going to see if the people in New York will choose the same one as you.

c) but you're not allowed any fruit …

d) fat or sugar?

e) it's got an exactly 50–50 mixture of fat and sugar.

f) that we find in so many processed foods.

g) or is it fat?

C Watch the video again and check.

D Work in pairs and discuss. Does the programme change how you feel about food? How might you change the way you eat?

The doughnut test: Which would you choose?

speakout a panel discussion

4 A Work in pairs. Write 6–8 questions to ask the twin brothers Chris (sugar) and Xand (fat), Hilary (a healthy eating expert) and a doctor. Use the words and phrases below to help.

About the diet
dangerous?
problems?
worst thing/best thing?
miss the most?
cheat?
About the future
eat more/less X?
change your diet?
do more exercise?
stop eating X?
recommend?

What was the worst thing about the diet?
Are you going to … ? Should we … ?

B 11.9 Listen to the discussion. How many questions were the same as yours?

C Listen again and tick the key phrases you hear.

KEYPHRASES

I've got a question for Chris/Xand/Hilary/the doctor.
What do you mean?
Do you agree with him/her?
Can you tell us more about that?
Could you give an example?
I don't understand. Could you explain?
Can I ask you about [your diet/the future/…] ?

D Work as a class. Four students are on a panel and are Chris, Xand, Hilary and the doctor. Other students: ask the panel members your questions.

writeback a website message

5 Work in pairs. Read the three questions from a forum posting. Choose one and complete Message 4 to give some advice. Use the key phrases to help.

Message 1 posted yesterday

Hi. I've got a real problem with chocolate. I can't stop eating it – after meals and in my coffee break and in the middle of the afternoon. I always have some in my bag or in my desk. How can I stop?

Posted by: Teresa, Spain
Reply | Previous Message | Next Message

Message 2 posted yesterday

Help! I started working from home three weeks ago. Now I've got terrible backache and my eyes hurt. I'm on the computer for about eight hours every day. Any advice?

Posted by: YuchenChi, China
Reply | Previous Message | Next Message

Message 3 posted yesterday

I stopped smoking a year ago and now I'm overweight. I often feel stressed and unhappy. I think I might start smoking again but I don't want to. What can I do?

Posted by: Great Amigo, Mexico
Reply | Previous Message | Next Message

Message 4 posted yesterday

Hi, ______. Don't worry! The same thing happened to ______, and I understand completely. Here are three pieces of advice I can give you:

- The best thing is ______.
- You should ______.
- And finally, ______.

I hope that helps!

All the best, ______.

Reply | Previous Message | Next Message

11.5 LOOKBACK

V THE BODY; HEALTH

1 A Complete the poems.

Poem 1

A: What's the matter?
What's wrong with you?

B: I've got a terrible co_ _ _,
A runny n_ _ _, a bad s_r_
thr_ _ _.

A: I can't stay here. I'm off!

Poem 2

A: My a_ _ _ hurt, my l_ _ _ hurt,
I think I've got bad flu.

B: Have you got a t_mp_r_t_ _ _?

A: Yes, what can I do?

Poem 3

A: I've got an awful h_ _d_ _ _ _.

B: My f_ng_ _ _ hurt a lot.

A: My e_e_ are t_r_d.

B: My b_ck_ _ _ _'s bad.

A & B: We don't know what we've got!

B Work in pairs. Read the poems.

G *SHOULD/SHOULDN'T*

2 A Read the situations and make a note of what the person *should/shouldn't do*.

a) My arm hurts so I can't use my computer. I have to finish a report by tomorrow.

b) I've got terrible backache. I'm going on holiday tomorrow and I've got two heavy bags to carry.

c) I've got a headache and a bad sore throat. I've got an important interview for a new job tomorrow.

d) My leg hurts so I can't walk very far. I'm going out tomorrow night and I want to dance.

B Work in pairs and take turns. Role-play the four situations above using your ideas.

V COMMUNICATION

3 Work in pairs. Match phrases 1–6 with a)–f). Then ask and answer the questions.

1 How many text messages *c*
2 Do you ever get
3 Can you have
4 What do you do when you forget
5 Do you remember
6 Do you ever turn off

a) a conversation and watch TV at the same time?
b) your phone? When?
c) ~~do you send a day?~~
d everyone's name in the class?
e) someone's name and they remember yours?
f) text messages in English?

G ADVERBS OF MANNER

4 A Write the opposite adverbs.

1 early – *late*
2 loudly
3 slowly
4 well
5 carelessly

B Complete the sentences with a verb from the box below and an adverb of your choice.

speak(s) eat(s) talk(s) drive(s) walk(s) go(es) to bed

1 I ______ too ______.
2 Everyone ______ too ______ on their phones.
3 My closest friend ______ too ______.
4 Everyone ______ too ______.

C Work in groups and take turns. One student: say one of your sentences. Other students: give advice or say your opinion using *should/shouldn't*.

A: Everyone talks too loudly on their mobiles.
B: Yes, they should speak quietly.

F OFFERING TO HELP

5 Work in pairs. What can you say in each situation?

1 You're at a friend's house and she breaks some glasses.
2 You're walking down the street and someone falls off his bicycle.
3 You're on a train and a woman next to you becomes ill.
4 You're at home and you pour hot coffee on a friend's shirt.
5 Your friend is cutting vegetables and cuts his finger badly.
6 Your friend wants a coffee, but she doesn't have enough money to buy one.

6 A Complete the conversation with the words in the box.

'll Shall me a 're you ~~help~~

A: Good morning. Can I *help* you?

B: Yes, the shower in my room doesn't work.

A: I send someone to look at it.

B: Thank. And when does the City Museum open?

A: Let look on the computer … It opens at ten today.

B: Thanks. And can you get me a taxi to go to the museum?

A: No problem. I phone for one now?

B: In about an hour, please.

A: Certainly.

B: Thanks lot.

A: You welcome.

B Work in pairs. Practise the conversation.

12 experiences

SPEAKING 12.1 Ask and answer questions about life experiences 12.2 Describe how you feel about different situations 12.3 Make telephone calls and say telephone numbers 12.4 Talk about an exciting or frightening experience

LISTENING 12.1 Listen to people talking about their experiences 12.3 Listen to phone conversations 12.4 Watch an extract from a documentary about sharks

READING 12.2 Read about a dangerous job

WRITING 12.1 Write an email using linkers 12.4 Write a story about an exciting or frightening experience

BBC INTERVIEWS

What's the most exciting thing you've done?

Ⓖ present perfect
Ⓟ sentence stress: present perfect
Ⓥ experiences

VOCABULARY

EXPERIENCES

1 A Complete the phrases below with the words in the box. Use the photos to help you.

~~be~~ ride do sleep climb meet go watch

1 ___be___ in a play/in a film
2 ______ a bungee jump/a parachute jump
3 ______ someone famous/a great new friend on a train or plane journey
4 ______ an elephant/a motorbike
5 ______ to a live sporting event/to a karaoke bar
6 ______ outside/in an unusual place
7 ______ a mountain/a volcano
8 ______ the sun rise/your favourite band or singer live in concert

B Work in pairs. Look at photos A–E and discuss the questions.

1 Which activities above can you see in the photos?
2 Which activities would you like to do? Why?
3 Which activities would you not like to do? Why not?

LISTENING

2 A ▶ 12.1 Listen to a survey about great experiences. Tick the things the speakers have done or seen.

	1	2	3
karaoke			
an elephant ride			
the sun rise			
a volcano			
a bungee jump			
being in a film			

B Look at these sentences. Which speaker might say each one? Write 1, 2 or 3.

1 'It's my favourite song!'
2 'I did it on holiday in Italy.'
3 'I'd like to try it. It looks fun but scary!'
4 'I wasn't very good, but lots of people watched it on YouTube.'
5 'Everyone in Japan does it.'
6 'I enjoyed it more than my husband did.'

C Listen again. Which sentences do the speakers actually say?

D Work in pairs. What does *it* mean in each sentence in Exercise 2B?

E Work in pairs and discuss. Which experience would you most like to have?

GRAMMAR

PRESENT PERFECT

3 A Look at the sentences and underline the verbs. Then choose the correct alternatives to complete the rules.

I've watched the sun rise. He's been in a film.

RULES	
	1 Use the present perfect to talk about a *present/past* action. **2** Use the present perfect to talk about general experiences in your life when you *say/ don't say* an exact time.

B 12.2 SENTENCE STRESS: present perfect
Listen and complete the table. Then listen again and repeat.

I	______ ______ never haven't	climbed watched ______	a volcano. the sun rise. outside.

______	you ever	ridden	an elephant?
No,	I	______.	

C Work in pairs and complete the information.

1 Make the present perfect with ______/______ and the past participle of the verb.
2 The past participle of regular verbs *(watch, climb)* is the same as the ______ of the verb.

▷ page 150 **LANGUAGEBANK**

4 A Complete the table with the correct past participles. Check in your dictionary or the irregular verbs list on page 127.

Regular Verbs	Past participle	Irregular Verbs	Past participle
1 watch	*watched*	7 do	*done*
2 climb	______	8 be	______
3 stay	______	9 have	______
4 try	______	10 meet	______
5 travel	______	11 go	______/ ______
6 use	______	12 see	______

B Use four of the past participles above to write sentences about you. Two sentences should be false.

I've had lunch with the President.

C Work in pairs and take turns. Student A: say your four sentences. Student B: guess which two are false.

speakout TIP

Look for patterns to help you remember. In your notebook, write the past participles: *meet – met, sleep … ride – ridden, write … grow – grown, know … swim – swum, drink … drive – driven, give …*

SPEAKING

5 A Complete the questions with your own ideas.

1 Have you ever been to ______?
2 Have you ever slept in a ______?
3 Have you ever had ______?
4 Have you ever met ______?
5 Have you ever ______?

B Work in groups. Ask and answer the questions above. Who has done most things in your group?

A: Have you ever been to the Sahara Desert?
B: Yes, I have.
C: No, I haven't, but I'd like to.

WRITING

LINKERS REVIEW

6 A Read the email below. Which country are the people visiting?

Dear Helena

This country is very different from what I expected. It's very hot in the day [1] *but* it's nice and cool at night, [2]______ I always carry a sweater in my bag. We sleep in tents, [3]______ sometimes on the boats, and every day we get up at six. We've seen the temples in Kom Ombo and Edfu, and [4]______ the ones at Abu Simbel. They were amazing! We haven't seen the Pyramids [5]______ we'll only get to Cairo on Saturday.

We've got two days in Cairo. On Saturday, [6]______ we're going to the museum, [7]______ we're going to visit a famous mosque and an old church [8]______. In the afternoon we're going to Khan Al-Khalili Market. We want to buy a lamp for Lily and one for us [9]______. Then [10]______ we're going to have dinner on a boat on the river. It's going to be a long day!

Speak soon

Ollie and Kriszti

B Complete the email with the linkers in the box.

~~but~~ also finally as well because then or so too first

C Write an email to another student about one of these topics: an amazing holiday, a live concert or an interesting experience. Write 80–100 words and include at least five different linkers.

D Work in pairs. Exchange your emails. Ask your partner questions about their experience.

12.2 AFRAID OF NOTHING

G present perfect and past simple
P irregular past participles
V prepositions

Eunice Huthart has accidents all the time. She's jumped off ships and fallen off buildings. She's driven cars very fast and crashed them, and she's loved every moment. Eunice is a stunt double in films and does things that most of us think are crazy.

Crashing a car at high speed, walking away, and then waking up the next morning with a few aches and pains is all part of the job for a stunt double.

Waking up with aches and pains is all part of the job.

Eunice has done stunts in Harry Potter and James Bond films. She's been Angelina Jolie's stunt double in many films, from the *Lara Croft: Tomb Raider* series to *Maleficent*.

Eunice has broken some bones, and perhaps her worst accident was during *Titanic* when she jumped off the ship onto some boxes and broke her cheek bone. Eunice worked on *Titanic* in her first year as a stuntwoman, in 1996.

Broken bones and other injuries are normal for stunt doubles. So why do they do it? Most talk about the excitement, the challenge and the big money.

Eunice now works more as a stunt director, directing other stunt performers. Altogether she has worked on over fifty films.

Eunice loves her job, but in the end she's a family person. When asked about the most memorable moment in her life, she talked about the birth of her daughter and Liverpool winning the European Cup.

Broken bones and other injuries are normal.

READING

1 A Read the definition of *stunt* below. Can you think of any famous stunts?

> **S** **stunt 1** /stʌnt/ *noun* a dangerous thing that someone does to entertain people, especially in a film: *There's a great stunt in which his car has to jump across a fifteen-metre gap.*

From Longman Wordwise Dictionary.

B Read the article. How many stunts does it mention? How many of the films in the article do you know?

C Read the article again. Are sentences 1–6 true (T) or false (F)?

1 She likes doing car stunts.
2 She started doing stunt work over fifteen years ago.
3 She gets angry when she hurts herself in her job.
4 She often works as a stuntwoman these days.
5 Stunt doubles get a lot of money for their work.
6 Her work is more important than her family.

D Circle four movement verbs in the first paragraph of the text. Write the verb, past simple and past participle. Use your dictionary or the irregular verbs list on page 127 to help.

(jumped) – jump jumped jumped

E Work with other students. What are three good things and three bad things about being a stunt performer? Would you like to have the job?

GRAMMAR

PRESENT PERFECT AND PAST SIMPLE

2 A Look at the sentences. Underline the correct tense of the verbs.

1 She has done stunts in Harry Potter films. *(past simple/present perfect)*
2 Eunice worked on *Titanic* in 1996. *(past simple/present perfect)*

B Underline the correct alternatives.

RULES	1 With the present perfect, you *say/don't say* the exact time in the past. 2 With the past simple, you *say/don't say* the exact time in the past.

▷ page 150 **LANGUAGEBANK**

3 A Write the questions in full. Use the present perfect and *ever*.

1 see / *Titanic*?
2 break / your arm?
3 eat / anything unusual?
4 swim / in a river?
5 make / anything to wear?
6 go / to a really hot or cold country?

B Look at the conversation. Which verb forms are used? Why?

A: *Have you ever seen Titanic?*
B: *No, I haven't. Have you?*
A: *Yes, I have. I saw it online last year.*
B: *What did you think of it?*

C Work in pairs and take turns. Ask and answer the questions in Exercise 3A. Remember to ask follow-up questions.

D Ask other students two questions about things you haven't done. How many students have done these things?

A: *Have you ever seen a live football match?*

4 A **IRREGULAR PAST PARTICIPLES** Work in pairs. Write the past participles of the verbs in the box under the correct sound below.

~~sleep~~ ~~sing~~ ~~speak~~ ~~drive~~ ~~buy~~ read write think fly win meet do give choose bring

/e/	/ʌ/	/əʊ/	/ɪ/	/ɔː/
slept	*sung*	*spoken*	*driven*	*bought*

B ▶ 12.3 Listen and check. Then listen and repeat.

VOCABULARY

PREPOSITIONS

5 A Look at the pictures. What is the man doing?

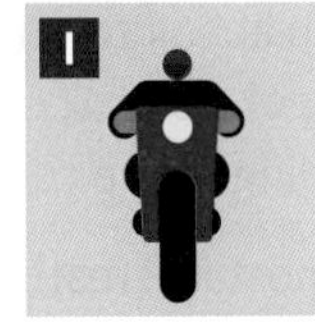

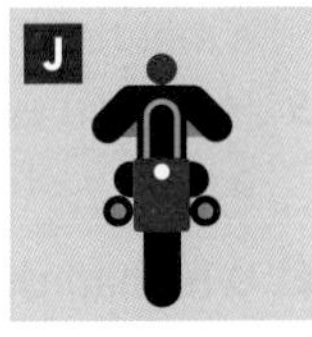

B Match the prepositions in the box with the pictures A–J.

down through up out of under towards away from across over into

C Some of the prepositions have opposites. Look at the pictures again and find the opposites of these prepositions: *down, over, away from, out of.*

D Complete the situations with a preposition of movement. More than one might be possible.

1 driving <u>*through*</u> a very long tunnel
2 going ______ in a glass lift
3 walking ______ a big dog
4 walking ______ a big park alone
5 going ______ a bridge when a train is going ______ the bridge
6 riding a bike fast ______ a big hill
7 walking ______ a rope bridge
8 walking ______ a room full of new people

SPEAKING

6 A How do you feel about the situations in Exercise 5D? Write one of the phrases in the box below next to each one.

I love it. It's not a problem. I really don't like it. I'm afraid of it. I've never done it.

B Work with other students and discuss your ideas.

A: *How do you feel about driving through a very long tunnel?*
B: *I really don't like it. In fact I really hate it. I feel sick.*
C: *Why? Have you had a bad experience?*
B: *Not really, I just don't like it.*

12.3 HELLO, I'VE GOT A PROBLEM

F telephoning
P sentence stress
V telephoning expressions

SPEAKING

1 A Work in pairs and take turns. Ask and answer questions 1–5. For each 'yes', ask your partner what happened.

1 Have you ever lost your …
keys? mobile? credit card?
2 Have you ever locked yourself out of your …
house? car? office?
3 Have you ever missed a …
train? bus? plane?
4 Have you ever been very late for …
a meeting? an appointment? a concert?
5 Have you ever got lost in …
a city? a building? the countryside?

B Who had the most interesting experience? Tell the class about it.

C In which of the situations did you use your phone to help with the problem?

VOCABULARY

TELEPHONING EXPRESSIONS

2 A Complete the sentences with words/phrases from the box.

~~take a message~~ leave a message call answer ring (someone) back

1 You answer the phone. It's a call for your colleague Patricia, but she's not in the office today so you _take a message_ for her.
2 You phone your friend Mark, but he's not at home so you _______ on his answerphone.
3 You want Mark to _______ you _______ this evening.
4 It's the evening. You _______ Mark, but he's having a shower.
5 Ten minutes later the phone rings and you _______ it. It's Mark.

B Work in pairs and compare your answers. Which two verbs mean *to phone*?

FUNCTION

TELEPHONING

3 A 12.4 Listen to three conversation extracts. Which situations from Exercise 1A are they?

B 12.5 Cross out the incorrect alternative. Then listen and check.

Extract 1
B: Hi, Sean. [1]*It's/I'm* Debbie.
A: Hi, Debbie. What's up?
B: [2]Is Kevin *there/here*?
A: No, he's not. He went out about ten minutes ago.

Extract 2
B: [3]Could I *leave/have* a message for him?
A: Of course.
B: [4]Just *ask/say* him to *mobile/call* me.

Extract 3
B: Hello. [5]Could I *speak/chat* to customer services, please?
A: [6]Just a *hold/moment*.
C: Customer services.
B: Hello. [7]*I am/This is* Alan Simpson. I've got a problem.

Extract 4
B: [8]Could you *ring/answer* me back?
C: Of course. Could you give me the number there?
B: Just a moment … It's 34 for Spain, 91 for Madrid, then 308 5238.
C: [9]Let me *check/buzz* that. 34 91 308 5238.
B: That's right.
C: Fine. Hang up and [10]I'll call you *up/back* straightaway.

C Match the conversation extracts 1–4 with descriptions a)–d) below.

a) Asking someone to call back *4*
b) Starting a call to a business
c) Starting a call to a friend
d) Leaving a message

D Underline the key stressed words in telephoning phrases 1–10 in Exercise 3B.

E 12.6 SENTENCE STRESS Listen and check. Then listen and repeat.

▷ page 150 LANGUAGEBANK

4 A Work in pairs. Look at the flowchart and write the conversation in full.

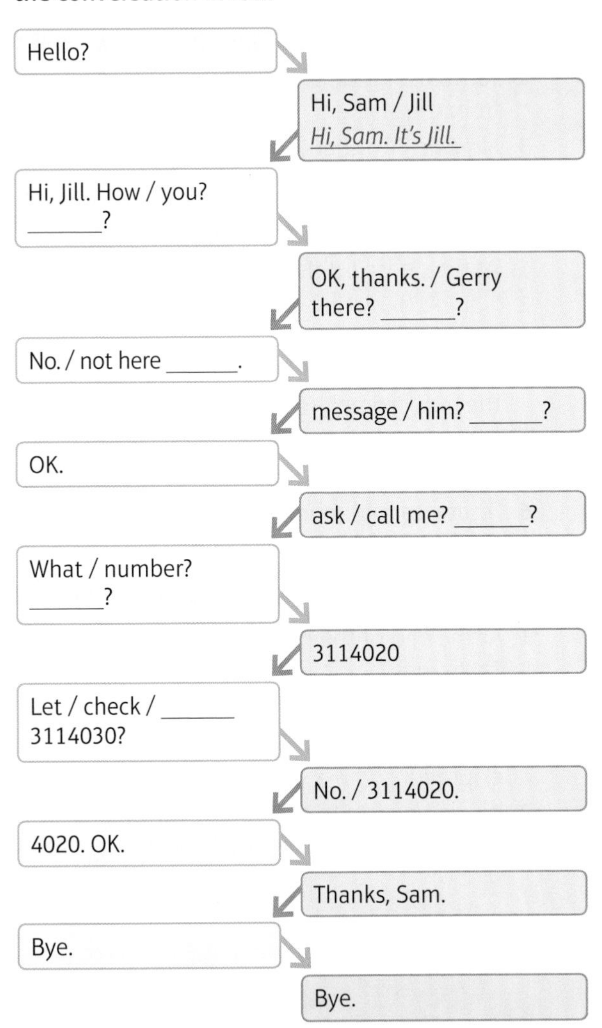

Hello?
Hi, Sam / Jill
Hi, Sam. It's Jill.
Hi, Jill. How / you?
_______?
OK, thanks. / Gerry there? _______?
No. / not here _______.
message / him? _______?
OK.
ask / call me? _______?
What / number?
_______?
3114020
Let / check / _______ 3114030?
No. / 3114020.
4020. OK.
Thanks, Sam.
Bye.
Bye.

B Work in pairs. Read out your conversation.

LEARN TO
SAY TELEPHONE NUMBERS

5 A 12.7 Complete the phone number. Then listen and check.

07663114020 = _______ seven _______ six three _______ one four _______ two _______

B Listen again. Draw a line between the words where you hear a short break.

speakout TIP

In telephone numbers:
- say '*oh*' for the number zero.
- when there are two of the same number, e.g. 77, say '*seven seven*' or '*double seven*'.
- group the numbers so they're easier to remember, for example, in the UK: 07663 (pause) 114 (pause) 020.

How do you pronounce numbers in your country?

C Work in pairs. Draw a line between the numbers where you think a pause is good. Practise saying the numbers.

1 07996072531
2 08355842706
3 81013005492
4 4478051349

D Work in pairs and take turns. Student A: look at page 163. Student B: look at page 166.

SPEAKING

6 Work in pairs. Student A: look at page 165. Student B: look at page 162. Role-play the situations.

SHARK THERAPY

DVD PREVIEW

1 Work in pairs. Look at the photos and discuss the questions. Are you afraid of any of these animals? Which ones? Why?

2 A Complete the sentences with words from the box.

~~frightened~~ nervous excited upset proud afraid

1 Some people are _frightened_ or ________ of the dark.
2 When you are positive and happy before your birthday or a party, you feel ______.
3 When you are happy about something you've done, often something difficult, you feel ______.
4 Before an exam or going to the dentist, you feel ______.
5 When you fail an exam, you feel ______.

B Complete sentences 1–6.

1 I'm afraid of ______.
2 I get very excited before ______.
3 I'm not frightened of ______.
4 I felt very proud when I ______.
5 I get nervous when I have to ______.
6 I last felt upset when ______.

C Work in pairs and compare ideas. Are any the same?

DVD VIEW

3 A Read the programme information. Why does Tanya go to the Bahamas?

Shark Therapy

BBC

Tanya Streeter is a world-famous diver, but she's got one big problem. She's afraid of sharks! To overcome her fear, she needs help or 'therapy' and travels to the Bahamas to get it. Here, she learns how to swim with them ... and comes face-to-face with a dangerous tiger shark.

B Watch the DVD. When do you think Tanya feels the most afraid?

C Underline the correct alternatives. Then watch again and check.

1 It's safer to wear a *black/green/shiny* wetsuit.
2 Tanya uses a *knife/stick/gun* to protect herself from the sharks.
3 *No/One/Two* shark(s) *try/tries* to bite Tanya.

D Look at the programme extracts below. Watch the DVD again and correct the mistakes.

1 'At first, it isn't ~~difficult~~.' *easy*
2 'I didn't think that they were going to be ... quite so ... friendly.'
3 'I noticed the mask and I think we should change the mask completely.'
4 'Jim throws meat into the water to attract the sharks.'
5 'Tanya, look behind you over on your right.'
6 'That was frightening! Tanya did great.'
7 'I've started to overcome my very real feeling.'

E Work in pairs and answer the questions.

1 At the end of the programme do you think Tanya was:
   a) frightened?
   b) excited?
   c) proud?
2 Would you like to try therapy with sharks or with any animals from Exercise 1? Why/Why not?

speakout a frightening experience

4 A Think about an exciting or frightening experience you've had. Look at the questions below and make notes:

- How old were you?
- Where was it?
- What happened? (write the verb phrases)
- How did you feel?
- What happened in the end?
- How did you feel in the end?

B 12.8 Listen to a man talk about an experience. Was it exciting or frightening? What happened?

C Listen again and tick the key phrases you hear.

KEYPHRASES

This happened in [time/place] when I was [age].
One day, … Then, … After that, …
I felt [excited/nervous/frightened/…]
I got [hot/hungry/tired/…]
In the end, …
It was [one of] the most [exciting/amazing/frightening/…] experiences I've ever had.

D Work in groups and take turns. One student: talk about your experience. Use the key phrases and your notes to help. Other students: listen and ask two follow-up questions about each event.

writeback a short story

5 A Before he talked about his experience, the man made some notes. Look at the notes below and number the events in the correct order.

went for a walk 1
one dog bit my arm
didn't move, didn't look at the dogs
remembered advice
dogs ran towards me
heard some dogs
realised I was in a new place
dogs jumped and barked

B Work in pairs and compare your answers.

C Use your notes from Exercise 4A and write about your experience in 80–100 words. Remember to use some of the key phrases to help.

V EXPERIENCES

1 A What are the activities? Add the vowels.

1 w_tch the s_n r_s_
2 sl_ _p _ _ts_d_
3 r_d_ an _l_ph_nt
4 m_ _t someone f_m_ _s
5 g_ to a l_v_ sp_rt_ng _v_nt
6 d_ a p_r_ch_t_ j_mp
7 cl_mb a m_ _nt_ _n
8 b_ in a f_lm

B Work in pairs and discuss.

1 Which activities above can you do in your country? Where can you do them?
2 Which activities above do you think are special/boring/exciting?
3 Which activities above would you like to do/try? Why?

G PRESENT PERFECT

2 A Write the sentences in full.

1 I / never / eat / fish eyes.
2 I / never / go / to an art gallery.
3 I / never / see / the sun rise.
4 I / never / drive / a Mercedes.
5 I / never / drink / tea with milk for breakfast.
6 I / never / play / golf.
7 I / never / cook / dinner for my parents.
8 I / never / speak / English on the phone.
9 I / never / go / to an outdoor festival.
10 I / never / hear / Adele live.

B Change the last part of each sentence so that it is true for you.

I've never eaten cabbage.
I've never been to an art gallery, but I'd like to.

C Work in pairs and compare your answers.

G PRESENT PERFECT AND PAST SIMPLE

3 A Complete the questions. Use the correct form of the verbs in brackets.

Have you ever …

1 _ridden_ a horse? (ride)
2 ______ in a small plane? (fly)
3 ______ in a lake? (swim)
4 ______ a long distance? (cycle)
5 ______ on a train? (sleep)
6 ______ a mountain? (climb)

B Work in pairs and take turns. Ask and answer the questions in Exercise 3A and ask follow-up questions.

A: Have you ever … ?
B: Yes, I have.
A: Oh, when was that?

V PREPOSITIONS

4 A Look at the word webs and cross out the place/thing which does not go with the preposition of movement.

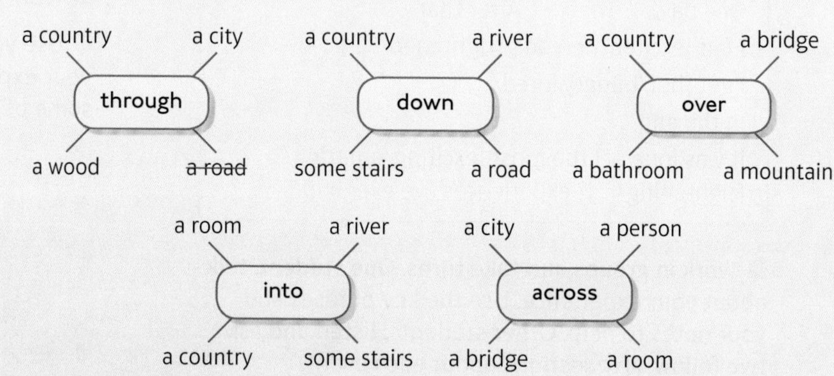

B Work in pairs. Student A: choose one of the prepositions. Say three things that can come after it. Student B: guess the preposition.

A: A country, a mountain, a bridge
B: Over?

F TELEPHONING

5 A Complete the telephone conversation. Write two words in each gap.

A: Hello, the Learn English Centre.
B: Hello, [1]______ Sofia Mitsotakis. [2]______ speak to my teacher, Rachel, please?
A: [3]______ moment. [4]______ check … I'm afraid she's in class at the moment.
B: I see. Could [5]______ a message for her?
A: Sure. Go ahead.
B: Could you [6]______ to call me this afternoon?
A: Yes, could you [7]______ your number?
B: It's 0853 58230.
A: OK. She'll [8]______ back.
B: Thank you.

B Work in pairs. Student A: Phone the school to speak to your English teacher. Student B: you are the receptionist. The teacher can't come to the phone. Continue the conversation with your ideas.

IRREGULAR VERBS

Verb	Past simple	Past participle
be	was	been
become	became	become
begin	began	begun
bite	bit	bitten
blow	blew	blown
break	broke	broken
bring	brought	brought
build	built	built
buy	bought	bought
catch	caught	caught
choose	chose	chosen
come	came	come
cost	cost	cost
cut	cut	cut
do	did	done
draw	drew	drawn
drink	drank	drunk
drive	drove	driven
eat	ate	eaten
fall	fell	fallen
feel	felt	felt
find	found	found
fly	flew	flown
forget	forgot	forgotten
freeze	froze	frozen
get	got	got
give	gave	given
go	went	gone
grow	grew	grown
have	had	had
hear	heard	heard
hide	hid	hidden
hit	hit	hit
hold	held	held
hurt	hurt	hurt
keep	kept	kept
know	knew	known
learn	learned/learnt	learned/learnt
leave	left	left

Verb	Past simple	Past participle
lend	lent	lent
let	let	let
lie	lay	lain
lose	lost	lost
make	made	made
mean	meant	meant
meet	met	met
pay	paid	paid
put	put	put
read	read	read
ride	rode	ridden
ring	rang	rung
run	ran	run
say	said	said
see	saw	seen
sell	sold	sold
send	sent	sent
shine	shone	shone
show	showed	shown
shut	shut	shut
sing	sang	sung
sit	sat	sat
sleep	slept	slept
smell	smelled/smelt	smelled/smelt
speak	spoke	spoken
spend	spent	spent
spill	spilled/spilt	spilled/spilt
stand	stood	stood
swim	swam	swum
take	took	taken
teach	taught	taught
tell	told	told
think	thought	thought
throw	threw	thrown
understand	understood	understood
wake	woke	woken
wear	wore	worn
win	won	won
write	wrote	written

GRAMMAR

1.1 present simple: *be*

Positive			
+	I	am 'm	fine, thanks.
+	He/She/It	is 's	in class 3A.
+	You/We/They	are 're	students.
Negative			
–	I	'm not	very well.
–	He/She/It	isn't	here.
–	You/We/They	aren't	students.

Use a subject pronoun (*I*, *you*, *she*, etc.) with a verb.
***She is** British.* NOT ~~*Is British.*~~
You is singular and plural.
Use contractions in speaking and in emails and letters to friends.
An apostrophe (') = a missing letter.
*I **am** Indian.* → *I'**m** Indian.* *You **are not** Greek.* → *You **aren't** Greek.*
In the negative, it is also possible to use: *He/She/It's not* and *You/We/They're not*.
***She's not** here.*

Use *be* to talk about:

- who a person is or what an object is. *I'**m** James. It'**s** a pen.*
- where a person or a thing is from. *She'**s** American. Spaghetti **is** Italian.*
- people's jobs. *I'**m** a student. My mother'**s** a teacher.*
- a person's age. *I'**m** eighteen. Mark'**s** twenty-four.*
- where something is. *The Eiffel Tower **is** in France.*
- prices. *It'**s** twelve euros.*

Questions and short answers						
?	Am	I	a teacher?	Yes,	I	am.
				No,		'm not.
	Are	you/we/they	tourists?	Yes,	you/we/they	are.
				No,		aren't.
	Is	he/she/it	OK?	Yes,	he/she/it	is.
				No,		isn't.

Use *be* + subject for the question.
It is good. ***Is it** good?*
You are from Italy. ***Are you** from Italy?*
Don't use contractions in positive short answers.
Yes, she is. NOT ~~*Yes, she's.*~~

1.2 *this/that, these/those*

	near	far
singular	this bag	that bag
plural	these bags	those bags

possessive *'s*

Akira's Chris's The teacher's	bag magazines books

Use *Akira's bag* NOT ~~*the bag of Akira*~~.
It is also possible to say *Akira's* without repeating the noun.
*Is this **John's** bag? No, it's **Akira's**.*

Possessive pronouns

Subject pronoun	Possessive adjective	Possessive pronoun
I	It's my mobile.	It's mine.
You	It's your pen.	It's yours.
He	It's his diary.	It's his.
She	It's her book.	It's hers.
We	It's our car.	It's ours.
They	It's their house.	It's theirs.

Use a possessive adjective (*my/your*, etc.) + noun.
my mobile, his name
Use a possessive pronoun (*mine/yours*, etc.) + no noun in short answers.
*Is this Ben's **mobile**? No, it isn't Ben's. It's **mine**.*
NOT ~~*It's mine mobile*~~.

1.3 making requests

Can Could	I	have	a sandwich, please? one of those batteries, please? a return ticket to Paris, please?

Use *Can/Could* + *I* + infinitive to make requests.
Note: *could* is often more formal and polite than *can*.
Reply. *Yes, of course. Here you are.*

PRACTICE

1.1

A **Complete the sentences with positive forms of *be*. Use contractions.**

1 I _______ Sonia D'Angelo.
2 They _______ at university.
3 It _______ Tuesday today.
4 Julio _______ on holiday.
5 We _______ from the BBC.
6 You _______ in my class, Yasmin.

B **Complete the conversation. Use the correct forms of *be*.**

Farah: [1]_______ you Cindy?
Jenny: No, I [2]_______. I [3]_______ Jennifer.
Farah: [4]_______ you a student?
Jenny: No, I [5]_______ the teacher! [6]_______ you a student?
Farah: Yes, I [7]_______.
Jenny: OK, please sit down.

C **Put the words in the correct order. Start with the underlined word.**

1 in / Debra / the / café / isn't.
2 name / your / Is / Khan?
3 at / Mrs / aren't / Mr / airport / and / Cabrera / the.
4 friend / is / Paolo / This / my.
5 their / What / names / are?
6 centre / 's / Where / health / the?

1.2

A **Complete the conversations. Use *this*, *that*, *these* or *those*.**

Conversation 1
A: Brigitte, [1]_______ is Phil.
B: Hello, Phil. Nice to meet you.
A: And [2]_______ are my children. [3]_______ is Tom and [4]_______ is Alice.
B: Hi!

Conversation 2
A: Is [5]_______ your car over there?
B: Yes, it is. It's great! And very fast!

Conversation 3
A: One of [6]_______ cakes, please.
B: [7]_______ one here?
A: No, [8]_______ one there.

B **Add an apostrophe (') in the correct place.**

1 This is Megans laptop.
2 These are Vickys keys.
3 Those books are my teachers.
4 Where are Boriss friends?
5 Are those sunglasses Ralphs?

C **Change the conversations so they don't repeat the nouns.**

Conversation 1
A: Hey! That's my pen!
B: No, it isn't. It's ~~my pen~~ *mine*, not ~~your pen~~ *yours*.

Conversation 2
A: I think these are Stefan's keys.
B: No, they aren't Stefan's keys. They're Daniela's keys.

Conversation 3
A: Is this your book?
B: No, it's your book. My book is in my bag.

Conversation 4
A: Are these Tanya's bags?
B: No, they aren't her bags. They're our bags.

1.3

A **Complete the conversation with the words in the box.**

you	That's	postcard	too	could	Can	Here	stamps	Thanks

A: [1]_______ I help you?
B: Yes, [2]_______ I have this [3]_______, please?
A: Here you are. Anything else?
B: Yes, can I have two [4]_______ for Australia, please?
A: [5]_______ £2.50.
B: [6]_______ you are.
A: Thank [7]_______. Have a good day!
B: [8]_______. You [9]_______.

2 LANGUAGE BANK

GRAMMAR

2.1 present simple: *I/you/we/they* positive and negative statements

+	I You We They	love go listen	films. running every day. to music on the bus.
–		don't read	books.

Use the present simple to talk about:
- things which are always true. *I **come** from Spain. I **like** cats.*
- habits and routines. *We **play** tennis on Sundays.*

In the negative, use *don't* + infinitive. *I **don't work** at the weekend.*
When speaking, and in emails and letters to friends, use the contraction *don't* (= *do not*).
After *love*, *like*, *enjoy*, *don't like* and *hate*, use infinitive + *-ing*. *I don't like eat**ing** junk food. I enjoy do**ing** nothing.*

present simple: *I/you/we/they* questions and short answers

?	Do	I/you/we/they	drink like	coffee? watching films?	+	Yes,	I/you/we/they	do.
					–	No,		don't.

Use *Do* + subject + infinitive for a question.
***Do you have** lunch at home?*
In short answers, use *Yes, I do* and *No, I don't*. NOT ~~*Yes, I like*~~ or ~~*No, I don't like*~~.

2.2 present simple: *he/she/it* positive and negative statements

+	He She It	comes watches does flies has	from Japan. TV. everything. to Peru. lunch.	verb + *-s* verb ending in *-ch*, *-sh*, *-s*, *-x* + *-es* *do* and *go* + *-es* verb ending in a consonant + *-y*, change *-y* to *-ies* *have* change to *has*
–	He/She/It	doesn't like		cats.

In the negative, use *doesn't* + infinitive. *He **doesn't want** to come.*
When speaking, or writing emails or letters to friends, use the contraction *doesn't* (= *does not*).

present simple: *he/she/it* questions and short answers

?	Does	he/she/it	come	from Italy?	+	Yes,	he/she/it	does.
					–	No,		doesn't.

Use *Does* + subject + infinitive to make a question. ***Does she get** home late?*
In short answers, use *Yes, it does* and *No, it doesn't* NOT ~~*Yes, it comes*~~ or ~~*No it doesn't come*~~.

2.3 asking for information

What time When	does	it the tour	start? finish?
Where			leave from?
How much			cost?

Do	you	take	credit cards?

answering with *in/at/on*

in	at	on
the morning the afternoon the evening	9 o'clock, 7.30 midnight night the weekend	Saturday Sunday

PRACTICE

2.1

A Complete the sentences with the correct form (positive or negative) of the verbs in the box.

~~go~~ eat read watch listen to drink work

1 I *don't go* running because I'm not very active!
2 We ________ sport on TV a lot because we really like it.
3 I ________ junk food because I don't like it.
4 They ________ on Sundays – they just relax all day!
5 I ________ books in English because it's good practice.
6 We ________ coffee late at night. We have milk or tea.
7 You ________ music a lot. What's your favourite band?

B Put the words in the correct order to make questions.

1 you / Do / classes / like / English / your ?
Do you like your English classes?
2 running / every day / go / they / Do ?
3 chat / you / friends / Do / with / a lot ?
4 junk / like / you / Do / food / eating ?
5 TV / on / watch / they / football / Do ?
6 cinema / the / to / go / you / Do / a lot ?

C Look at the short answers to the questions above and correct the mistakes.

1 Yes, I ~~like~~. *do*
2 No, they aren't.
3 Yes, we do chat.
4 No, I don't like.
5 No, they not.
6 Yes, we go.

2.2

A Write the *he/she/it* form of the verbs.

1 eat *eats* 2 study 3 understand 4 take 5 wash
6 chat 7 write 8 have 9 play 10 do

B Complete the texts with the verbs in the box. Use the present simple in the correct form.

go listen to watch study get up drink read meet work start have finish relax talk

Simona is a student. She [1]______ late, at 10a.m., [2]______ a black coffee and then [3]______ to classes at the university. In the afternoon, she [4]______ in the library. In the evening, she [5]______ TV or [6]______ music.

Beatrice is a businesswoman. She [7]______ breakfast at 6a.m. and [8]______ work at 8. In the morning, she [9]______ her emails and [10]______ to people on the phone. Beatrice's husband [11]______ near her office, so they [12]______ and have lunch together. She [13]______ work at 6p.m. and in the evening she just [14]______ at home.

C Correct the mistakes.

1 Dan likes dogs, but he no like cats.
2 Tariq drinks coffee, but he don't drink tea.
3 Sophia reads magazines, but she reads not books.
4 Lara works at the weekend, but she does work on Monday.
5 The hotel room has a television and a telephone, but it no have WiFi.

D Complete the conversation.

A: [1]______ you work?
B: No, I [2]______, but my wife [3]______.
A: Oh, what [4]______ she do?
B: She [5]______ English at a school.
A: Oh. And [6]______ she like it?
B: Yes, she [7]______. Well, she [8]______ like working in the evening, but she [9]______ her students.
A: And what [10]______ you do all day?
B: I [11]______ TV and [12]______ with my friend Bob on the phone.
A: Oh, and what [13]______ Bob do?
B: He's a film reviewer. He [14]______ about films on TV.

2.3

A Look at the table. Use the information to write questions for answers 1–6.

train	leaves arrives	8.30 10.15	$30
museum	opens closes	10.00 6.00	$15

1 8.30 2 10.15 3 $30 4 10.00 5 6.00 6 $15
What time/When does the train leave?

B Read the text and add *in*, *on* or *at* in ten more places.

At
The weekend we do a lot Saturday, but Sunday we have a relaxing day. We get up 10 o'clock the morning and have a late breakfast. We have lunch about 2 o'clock and then the afternoon we relax home. The evening we watch a DVD or something on TV and then we go to bed about 11.30 night.

GRAMMAR

3.1 *have/has got*

+	I/You/We/They	've (have)	got	three sisters.
	He/She/It	's (has)		
–	I/You/We/They	haven't		a phone. any coins.
	He/She/It	hasn't		

Use *have/has got* to talk about family and possessions.
Use contractions when speaking, or in emails or letters to friends. *I**'ve** got, she**'s** got.*
In the negative, use *any* before plural nouns.
*I haven't got **any brothers**.*

?	Have	I/you/we/they	got	a stamp? any aunts?	Yes,	I/you/we/they	have.
					No,		haven't.
	Has	he/she/it			Yes,	he/she/it	has.
					No,		hasn't.

In questions, use *a/an* before singular nouns, and *any* before plural nouns.
*Has she got **a car**?* *Have you got **any brothers**?*
In short answers use *Yes, I have* and *Yes, he has* NOT ~~*Yes, I've*~~ and ~~*Yes, she's*~~.

3.2 adverbs of frequency

never	hardly ever	sometimes	often	usually	always
0%	10%	40%	60%	80%	100%

I	often	listen to	the radio.
Keanu	hardly ever	has	breakfast.
They	are	never	late.
My phone	's	usually	here.

Use adverbs of frequency to say how often you do something.
*I **usually** have breakfast at home.*
*Leo is **always** very happy.*
Frequency adverbs go before most verbs: *He **never** listens to me,* but after the verb *be*: *Sarah is **usually** friendly.*
Usually and *sometimes* can also go at the beginning of a sentence.
***Sometimes** Ahmed phones me after midnight.*

3.3 making arrangements

Are	you free tonight?	
What	would you like	to do?
What time When		to go?
What time	's	good for you?
	does it	start?

ARE YOU FREE TONIGHT?
HMMM

making suggestions

How about	going	to the cinema?
Would you like	to go	

Use *How about* + infinitive + *-ing*.
Use *Would you like* + *to* + infinitive.
Would you like to = *Do you want to.*
***Would** you like **to play** tennis tomorrow?*
Do you like + *-ing* = in general.
***Do** you like **playing** tennis?*

responding to suggestions

+	Great. Sounds good. That's a good idea. OK.	–	Hmm. That's a problem. Sorry, I'm busy.

PRACTICE

3.1

A Complete the conversation with *have/has got*.

A: [1]__________ you [2]__________ any brothers or sisters?

B: Yes, I [3]__________ one sister, but I [4]__________ any brothers.

A: [5]__________ you [6]__________ any children?

B: Yes, I [7]__________. I [8]__________ three sons and a daughter, Annie. She [9]__________ a son and a daughter. And two of my sons [10]__________ two children each. Charlie [11]__________ two sons, and Andy [12]__________ two daughters.

A: And your sister? [13]__________ she [14]__________ any children?

B: Yes, Maggie [15]__________ a son and a daughter too.

B Complete the questions. Use the correct form of *be* or *have got*.

1 ___*Are you*___ (you) married?
2 __________ (you) a mobile?
3 __________ (your classroom) a TV?
4 __________ (your teacher) British?
5 __________ (you) usually early or late for class?
6 __________ (you) a diary with you?
7 __________ (you) cold?
8 __________ (your brother) twenty or twenty-one?
9 __________ (your home) WiFi?
10 __________ (the keys) in your bag?

3.2

A Put the words in the correct order to make sentences.

1 late / students / The / never / are
2 homework / their / always / They / do
3 hardly / ever / rains / here / It
4 TV / the morning / in / usually / We / watch / don't
5 quiet / I / am / very / sometimes
6 eat / We / ever / meat / hardly
7 does / finish / lesson / What / usually / the / time?
8 half / The / past / doctor / at / is / here / seven / often
9 never / here / tour / boat / leaves / The / from
10 that / Do / go / to / snack / often / bar / you?
11 up / the / At / gets / sometimes / eleven / weekend / at / Kim
12 watch / always / My / correct / isn't

B Add an adverb of frequency to each sentence. Use the information in brackets to help.

1 I get up early. (0%)
I never get up early.
2 I have breakfast with my family. (100%)
3 My father reads a newspaper on Sundays. (80%)
4 We're tired in the morning. (60%)
5 I go to bed up before 11p.m. (10%)
6 I drink coffee. (0%)
7 Nicola's late. (40%)
8 My sister phones me in the evening. (60%)
9 The hotel receptionist is friendly (100%)
10 The coffee here is hot! (0%)

3.3

A Complete the conversation.

Paolo: Hi, Carl. [1]_______ _______ free on Thursday evening?
Carl: No, but [2]_______ about Friday or Saturday?
Paolo: What time's [3]_______ _______ you?
Carl: Saturday evening's good. [4]_______ _______ _______ like to do?
Paolo: [5]_______ _______ going to the theatre?
Carl: Great. What's [6]_______?
Paolo: It's Macbeth by the Royal Shakespeare Company.
Carl: [7]_______ good. When [8]_______ the play _______?
Paolo: At half past seven. When [9]_______ you _______ to meet?
Carl: How [10]_______ _______ at seven o'clock? At the theatre?
Paolo: OK. See you there.

4 LANGUAGE BANK

GRAMMAR

4.1 *there is/are*

+	There	's	a balcony.	
		are	three bedrooms. some pictures.	
–	There	isn't	a	garden.
		aren't	any	chairs.

Is	there	a TV in the bedroom?	Yes,	there	is.
			No,		isn't.
Are	there	two bedrooms? any shelves?	Yes,	there	are.
			No,		aren't.

Use *there is* and *there are* to say that something exists.
Use t*here is* and *there are* to talk about places, and things and people in places.
There's *a health centre five minutes from here.*
There's *a spider in the bathroom!*
There are *only five students in class today.*
Use *there are* + *some* for no exact number.
There are ***some*** *books.*
In plural negatives and questions use *there aren't/are there* + *any* + noun.
There aren't ***any tables****.*
Are there ***any chairs****?*
In short answers, use *Yes, there is.* NOT ~~*Yes, there's*~~.
In negatives it's also possible to use *there's no* + noun.
There's no WiFi.

4.2 *can* for possibility

+	I/You/He/She/It/We/They	can	come to the party.
–		can't	

?	Can	I/you/he/she/it/we/they	buy English food?	Yes,	I/you/he/she/it/we/they	can.
				No,		can't.

Use *can* + infinitive to say something is possible.
You ***can buy*** *stamps at that shop.*
Use *can't (cannot)* + infinitive to say something is impossible.
You ***can't buy*** *medicine at this supermarket.*
Can is the same for all persons (*I*, *you*, *he*, *she*, etc.). *I can, she can* NOT ~~*she cans*~~.
Don't use *to* after *can*. *We can eat here.* NOT ~~*We can to eat here.*~~

4.3 shopping

It's	too very	big. small. expensive. long.
They're		

Use *very* + adjective with positive and negative ideas.
It's ***very*** *good.* *It's* ***very*** *expensive.*
Use *too* + adjective with negative ideas.
It's ***too*** *small.* = It's a problem for me.
Don't use *too* in place of *very*. *It's very nice.* NOT ~~*It's too nice.*~~

Have you got it in	extra large/large/medium/small? green/blue?
How much	is it? are they?

PRACTICE

4.1

A Write sentences with the prompts below. Use *there is/are* or *there isn't/aren't*.

1 2 / table / kitchen
There are two tables in the kitchen.
2 4 / chair / living room
3 2 / bedroom / my flat
4 0 / sofa / my living room
5 a bathroom / upstairs
6 0 / any shelves / the bathroom
7 a / television / our kitchen
8 0 / garden

B Complete the questions with *is/are there*.

1 How many chairs ____________ in the living room? 6
2 ____________ a desk in your bedroom? ✓
3 How many bedrooms ____________ in your flat? 3
4 ____________ a study? ✗
5 ____________ a separate dining room? ✓
6 How many bathrooms ____________ in your flat? 1

C Complete the answers to the questions in B.

1 *There are six chairs.*
2 ____________
3 ____________
4 ____________
5 ____________
6 ____________

4.2

	1	2	3	4	5
seaside hotel	a) no	b) yes	c) no	d) no	e) no
beach apartment	f) yes	g) no	h) no	i) yes	j) yes

A Write questions about a hotel/apartment for pictures 1–5. Use *Can you … there?*

1 *Can you cook there?*
2 ____________
3 ____________
4 ____________
5 ____________

B Look at the table. Complete the sentences below with *can* or *can't*.

At the seaside hotel …
a) *you can't cook.*
b) ____________
c) ____________
d) ____________
e) ____________

At the beach apartment …
f) ____________
g) ____________
h) ____________
i) ____________
j) ____________

4.3

A Complete the conversation.

Customer: Excuse me. [1]_______ _______ _______ this _______ medium?
Assistant: Hold on. I'll check. Yes, here you are.
Customer: Oh, blue. [2]_______ _______ _______ it _______ green?
Assistant: Medium in green? No. Here's a large. Is that OK?
Customer: Oh, no! That's [3]_______ _______.
Assistant: Ah, here's a medium in purple.
Customer: Great. [4]_______ _______ is it?
Assistant: £59.99.
Customer: Oh … that's too [5]_______, sorry. _______ anyway.

GRAMMAR

5.1 Countable and uncountable nouns

There are two types of nouns in English: countable nouns and uncountable nouns.

- Countable nouns are things you can count in English. They are singular or plural.
  a** banana, **an** apple, potato**es
- Uncountable nouns are things you **can't** count in English, e.g. *water, rice, bread*. They are never plural.
  NOT ~~one water~~, ~~two rices~~, ~~three breads~~
- Drinks are usually uncountable, e.g. *coffee, tea, juice* but you can say *a juice* (= a glass of juice) or *three coffees* (= three cups of coffee).
- It is also possible to use containers or amounts with the noun to show quantity, e.g. *a glass of water, two kilos of rice*
- Use a singular verb with uncountable nouns.
  ***Water is** good for you.* NOT ~~*Water are …*~~
  *There**'s sugar** in this coffee.* NOT ~~*There are sugar …*~~

Nouns with *a/an, some, any*

		Countable	Uncountable
+	We've got	a banana. some bananas.	some rice.
–	We haven't got	an apple. any apples.	any bread.
?	Have we got	a pear? any pears?	any pasta?

- Use *a/an* + singular countable nouns.
  *I need **an egg**.*
- Use *some* + plural countable nouns or uncountable nouns.
  *We've got **some vegetables**.*
  *There's **some butter** in the fridge.*
  (*Some* = not an exact number)
- Use *any* + plural countable nouns or uncountable nouns in questions and negatives.
  *Have you got **any sweets**?*
  *There isn't **any milk**.*
- Usually use *some* (NOT ~~*any*~~) to ask for things or to offer something to a person.
  *Can I have **some** coffee?*
  *Would you like **some** tea?*

5.2 *How much/many*; quantifiers

Countable	Quantifiers		Uncountable	Quantifiers	
How many apples do you eat?	A lot./Lots. Quite a lot. Not many. None.		How much coffee do you drink every day?	A lot./Lots. Quite a lot. Not much. None.	

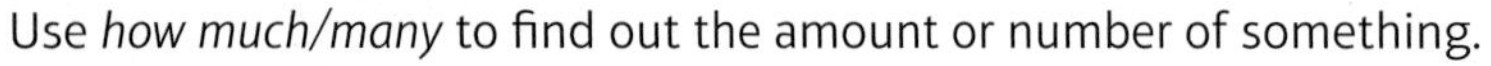

Use *how much/many* to find out the amount or number of something.

- Ask questions with *how much* + uncountable nouns.
  ***How much** sugar have we got?* ***How much** milk is there in the fridge?*
- Ask questions with *how many* + plural countable nouns.
  ***How many** tomatoes are there in that bag?* ***How many** vegetables do you eat in a week?*

Use quantifiers for short answers to *How much/many …* ?
***How much** cheese have we got? None.*
Use *a lot/lots (of), quite a lot (of), not much/many* + noun.
*I eat a **lot of** fruit.* *I do**n't** drink **much** water.*
We use *no* + noun. *There's **no milk**.* NOT *There's ~~none~~ milk.*

5.3 Ordering in a restaurant

Could I	have	a glass of water, some vegetable soup,	please?	+	Yes, of course. Yes, certainly.
Can I					
I'd	like		please.	–	I'm sorry, we haven't got any soup.

PRACTICE

5.1

A Look at the sentences and correct the mistakes in six sentences.

1 Do you often eat chickens?
2 Garlics are good for you.
3 Sylvie hardly ever eats fruit.
4 My parents never drink wines.
5 Does she eat prawn?
6 I usually put butters on my bread, not margarines.
7 Ken doesn't have sugar in his tea.
8 There are water on the table.

B Look at the picture. What does the customer buy? Write *a/an* or *some* and the types of food.

E = some bread

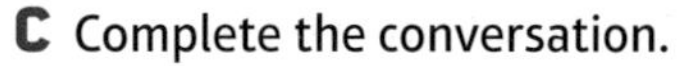

C Complete the conversation.

Man: What's for dinner?
Woman: Well, let's see. Oh no, we haven't got [1] ________ eggs.
Man: So I can't make an omelette. [2] ________ there ________ spaghetti?
Woman: Yes, there's [3] ________ packet of spaghetti.
Man: Have we got [4] ________ tomatoes?
Woman: Yes, but there [5] ________ only one.
Man: Oh. [6] ________ there ________ butter?
Woman: Yeah, we've got [7] ________ butter.
Man: Great. So dinner is … spaghetti with butter on it!

5.2

A Complete the questions with *How much/many*.

1 ________ tea or coffee do you drink in the evening?
2 ________ people are there in this room?
3 ________ homework do you do every day?
4 ________ eggs are there in an omelette?
5 ________ hours do you sleep every night?
6 ________ children have you got?

B Complete the sentences about the picture. Use *is/are* + *a lot of*, *quite a lot of*, *not much/many*, *none* or *no*.

1 There *'s quite a lot of* water.
2 There ________ women.
3 There ________ men.
4 There ________ empty glasses.
5 There ________ food.
6 There ________ fruit juice.

5.3

A Complete the conversation in a restaurant.

Waiter: Are you ready to order?
Customer: Yes, [1] ________ I have some tomato soup, ________?
Waiter: And for the main course?
Customer: I [2] ________ like roast beef.
Waiter: What sort of vegetables [3] ________ you ________?
Customer: [4] ________ I have potatoes and green peas?
Waiter: [5] ________ you ________ a salad with that?
Customer: No, thank you.
Waiter: And something to drink?
Customer: [6] ________ like a mineral water, please.
Waiter: Yes, of course.

GRAMMAR

6.1 past simple: *was/were*

+	I/He/She/It	was	happy. born in 2004.
	You/We/They	were	
–	I/He/She/It	wasn't	
	You/We/They	weren't	

?	Was	I/he/she/it	at home?	Yes,	I/he/she/it	was.
				No,		wasn't.
	Were	you/we/they		Yes,	you/we/they	were.
				No,		weren't.

The past simple of *be* is *was/were*. Use *was/were* to talk about things which started and finished in the past.
*I **was** five years old.* *The people in Colombia **were** very friendly.*
When speaking or writing emails and letters to friends, use contractions: *wasn't = was not, weren't = were not.*

6.2 past simple

regular verbs				
+	I/You/He/She/It/We/They	started	a new school.	most verbs + *-ed*
		lived	in Spain.	verb ending in *-e* + *-d*
		studied	English.	verb ending in a consonant + *-y*, change to *-ied*
		travelled	a lot.	verb ending in a consonant–vowel–consonant, double the final consonant + *-ed*

Use the past simple to talk about things which started and finished in the past.
*I **travelled** to China last year.* (I'm not in China now.) *We **lived** in Turkey for three years.*

irregular verbs			
+	I/You/He/She/It/We/They	went	home.
		had	a big meal.

Many common verbs have an irregular past simple form. Look at the list on page 127.

negatives with regular and irregular verbs				
–	I/You/He/She/It/We/They	didn't	like	the food.
			have	a DVD player.

The negative is the same for regular and irregular verbs.
Use *didn't* + infinitive. *I **didn't work**.* (regular) NOT ~~*I didn't worked.*~~
*We **didn't eat**.* (irregular) NOT ~~*We didn't ate.*~~

Questions and short answers					
Did	I/you/he/she/it/we/they	stop? come? like it?	Yes,	I/you/he/she/it/we/they	did.
			No,		didn't.

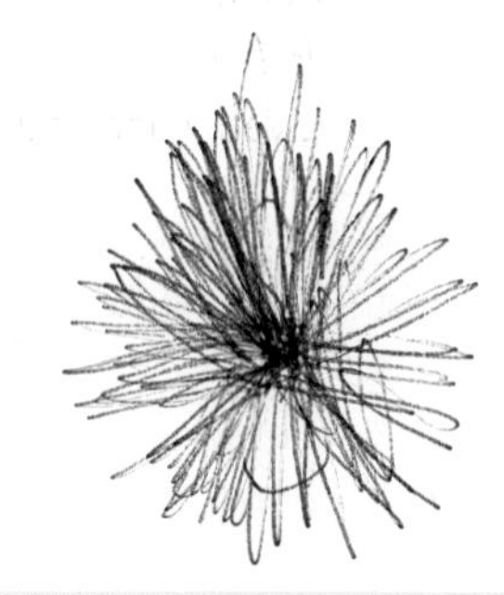

In questions, use *Did* + subject + infinitive. ***Did you like** it?* NOT ~~*Did you liked it?*~~
WH questions begin with *what, where, when, what time, who, why* or *how*.
In *WH* questions in the past simple, use *WH* question word + *did* + subject + infinitive.
***When did** you **go**?* *How **did** you **travel**?* NOT ~~*When did you went?*~~ ~~*How did you travelled?*~~

6.3 Ask follow-up questions

Opening questions	Answers	Showing interest
How was your weekend? What did you do at the weekend?	It was great/terrible! Not bad./It was OK./So-so. Nothing special/much.	Really? That sounds nice/great/lovely/ good/interesting/terrible. That's interesting/a shame.

Follow-up questions
Why, what happened? Why was that? Where did you go? What did you do? Who did you go with?

In spoken English, when you show interest, it's possible to leave out *That* in *That sounds …*, e.g. *Sounds great/terrible!*

PRACTICE

6.1

A Put the words in the correct order. Add capital letters.

1 child / were / a / you / happy?
2 was / holiday / your / how?
3 yesterday / concert / at / Jack / was / the?
4 were / last / night / the / open / windows?
5 people / the / many / at / there / how / were / party?

B Complete the answers to the questions in Exercise A.

1 Yes, I ________.
2 It ________ great, thanks.
3 No, he ________.
4 Yes, they ________.
5 There ________ about fifty.

6.2

A Complete the sentences with the verbs in the box. Use the past simple.

dance	play	love	study	listen to	work

1 Mick Jagger ________ economics in London in 1961.
2 When she was four, Shakira ________ on the table to some Arab music.
3 Brad Pitt ________ as a driver before he was a film star.
4 Cate Blanchett ________ the piano every day when she was young.
5 Shizuka Arakawa ________ swimming and ballet when she was young.
6 Ronaldinho ________ samba music when he was young.

B Read the text. Then complete the story about yesterday with the verbs in brackets in the correct form.

Tom usually gets up at six, does some exercise and walks to work. He eats lunch alone, leaves work at five and meets his girlfriend for dinner. Then he reads a book in the evening, drinks a cup of tea and goes to bed early.

But yesterday was different. He [1] *didn't get up* (not get up) at six, he [2] ________ (get up) at eight. He [3] ________ (not do) any exercise and he [4] ________ (drive) to work. He [5] ________ (not have) lunch alone – he [6] ________ (meet) his friend Sally at a restaurant. She [7] ________ (tell) him about her problems, but he [8] ________ (not listen). He [9] ________ (not meet) his girlfriend for dinner – he [10] ________ (eat) alone, then [11] ________ (watch) a DVD. Two things [12] ________ (not change): he [13] ________ (drink) a cup of tea and [14] ________ (go) to bed early as usual.

C Complete the questions using the answers to help. Who is the famous person?

1 Born? When *was he born*?	In 1963. He was born in Kentucky, USA.
2 Lived when young? Where ________?	In a lot of different places. His family moved twenty times.
3 Began film work? When ________?	He began acting in films in 1984. His first film was *A Nightmare on Elm Street*.
4 What role had most fun playing? What ________?	Captain Jack Sparrow in *Pirates of the Caribbean*.

6.3

A Complete the conversation.

A: Hi, Chris. How [1] ________ weekend?
B: Not bad.
A: What [2] ________ do?
B: I stayed at home on Saturday and did my homework. On Sunday we went swimming.
A: [3] ________ good. Who did [4] ________ with?
B: With my sister and her family. They've got three kids.
A: Really? Where [5] ________ go?
B: Oh, just to the swimming pool. And you? What did you [6] ________ the weekend?
A: Liz and I went clubbing on Friday night. Then I stayed in bed on Saturday.
B: [7] ________ great!
A: It wasn't great – I was ill.
B: Oh, [8] ________ a shame!

GRAMMAR

7.1 comparatives

adjective		comparative	rule
one-syllable adjectives some two-syllable adjectives	cold quiet	colder quieter	adjective + *-er*
adjectives: ending in *-e* ending in *-y* ending in a consonant + vowel + consonant	 large noisy hot	 larger noisier hotter	 adjective + *-r* adjective ~~*y*~~ + *-ier* double the final consonant of the adjective + *-er*
many two-syllable adjectives all longer adjectives	boring expensive	more boring more expensive	*more* + adjective
irregular adjectives	good bad far	better worse further/farther	

Use comparatives (+ *than*) to compare things and people.

*My sister's **taller than** me.* *A restaurant is **quieter than** a disco.*

7.2 superlatives

adjective	superlative	rule
cold nice friendly big	the coldest the nicest the friendliest the biggest	*the* + adjective + *-est* *the* + adjective + *-st* *the* + adjective ~~*y*~~ + *-iest* double the final consonant of the adjective + *-est*
boring interesting	the most boring the most interesting	*the most* + adjective
good bad far	the best the worst the furthest/farthest	

Use superlatives to talk about the number one thing in a group.

*Maria's spelling is **the best** in the class.*

Note: The spelling rules for superlatives are the same as for comparatives.

7.3 giving directions

Asking for directions		
Excuse me,	can you tell me the way to could you tell me the way to how can I get to	the station, please? Oxford Street, please?
	is there a	sports shop near here?

Giving directions		
Go	straight on/ahead.	
It's	past	the bank.
Turn	left/right	at the crossroads. into Lake Road.
It's	on	the left/right. the corner of …

Use imperatives (e.g. *Turn*, *Go*, *Stop*) or *You* + infinitive to give directions.

***Go** straight on at the traffic lights.*

***You turn** right at the post office.*

When speaking, check information by repeating what you hear.

*The **third** right?*

*So, I take the next **left**?*

Correct information by stressing the correction.

*No, the **first** right.*

*No, the next **right**.*

PRACTICE

7.1

A Write the comparative of the adjectives.

1 fast ___*faster*___
2 close ______
3 big ______
4 beautiful ______
5 easy ______
6 cheap ______
7 important ______
8 happy ______
9 intelligent ______
10 late ______

B Complete the sentences with comparatives. Use the adjectives in brackets.

1 A café is ______ ______ a nightclub. (quiet)
2 It's ______ in south India ______ in north India. (hot)
3 My brother is ______ ______ you. (funny)
4 Your job is ______ ______ ______ mine. (interesting)
5 The people here are ______ ______ the people in my town. (kind)
6 Winter this year was ______ ______ winter last year. (bad)
7 When I was young I was ______ ______ ______ I am now. (serious)
8 These earphones are ______ ______ those ones. (good)
9 The beach is ______ ______ the swimming pool. (far)
10 The museum's ______ ______ the art gallery. (near)

7.2

A Write the superlative of the adjectives.

1 great ___*the greatest*___
2 quiet ______
3 comfortable ______
4 close ______
5 noisy ______
6 cheap ______
7 interesting ______
8 hot ______
9 fast ______
10 crowded ______

B Complete the sentences. Use the superlative of the adjectives in the box.

~~long~~ busy big high good old deep popular

1 ___*The longest*___ bridge in the world is the Pearl Bridge in Japan. It's 1,991 metres.
2 ______ tourist destination in Europe is Disneyland Paris. Over twelve million people visit it in a year.
3 ______ and ______ lake in the world is Lake Baikal, in southern Siberia, Russia. It's 1,600 metres deep and over twenty-five million years old.
4 ______ rainforest in the world is the Amazon. It's four million square kilometres.
5 ______ mountain in the USA is Mount McKinley. It's 6,194 metres. ______ view is at the top.
6 ______ train station in the world is Shinjuku Station in Tokyo. Over three million people use it every day and it has over 200 exits.

7.3

A Read the conversation. Add six more missing words.

A: Excuse *me*. Can you tell me way to the beach?

B: Yes, you turn right the cinema. Then straight on for about fifteen minutes.

A: Fifty minutes?

B: No, fifteen minutes. Then turn left Menier Avenue. Go the café your right. You can see the beach straight ahead. You can't miss it.

A: Thank you very much.

GRAMMAR

8.1 Present continuous

+	I	'm	having	a great time.
	He/She/It	's	sitting	on the balcony.
	You/We/They	're	waiting	for a train.
–	I	'm not	enjoying	this food.
	He/She/It	isn't	working	at the moment.
	You/We/They	aren't	doing	anything.

?	Am	I	leaving?	Yes,	I	am.
					you/we/they	are.
	Are	you/we/they		No,	I	'm not.
					you/we/they	aren't.
	Is	he/she/it	working?	Yes,	he/she/it	is.
				No,		isn't.

Use the present continuous to speak about something happening now/at this moment.
In speaking or in emails and letters to friends, usually use the contracted form: *I am reading.* = *I**'m** reading.*
In the negative, it is also possible to use
*He**'s not** working.* *They**'re not doing** anything.*
Don't use contractions in positive short answers: *Yes, **we are***. NOT ~~*Yes, we're.*~~

Spelling the *-ing* form

Most verbs + *-ing*	wait do	waiting doing
Verbs ending in *-e*, ~~e~~ + *-ing*	write take	writing taking
Most verbs ending in a consonant–vowel–consonant, double the final consonant *-ing*	swim run	swimming running

8.2 Present simple and present continuous

Mario usually	wears	a jacket and tie.
Now he	's wearing	jeans and a T-shirt.

What	do	you	do?	I'm a police officer.
	are		doing?	I'm writing down your number!

Use the present simple to talk about habits or routines.
***We often watch** DVDs on Friday evenings.*
Also use it to talk about things which are always true or true for a long time.
***Eva works** in the city centre.*
Use the present continuous to speak about something happening at this moment.
*Sorry, I can't chat now. **I'm cooking** dinner.*

8.3 Asking for a recommendation

Can you recommend	a good an interesting	film? book?
I don't really like I really like I love/hate		romantic films. sci-fi books.
What's it about? Who's in it? (for a film)		

Giving a recommendation

What kind of	films books	do you like?
I think	you'd like	*Gold River.* it.
How about What about Do you know	*X-Men?* *A Tale of Two Cities?*	
It's about …		

PRACTICE

8.1

A Write the *-ing* form of the verbs.

1 live ____________
2 go ____________
3 come ____________
4 put ____________
5 feel ____________
6 make ____________
7 get ____________
8 stand ____________
9 drive ____________
10 meet ____________

B Write a phone conversation using the prompts below.

Bruno: Hi, Gerald. It's me. you / sleep? *Are you sleeping?*
Gerald: No, I'm at work. I / read.
Bruno: What / you / read?
Gerald: I / read some reports. What / you / do?
Bruno: Karl and I / play cards and listen / to music.
Gerald: So / you / not / work / today.
Bruno: Well / we / take a break.
Gerald: Uh-oh. I / talk / on the speaker phone. My boss / listen.
Bruno: you / joke?
Boss: No, he / not / joke!

8.2

A Complete the sentences with the verbs in the box in the correct form.

listen to (x2) write have (x2) phone stay (x2) watch (x2) ~~wear~~ (x2)

1 I *wear* glasses, but I *'m not wearing* them now.
2 I don't normally ____________ TV, but I ____________ it now.
3 We usually ____________ salad for lunch, but today we ____________ sandwiches.
4 I ____________ an email to my mother at the moment – usually I ____________ her.
5 We often ____________ classical music in the office, but today we ____________ pop.
6 He usually ____________ in a five-star hotel, but now he ____________ in a self-catering apartment.

B Complete the questions with the verbs in brackets. Use the present simple or the present continuous.

1 *Do* you *study* English every day? (study)
2 ______ you ____________ English now? (study)
3 ______ your friend ____________ every day? (work)
4 ______ your best friend ____________ at the moment? (work)
5 ______ your teacher ____________ blue today? (wear)
6 ______ your teacher often ____________ blue? (wear)
7 ______ you usually ____________ grammar exercises alone? (do)
8 ______ you ____________ this exercise alone? (do)
9 ______ you ____________ to music a lot? (listen to)
10 ______ you ____________ to music at the moment? (listen to)

8.3

A Read the conversation and correct six mistakes.

Ines: Do you recommend a good film?
Jim: What kind of films you like?
Ines: Action films, mostly, and I really like comedies.
Jim: Do you know it *Rush Hour*?
Ines: No, I don't. Who's on it?
Jim: Jackie Chan and Chris Tucker.
Ines: What it's about?
Jim: Jackie Chan is a detective and he comes to New York to help a friend.
Ines: It sounds interesting.
Jim: I think you like it.

9 LANGUAGE BANK

GRAMMAR

9.1 *can/can't, have to/don't have to*

I/You/He/She/We/They	can	use	the bikes for free.
	can't	park	in the city centre.
I/You/We/They	have to	pay	ten euros.
He/She/It	has to		
I/You/We/They	don't have to	pay	anything – it's free.
He/She/It	doesn't have to		

Use *can* when something is OK/permitted.
Use *can't* when something is not OK/not permitted.
Use *have to* when something is necessary/obligatory.
Use *don't have to* when something is not necessary/obligatory.

Compare:
You ***can't*** *come to the party.* (You didn't get an invitation.)
You ***don't have to*** *come to the party.* (You got an invitation, but it's OK to stay at home.)

Make the question with *Do you have to* + infinitive, *Does he/she have to* + infinitive.

9.2 articles

no article		
usually use no article	before plural nouns when we speak in general	I like cats, but I don't like dogs. Sweets are bad for you.
	before cities and most countries	Shanghai is in China. I went to Russia last year.
	in some phrases	go by car/train/bus/taxi go on foot go/get home/to work/ to school be at home/work/school have breakfast/dinner/lunch

a/an		
usually use *a/an*	before singular countable nouns	It's a new car. I've got a younger brother. There's an apple in the fridge.
	before jobs	My sister's a teacher.

the		
usually use *the*	before nouns when there's only one	The President visited us last year. Could you close the door, please?
	in some phrases	in the morning/afternoon/ evening at the weekend in the town/city centre on the right/left

9.3 apologising

Apologising				**Responding**	
I'm	very really terribly so	sorry	I'm late. I missed the meeting. to be late.	+	That's OK. No problem. Don't worry about it. No, really. It's fine.
Sorry					
I'm afraid			(+ reason) I missed the bus. I didn't hear my alarm clock. I lost my keys.	–	I don't believe you. Don't let it happen again.

When you apologise, say how you feel: *feel* + adjective.
I ***feel*** *really* ***bad*** *about it.*

When someone apologises too much, use *No, really. It's fine.*

A: *I'm so sorry I'm late.*
B: *Don't worry about it.*
A: *But I feel terrible …*
B: ***No, really. It's fine.***

Use *Don't let it happen again.* only when you're really angry.

PRACTICE

9.1

A Look at signs A–F. What do they mean? Underline the correct alternative.

1 Motorbikes *don't have to/can't* go here. They *have to/don't have to* go on another road.
2 You *can/have to* park here for free. You *can't/don't have to* pay for fifteen minutes' parking.
3 Bikes *have to/can* keep left. People on foot *don't have to/ can't* walk on the left.
4 You *can/can't* catch the bus here. You *have to/don't have to* wait more than ten minutes.
5 You *can't/don't have to* ride your bike. You *can/have to* get off and walk.
6 You *can/can't* take a taxi here. You *can/can't* park here.

A

B

C

D

E

F

B Complete the conversations. Use the correct form of *can/can't*, *have to/don't have to* and the verbs in brackets.

Conversation 1

A: You [1] ___*have to wear*___ (wear) a jacket and tie to this dinner. It's a very formal party.
B: But it's so hot!
A: Well, you [2] ________ (wear) your light jacket.

Conversation 2

A: You [3] ________ (come) to the meeting. It's not very important.
B: That's good because I [4] ________ (come) – I'm too busy.

Conversation 3

A: I [5] ________ (get) a birthday present for Sandra. I completely forgot yesterday.
B: It's OK. You [6] ________ (get) anything. I bought her a present from both of us.
A: Thanks! What did you buy?

9.2

A Complete the text with *a/an*, *the* or no article (-).

Lucio is from [1] ___-___ Italy and he's [2] ______ doctor. He was born and grew up in [3] ______ Venice, but now he lives just outside [4] ______ small town in the south. Every day, early in [5] ______ morning, he leaves [6] ______ home and drives to his clinic in [7] ______ town centre. He usually has [8] ______ lunch with [9] ______ colleagues and sometimes teaches in [10] ______ afternoon. At [11] ______ weekend, he often visits his brother's family. They live in the countryside, about two hours away by [12] ______ car.

B Complete the sentences with *a/an*, *the* or no article (-).

1 I think ___-___ cars are safer than motorbikes.
2 I'd like ______ scooter for my birthday.
3 It's the best airline in ______ world.
4 I rode ______ bike to school when I was younger.
5 I hate ______ boats. I'm always sick!
6 I live in a small village and walk to ______ train station every day.

C Read the conversation. Find and correct six mistakes with *the*. (Two are correct.)

Pedro: Mrs Thorpe, where can I buy the dictionary?
Mrs T: There's the bookshop in South Street. I think they sell the dictionaries. What kind do you want?
Pedro: I need the English–Spanish dictionary for my English class. The teacher said we have to get one. The only problem is that books are very expensive here.
Mrs T: Maybe you can borrow one. Does your school have the library?
Pedro: Yes, it does. That's the good idea. I can ask there.

9.3

A Read the conversation and correct the six mistakes.

Teacher: Can I have your homework?
Student: Oh, I really sorry. I'm afraid of left it at home.
Teacher: Don't worry it. Did you do it?
Student: Yes, of course.
Teacher: Which part did you think was difficult?
Student: I don't remember.
Teacher: Did you *really* do it?
Student: Er … I afraid I forgot to do it. I'm feel bad about it.
Teacher: Don't left it happen again!

GRAMMAR

10.1 *be going to*

+	I	'm	going to	be there start leave	soon. tonight. tomorrow.
	He/She/It	's			
	You/We/They	're			
–	I	'm not			
	He/She/It	isn't			
	You/We/They	aren't			

Use *be going to* + infinitive to talk about plans and intentions.
*I'**m going to do** my homework tonight.*
With *be going to* + *go*, you don't need to repeat *go*.
*She'**s going** ~~(to go)~~ to the post office.*
Use *be going to* with future time phrases, e.g. *tomorrow, soon, this weekend, next week, in two years.*
***In two weeks'** (time) **I'm going to be** on holiday!*

?	Am Is Are	I he/she/it you/we/they	going to	finish today?	+	Yes,	I	am.
							he/she/it	is.
							we/you/they	are.
					–	No,	I	'm not.
							he/she/it	isn't.
							we/you/they	aren't.

would like to

+	I/You/ He/She/It/ We/They	would 'd	like to	go. eat.
–		wouldn't		

Use *I'd like to* + infinitive to talk about what you want to do.
*It's hot. I'**d like to go** for a swim.*
You can also use *want to* + infinitive for the same idea.
*I **want to go** to the gym.*
Note: *I'd like to* is more polite than *I want*.

?	Would	I/you/he/she/it/we/they	like to	drink some tea?	+	Yes,	I/you/he/she/it/we/they	would.
					–	No,		wouldn't.

10.2 *will/might (not)/won't*

+	I/You/ He/She/It/ We/They	'll (will)	be cold. come.
		might	
–		might not	
		won't (will not)	

Use *will* + infinitive and *won't* + infinitive to predict the future when you are sure about something.
*Your book **will be here** tomorrow.*   *I'm sure he **won't come**.*
Use *might* + infinitive to predict the future if you are not sure.
*I **might see** Yuki tonight.* (= it's possible, but I'm not sure)
It is also possible to use *will, might, might not* and *won't* with *there*.
*I think **there will be** a lot of people at the party.*

?	Will	I/you/he/she/it/we/they	win?	+	Yes,	I/you/he/she/it/we/they	will.
				–	No,		won't.

10.3 making suggestions

How about	going	to a concert?
Why don't you/we Shall we	watch	a film?
Let's	cook	something.

Use *How/What about* + infinitive + *-ing* in questions. ***What about** having lunch now?*
Use *Why don't* + subject + infinitive in questions. ***Why don't we watch** a film?*
Use *Shall we* + infinitive in questions. ***Shall we watch** a film?*
Use *Let's* + infinitive in positive sentences. ***Let's go** to the beach.*

responding to suggestions

+	Cool/Great! (That) sounds interesting/good. I'd like to go. (That's a) good idea.
–	I don't (really) feel like doing that/going. That/It doesn't sound very good. It's not for me.

PRACTICE

10.1

A Complete the sentences with the correct form of *be going to*. Use the verbs in brackets.

1 I ________________ the cinema tonight. (go)
2 We ________________ a flat next week. (look at)
3 ________________ ready in time? (you / be)
4 We ________________. (not wait)
5 They ________________ a new car. (buy)
6 When ________________ to Rome? (Steve / go)

B Underline the correct alternative.

1 I *'d like to go/'m going* to the theatre, but there are no more tickets.
2 I *'d like to go/'m going* to a concert tonight. I've got the tickets here.
3 We *'d like to/'re going to* buy a bigger flat, but we don't have enough money.
4 I *'d like to/'m going to* take a trip to Zurich tomorrow. My train leaves at 7a.m.

C Complete the sentences with the words in the box.

like (x2) don't 'd (x2) would (x2) want

A: Would you [1]______ to go to the party?
B: Yes, I [2]______ , but I've got too much work.

A: Would you [3]______ to dance?
B: No, thanks. I [4]______ like to sit down for a minute!

A: What [5]______ you like to do on your birthday tomorrow?
B: I don't know, I [6]______ want to think about it. I feel quite old!

A: Do you [7]______ to have dinner with me tonight?
B: I [8]______ love to!

10.2

A Complete the conversation with *'ll, will, won't* or *might*.

A: Oh, no. The dog ran away again!
B: Don't worry – he [1]______ come back.
A: Are you sure he [2]______?
B: OK, he [3]______ not come back today – that's possible. But I'm sure he [4]______ come back tomorrow.
A: I don't believe you! He [5]______ come back. We [6]______ never see him again – I'm sure.
B: Oh, look … Here he is now!

B Circle the two correct alternatives.

1 He *will* / *won't* / *might* eat it – I'm sure!
2 It *might* / *'ll* / *won't* rain, so bring an umbrella.
3 There *might not* / *won't* / *might* be enough time to watch all the film, so let's not start.
4 I *might not* / *'ll* / *won't* go by train. It's quicker by car.
5 She *might* / *won't* / *'ll* phone tomorrow so please take a message.
6 We *might* / *'ll* / *won't* be late, so don't wait for us.

10.3

A Put the words from the box in the correct places in the conversation.

~~about~~ good idea sound don't like have we

Sam: I'm tired. How *about* having a break now?

Jim: I don't feel stopping.

Sam: Oh, come on! Let's a coffee.

Jim: Why *you* make some coffee? I'll go on working.

Sam: That's a good. Shall have a sandwich?

Jim: No, thanks, I want to finish this.

Sam: OK. You work, I'll have lunch.

Jim: That doesn't good.

Sam: Really? Sounds to me.

GRAMMAR

11.1 *should/shouldn't*

+	I/you/he/she/it/we/they	should	sleep.
			drink lots of water.
–		shouldn't	take antibiotics.
			eat late at night.

?	Should	I/you/he/she/it/we/they	stay	inside?	Yes,	I/you/he/she/it/we/they	should.
					No,		shouldn't.

Use *should* + infinitive to give advice.
You ***should*** *take an aspirin.*
Use *should* to recommend something.
You ***should*** *see that film.*
Use *have to* not *should*, when something is necessary.
You ***have to*** *drive on the right.* NOT ~~*You should drive on the right.*~~
Note: *You* ***should try*** *this soup.* NOT ~~*You should to try this soup.*~~

11.2 adverbs

	adjective	adverb
Most adjectives, add *-ly*	bad loud careful	badly loudly carefully
Adjectives ending in *-y*, ~~-y~~ + *-ily*	easy angry	easily angrily
Adjectives ending in *-le*, change to *-ly*	terrible	terribly
Irregular adverbs	good fast hard (= difficult) early late	well fast NOT ~~fastly~~ hard NOT ~~hardly~~ early late

Use adverbs of manner to say how you do something. *I can swim* ***well****.* *She spoke* ***quietly****.*
Use adverbs of time to say when you did something. *I went to bed* ***early****.* *She had lunch* ***late****.*
Use adverbs with verbs. *He* ***drives badly****.*
Use adjectives with nouns. *He's a* ***bad driver****.*
With *be* and *feel*, use adjectives. *The film* ***was terrible****.* *I* ***feel terrible****.*
Adverbs usually go after the verb. *I* ***arrived*** *early.*
OR after the verb phrase. *I* ***started work*** *early.* *She* ***drove her car*** *quickly.*
OR at the end of a sentence or phrase. *I* ***arrived at work*** *early.* *She* ***drove to the shops*** *quickly.*

11.3 offering to help

Problems	Offers		Thanking	Responses
I can't lift this case. It's hot in here.	I'll Let me	do it. try.	Thank you very much. Thanks a lot. Thanks so/very much. That's kind of you.	You're welcome. No problem. That's OK.
	Shall I	do it? try?		

Use *I'll* (NOT ~~*I will*~~), *Let me* and *Shall I* + infinitive to offer help.

PRACTICE

11.1

A Complete questions 1–6. Then match them with replies a)–f).

1 I don't have much time. _Should I_ send Kirsten an email? *d)*
2 Ben doesn't like the colour of his mobile. ____________ get a new one?
3 Look at my hair – it's a mess! ____________ get a haircut?
4 Some students never say anything in class. ____________ speak more?
5 My daughter wants to travel in South America. ____________ learn Spanish?
6 There are so many words we don't know. ____________ buy an electronic dictionary?

a) Yes, you should. It's too long.
b) Yes, they should. It's important to practise.
c) No, he shouldn't. The old one is fine.
d) No, you shouldn't. Phone her – it's quicker.
e) Yes, she should if she has enough time.
f) Yes, you should get an English–English one.

B Complete the sentences with *should* or *shouldn't* and a verb from the box.

~~get~~ go have stay try wear change

1 My camera's very old. I _should get_ a new one.
2 You ____________ this drink. It's delicious!
3 Do you think I ____________ my money here or at the airport?
4 You ____________ black. I think it doesn't look good on you – sorry!
5 They ____________ by taxi. It's too expensive.
6 She looks tired. She ____________ a holiday.
7 We ____________ out in the sun too long. We'll get sunburnt.

11.2

A Complete the sentences. Use the adjective or adverb form of the words in brackets.

1 The teacher was very ____________. She spoke to the students ____________. (angry)
2 She dances ____________. She's such a ____________ dancer. (beautiful)
3 I passed the exam ____________. It was ____________. (easy)
4 Shhh – be ____________. The baby's sleeping. We have to talk ____________. (quiet)
5 She's a ____________ teacher. She teaches ____________. (good)
6 I sing ____________. I'm a ____________ singer. (terrible)

B Complete the story. Use the adverb forms of the adjectives in the box.

~~early~~ late easy quick angry slow

The other morning, I woke up [1] _early_ because the neighbours were shouting [2] ____________. I didn't want to stay at home, so I made some breakfast [3] ____________ and ran out of the door to work. I forgot to take an umbrella and it started raining so I got very wet. I got to the station at 7.50 and caught the eight o'clock train [4] ____________. I was surprised when I looked round because the train was empty. Because of the rain, the train went very [5] ____________ so I arrived at the office [6] ____________. There was no one there. Then I realised that it was Sunday, and I didn't have to work!

11.3

A Complete the six conversations below. Use the verbs in brackets to help.

Conversation 1
A: I can't find the information anywhere.
B: I' ______ ______ on the computer. (check)

Conversation 2
A: I don't understand this homework.
B: ______ me ______ a look. (have)

Conversation 3
A: My hands are full. I can't carry all these things.
B: ______ I ______ something for you? (carry)

Conversation 4
A: The radio is too loud.
B: ______ I ______ it down? (turn)

Conversation 5
A: The top on this bottle is too tight.
B: ______ me try to ______ it. (open)

Conversation 6
A: I haven't got any change for the parking machine.
B: No problem. I ______ ______. (pay)

GRAMMAR

12.1 present perfect

+	I/You/We/They	've	climbed	Mount Everest.
	He/She/It	's	watched	the sun rise.
–	I/You/We/They	haven't	tried	milk in tea.
	He/She/It	hasn't	slept	outside.

Make the present perfect with have/has + past participle.
Use the present perfect to talk about past experiences in your life.
Usually you don't know or say when exactly these things happened.
For regular verbs, the past participles are the same as the past simple: verb + *-ed*, *-d* or ~~y~~ *-ied*.
*miss – miss**ed** – miss**ed**, move – mov**ed** – mov**ed**, stud**y** – stud**ied** – stud**ied***
For irregular verbs, look at the list on page 127.

?	Have	I/you/we/they	(ever) swum	in a river?	Yes, No,	I/you/we/they	have. haven't.
	Has	he/she/it			Yes, No,	he/she/it	has. hasn't.

ever = 'in your life'. We often use it for more unusual experiences.
*Have you **ever** met a famous person?* (Compare to *Have you met my husband?*)
In the negative you can use *never*. *I've **never** played golf.*

Go has two past participles: *been* and *gone*:

*She's **gone to** India. = She went there and she's there now.*

*She's **been** to India. = She went there in the past and she came back.*

12.2 present perfect and past simple

Use the present perfect to talk about past experiences in your life. You don't say exactly *when*.
***I've been** to Egypt. **I've seen** the Great Pyramid.*
Use the past simple if you say *when* something happened.
*I **went** to Egypt three years ago. I **saw** the Great Pyramid when I **was** there.*
When speaking, it is possible to start a conversation by asking a question in the present perfect and then asking about more details in the past simple.
A: ***Have** you **ever been** to Egypt?*
B: *Yes, I have. I **went** there three years ago.*
A: ***Did** you **like** it?*
B: *Yes, it **was** great!*

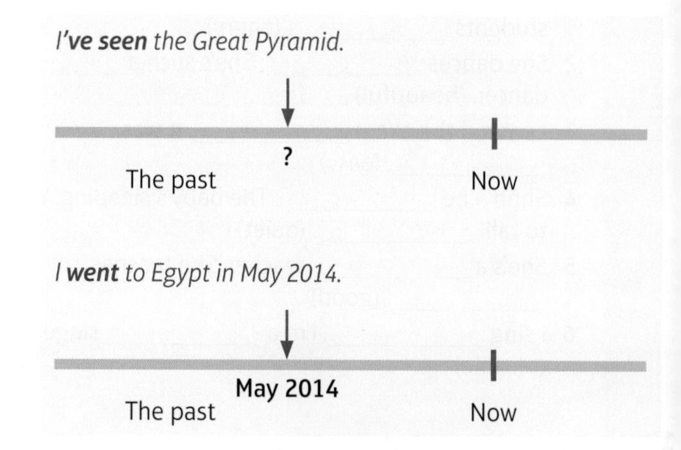

12.3 telephoning

Calling a friend	Hi, Philippe. It's Debbie. Is Lise there?
Calling a business	Hello. This is Carla Rimini. Could I speak to Harry Jones, please?
Calling back	Could you ring/phone/call (me) back? Just ask him/her to ring/phone/call me. I'll call you back.
Leaving/taking a message	Could I leave a message for him/her? Just a moment. Let me get a pen. Let me check that.

Use *It's* + name (informal) or *This is* + name (formal) NOT ~~*I am*~~.
*Hello, **this is** Ali Hassan.*

PRACTICE

12.1

A Write sentences in the present perfect.

1 you / ever / eat / Japanese food?
2 I / eat / Thai food two or three times
3 We / never / sleep / in a four-star hotel before
4 They / drive / across Europe many times
5 he / ever / go / to the UK?
6 Lise / have / three husbands
7 I / never / lose / my mobile phone
8 She / learn / Arabic, Spanish and Chinese
9 you / ever / climb / a volcano?
10 My parents / never / use / a tablet computer

B Correct ten mistakes in the conversation.

A: You have ever been to Australia?
B: No, I have. And you?
A: Yes, I've.
B: And have you gone to China too?
A: No, but I been to Korea.
B: You've travel to many countries in your life …
A: Yes, I has. I've meeted a lot of people and I've try a lot of interesting food.
B: But you haven't learn to speak English perfectly!
A: Not yet …

12.2

A Read the email and underline the correct alternatives.

To

Hi Renata,

Thanks for the email. Lucky you … going to Italy next month! You asked me about Venice. Yes, [1] I *'ve been/went* there. [2] I *'ve been/went* there for a long weekend last year. [3] It *has been/was* beautiful. [4] I *'ve loved/loved* all the bridges and old squares. [5] I *'ve also visited/also visited* Rome. [6] We *have been/were* there in 2006. It's busier than Venice, but I know you like old buildings and churches, so maybe you'd like Rome better. [7] I *'ve never travelled/never travelled* in the Italian countryside but my friend Emily [8] *has driven/drove* around the south and she says it's lovely, but very hot at that time of year. Anyway, I'm sure you'll have a great time! Send me some photos.

Simone

B Complete the sentences using the prompts in brackets.

1 ___*Have you seen*___ *Gravity*? (you / see)
Yes, I _*saw*_ it a few months ago.
2 ______ Sarah? (you / meet)
Yes, we ______ last year.
3 ______ to Spain? (Lea / go)
Yes, she ______ there last month and she's going to stay for a year.
4 ______ an accident on his motorbike? (Paolo / ever have)
Yes, he ______ a small accident a month ago.
5 ______ *Anna Karenina*? (you / read)
Yes, I ______ it at university.
6 ______ school? (your children / finish)
Yes, they ______ a long time ago.

12.3

A Complete Judy's sentences.

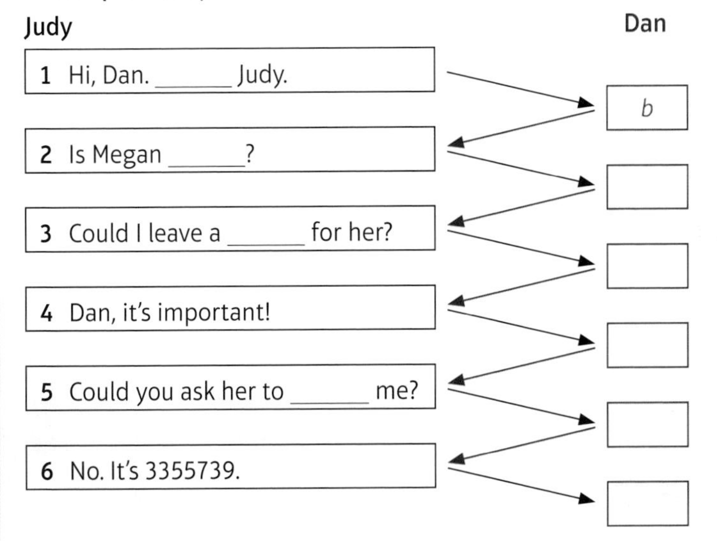

Judy
Dan
1 Hi, Dan. ______ Judy.
b
2 Is Megan ______?
3 Could I leave a ______ for her?
4 Dan, it's important!
5 Could you ask her to ______ me?
6 No. It's 3355739.

B Complete the conversation with the correct response from Dan.

a) A message … ? Oh, I can't find a pen. Could you ring me back?
b) Oh, hi Judy.
c) Has she got your number?
d) Let me just look … OK, I've got one.
e) 3355739. OK, got it. I'll tell her.
f) No, she's gone out somewhere.

PHOTO BANK

Lesson 1.1 COUNTRIES AND NATIONALITIES

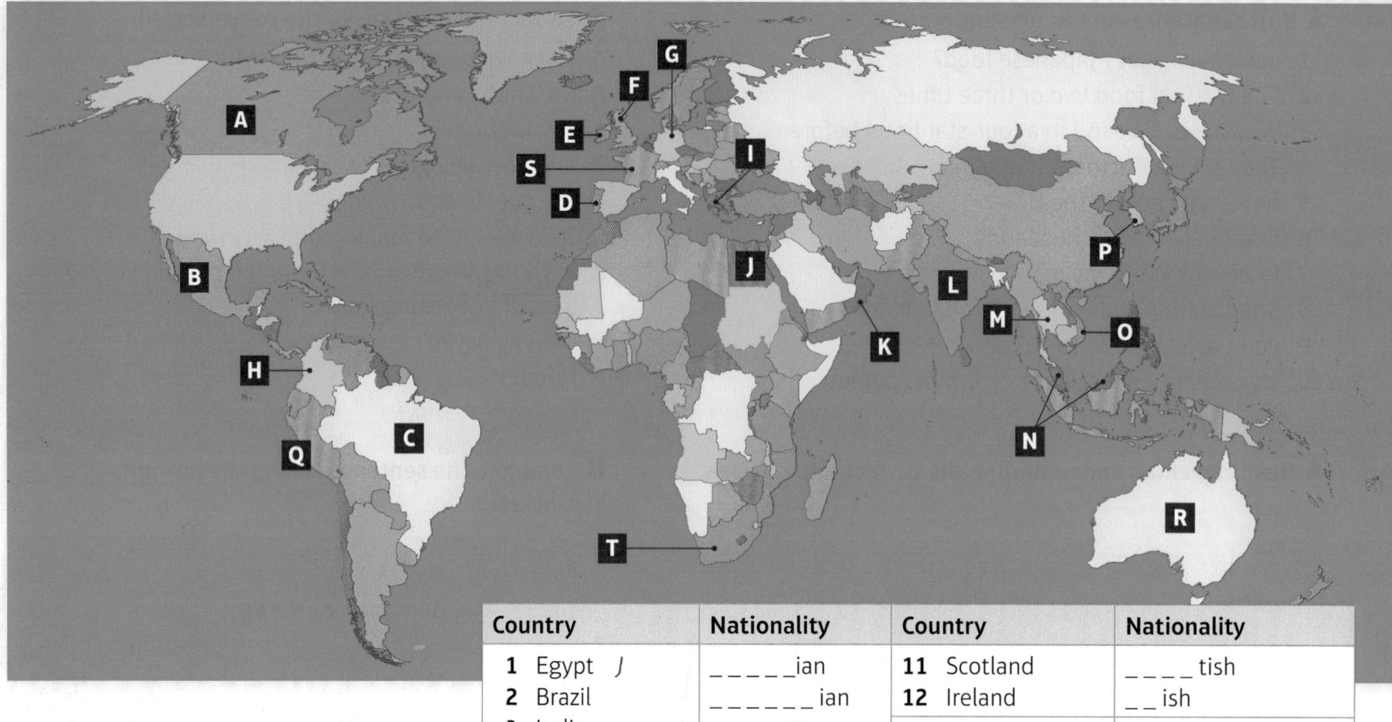

Country	Nationality	Country	Nationality
1 Egypt *J*	_ _ _ _ _ian	11 Scotland	_ _ _ _ tish
2 Brazil	_ _ _ _ _ _ ian	12 Ireland	_ _ ish
3 India	_ _ _ _ an	13 Portugal	_ _ _ _ _ _ uese
4 Australia	_ _ _ _ _ _ _ _ _ an	14 Vietnam	_ _ _ _ _ _ _ ese
5 Colombia	_ _ _ _ _ _ ian	15 Germany	_ _ _ man
6 Canada	_ _ _ _ _ ian	16 Greece	_ _ _ _ k
7 Korea	_ _ _ _ an	17 Thailand	_ _ _ i
8 Mexico	_ _ _ _ _ an	18 Oman	_ _ _ _ i
9 Malaysia	_ _ _ _ _ _ ian	19 France	_ _ _ _ ch
10 Peru	_ _ _ _ _ ian	20 South Africa	_ _ _ _ _ _ _ _ _ _ an

1 A Match the countries with the letters on the map.

B Complete the nationalities.

Lesson 1.2 EVERYDAY OBJECTS

1 A Match the everyday objects with the photos.

B Complete the gaps with *a*, *an* or -.

1 ___*a*___ dictionary *A*
2 ___-___ stamps
3 ______ identity card
4 ______ sweets
5 ______ file
6 ______ tissues
7 ______ umbrella
8 ______ glasses
9 ______ wallet
10 ______ comb
11 ______ driving licence
12 ______ chewing gum

A

B

C
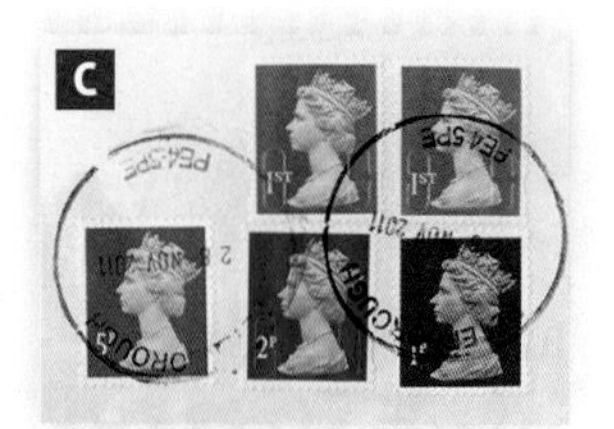

D

E F

G

H
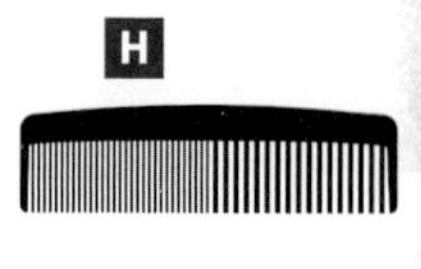

I

J

K
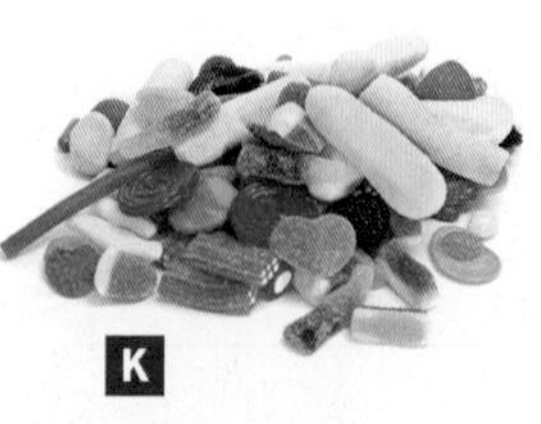

L

Lesson 2.2 JOBS

1 A Match the jobs with the pictures.

B Complete the gaps with *a* or *an*.

1 _____ lawyer
2 _____ teacher
3 _____ accountant
4 _____ police officer
5 _____ engineer
6 _____ politician
7 _____ hairdresser
8 _____ shop assistant
9 _____ chef
10 _____ doctor
11 _____ receptionist
12 _____ nurse
13 _____ personal assistant (PA)
14 _____ waiter/waitress
15 _____ sportsman/sportswoman
16 _____ actor/actress
17 _____ businessman/businesswoman

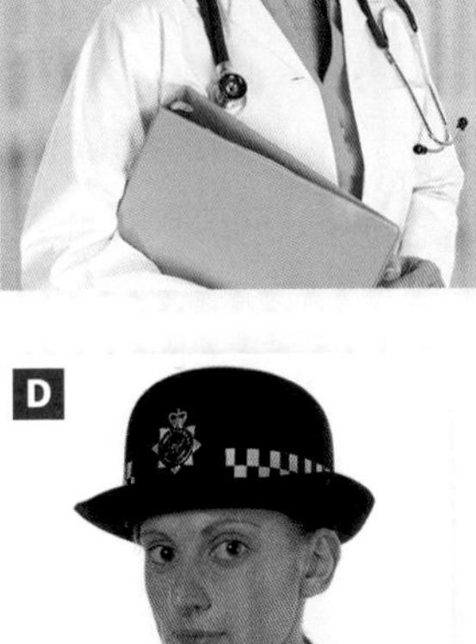

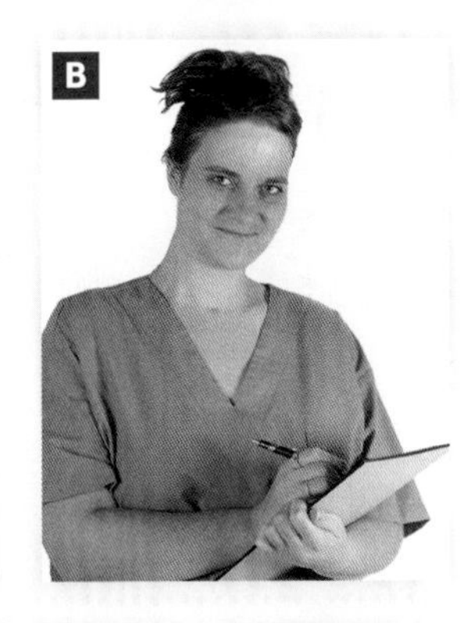

Lesson 3.1 FAMILY

A Frank Jackson

B Maggie Jackson

C Ann Barnes

D John Barnes

E Elizabeth Jackson

F Robert Jackson

G Katy Barnes

H Jake Barnes

I Mark Jackson

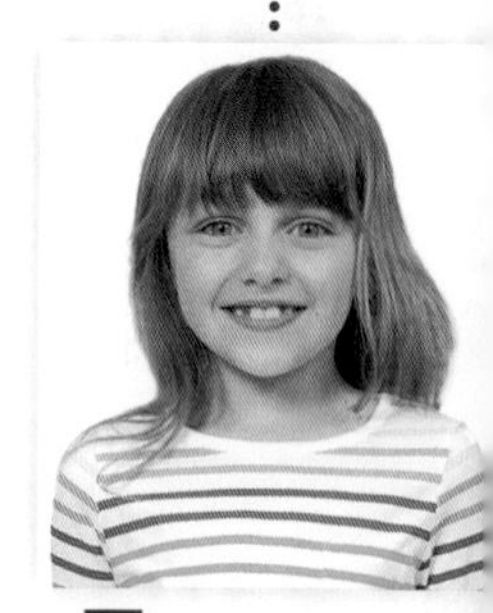
J Amy Jackson

1 A Look at the family tree and write the people in the correct space below.

1 ______________ are Jake's grandfather and grandmother.
2 ______________ are Jake's father and mother (parents).
3 ______________ is Elizabeth's husband.
4 ______________ is John's wife.
5 ______________ are Elizabeth and Robert's son and daughter.
6 ______________ is Jake's sister.
7 ______________ is Amy's brother.
8 ______________ are Katy's aunt and uncle.
9 ______________ are Mark's cousins.
10 ______________ are Ann's nephew and niece.

B Choose one person from the family tree. Then use the words in the box to write how he/she is related to the other people.

father mother wife husband parents grandfather grandmother son daughter brother sister uncle aunt cousin niece nephew

Robert is Maggie's son. He's Elizabeth's ...

Lesson 4.1 ROOMS AND FURNITURE

1 A Match the names of the rooms and places with the photos. A–K

1 garage
2 balcony
3 hall
4 kitchen
5 dining room
6 living room
7 stairs
8 home office
9 bedroom
10 bathroom
11 roof terrace
12 garden
13 upstairs
14 downstairs

B Match the items of furniture with the words in the box below.

armchair *k* bath bed carpet cupboard chair desk lamp plant rug television shower sink sofa shelves table wardrobe washbasin

2 Look at the pictures for thirty seconds. Then close your book and make a list of the furniture in each room.

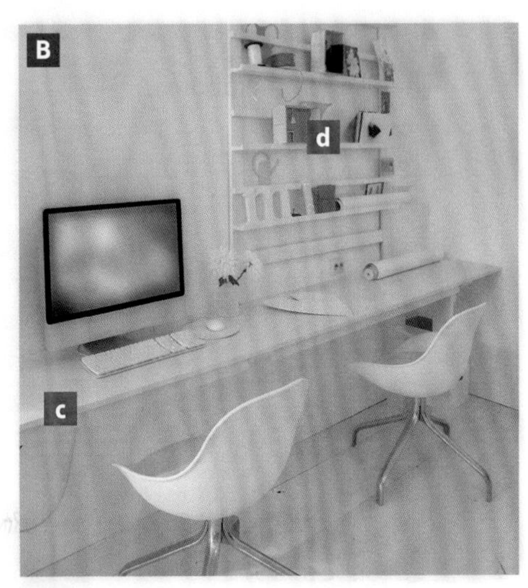

Lesson 4.3 SHOPS

1 Match the names of the shops with the photos.

1 baker's
2 bookshop
3 butcher's
4 clothes shop
5 dry-cleaner's
6 electronics shop
7 greengrocer's
8 hairdresser's
9 internet café
10 pharmacy/chemist's
11 newsagent's
12 shoe shop
13 sports shop
14 supermarket

Lesson 5.1 FOOD

1 A Match the names of the food with the photos.

1 an onion
2 beans
3 a cabbage
4 peas
5 a lettuce
6 spinach
7 an aubergine
8 corn on the cob
9 grapes
10 an orange
11 a lemon
12 tomatoes
13 oil
14 cake
15 biscuits
16 yoghurt
17 sugar
18 ice cream
19 bread
20 rice
21 pasta
22 cereal
23 noodles
24 beef
25 lamb
26 prawns

B Write countable (C) or uncountable (U) next to each word.

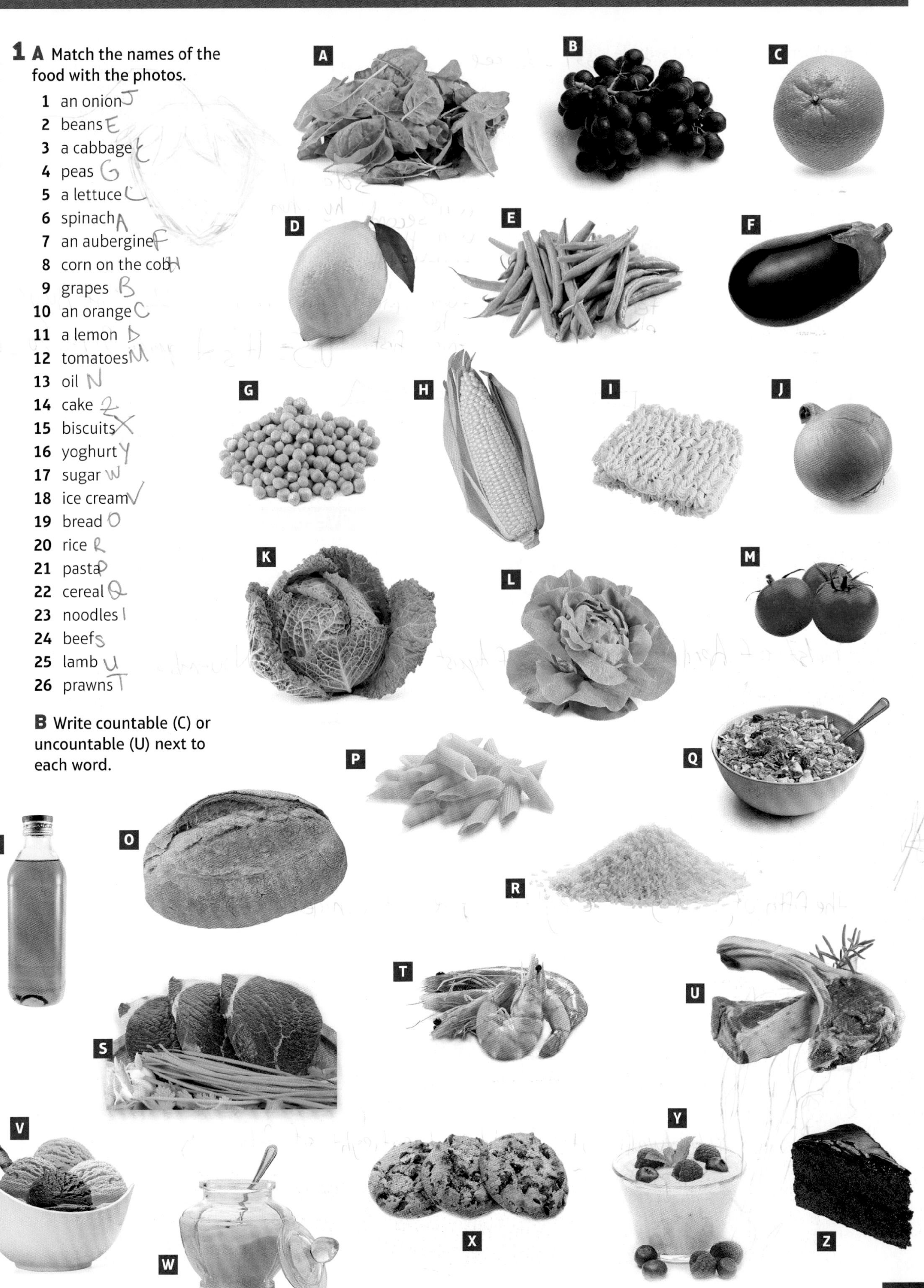

Lesson 6.1 MONTHS AND ORDINAL NUMBERS

1 A Underline the stressed syllable in each month.

The months	Ordinal numbers	
January	1st – first	13th – thirteenth
February	2nd – second	14th – ______
March	3rd – third	17th – ______
April	4th – fourth	20th – twentieth
May	5th – fifth	21st – twenty-first
June	6th – sixth	22nd – ______
July	7th – seventh	23rd – ______
August	8th – eighth	25th – ______
September	9th – ninth	28th – ______
October	10th – ______	29th – ______
November	11th – ______	30th – thirtieth
December	12th – twelfth	31st – ______

B Complete the ordinal numbers.

C Write the dates A–H. Most ordinal numbers are the number + *-th*, e.g. *fourth, thirteenth*. How are the numbers different in A–H?

A APRIL 1st ______

B 2nd AUGUST ______

C NOVEMBER 3rd ______

D 5th JANUARY ______

E JUNE 8th ______

F MAY 9th ______

G SEPTEMBER 12th ______

H FEBRUARY 20th ______

Lesson 8.2 APPEARANCE AND CLOTHES

1 A Look at the photos and find an example for each word or phrase in the box.

tall short slim* overweight** bald straight hair curly hair long hair short hair medium build

*also use *thin*, but *slim* is more positive
***fat* is also possible, but is very negative

B Match the names of the clothes with the letters A–N.

1 socks
2 jeans
3 suit
4 jacket
5 trousers
6 shirt
7 tie
8 top
9 skirt
10 sweater
11 shorts
12 dress
13 T-shirt
14 coat

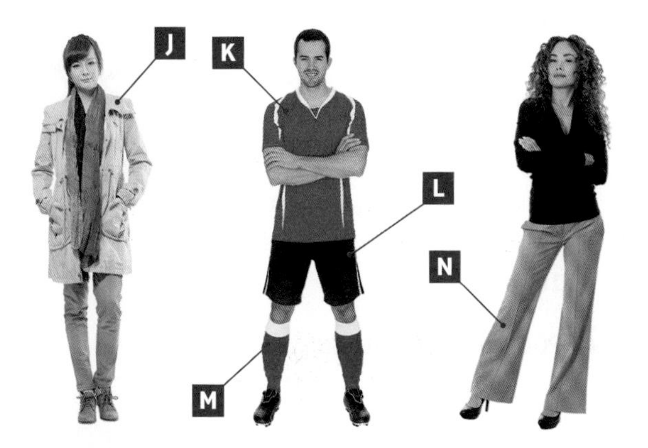

2 Write which words are adjectives (adj), uncountable nouns (U), countable singular nouns (C sing), countable plural nouns (C pl).

Lesson 11.1 BODY PARTS

1 Match the names of the body parts with the photos.

1 arm
2 back
3 ear
4 eye
5 face
6 finger
7 foot
8 hand
9 head
10 knee
11 leg
12 elbow
13 neck
14 nose
15 shoulder
16 mouth
17 thumb
18 toe

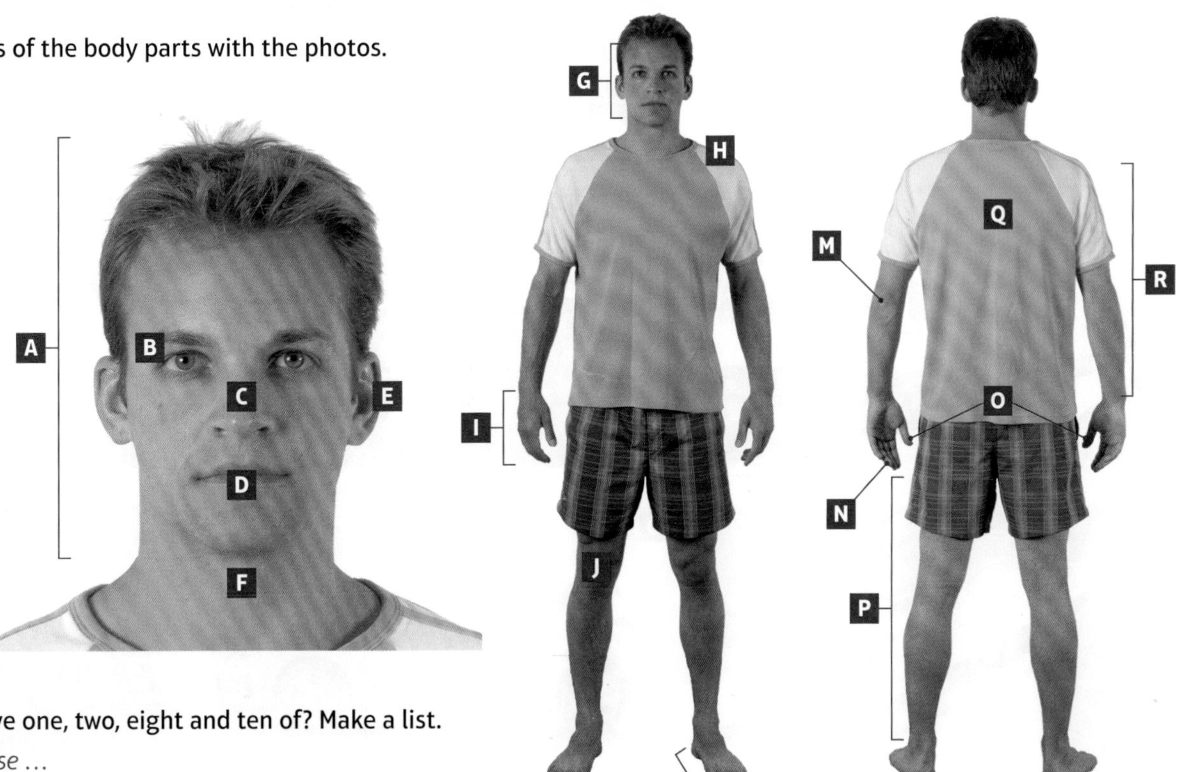

2 What do you have one, two, eight and ten of? Make a list.

1 = head, face, nose …

Lesson 9.2 TRANSPORT

1 Match the types of the transport with the photos.

1 a bike
2 a boat
3 a bus
4 a car
5 a ferry
6 a horse
7 a lorry/a truck
8 a motorbike
9 a plane
10 a scooter
11 a ship
12 a taxi
13 a train
14 a tram
15 an underground/ a subway train
16 a van

2 Put the words into the transport groups.

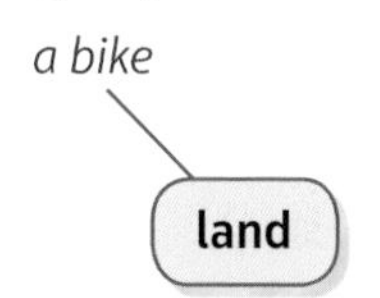

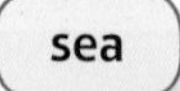

air

A

B

C

D

E

F

G

H

I

J

K

L

M

N

O

P

Lesson 5.3

6 C Student A

You are the waiter. Answer the customer's questions. Take his/her order.

A: *Are you ready to order?*
B: *Can I ask about today's specials? What's the Spring special?*

TODAY'S SPECIALS

Spring special –
Salad with cold chicken and fresh bread

Fisherman's platter –
Fish, rice and salad

Roman holiday –
Spaghetti with meatballs and a cucumber salad

Lesson 10.2

2 B Student B

How to be safe in an earthquake

Stay inside. Get under a strong table or desk and hold onto the furniture. Stay away from windows and mirrors because they might break. Stay away from bookshelves too. They might fall on you. If you are in bed, stay there and put a pillow over your head. Do not run outside. A building might fall on you. If you're in a car, drive away from buildings, bridges and trees and stay in your car. Wait until the end of the earthquake before you leave your car.

What to do if you get lost in a forest

First, stay calm, stay in one place and make a plan. A plan will help you to feel better. Build a simple shelter and make a fire so you can get warm and feel safer as well. Also remember that water is the most important thing, so look for water, but don't move far away from your starting place or you might get more lost. And don't be surprised about the mobile – in a forest a mobile often won't work because there's no signal.

Lesson 2.3

1 D Student A: ask and answer questions. Complete the times on the clocks.

A: *What's the time in number 1?*
B: *It's … What's the time in number 2?*
A: *It's …*

Lesson 11.2

5 Student B

A Read this list of ways of reducing stress. Put a tick (✓) for good ideas and a cross (✗) for bad ideas.

Have a technology-free hour every day. No computers, tablets or phones.
Don't sleep with your phone.
Do a five-minute meditation every day.
Take a short sleep after lunch – twenty minutes a day.
Eat meat only one day a week.
Spend more time with friends.
Do exercise or sport for one hour a day.
Watch comedy films.

B Work with other Student Bs and compare your ideas. Choose the top three good ideas.

A: *Which ideas do you think are good?*

C Work with a Student A and tell each other your top three ideas. Choose the best three ideas.

A: *What are your top ideas?*
B: *Well first I think you should/shouldn't …*

D Work with all the other students and choose the best three ideas.

Lesson 1.3

7 Student A: ask Student B the prices to complete your table. Then answer Student B's questions.

A: How much is a sandwich and a tea?
B: Three twenty-five. How much is a burger and a coffee?

	tea	juice	coffee
muffin	1.75		
burger		4.15	
chips	1.95		2.20
sandwich		3.75	3.50

Lesson 9.1

6 A Student B

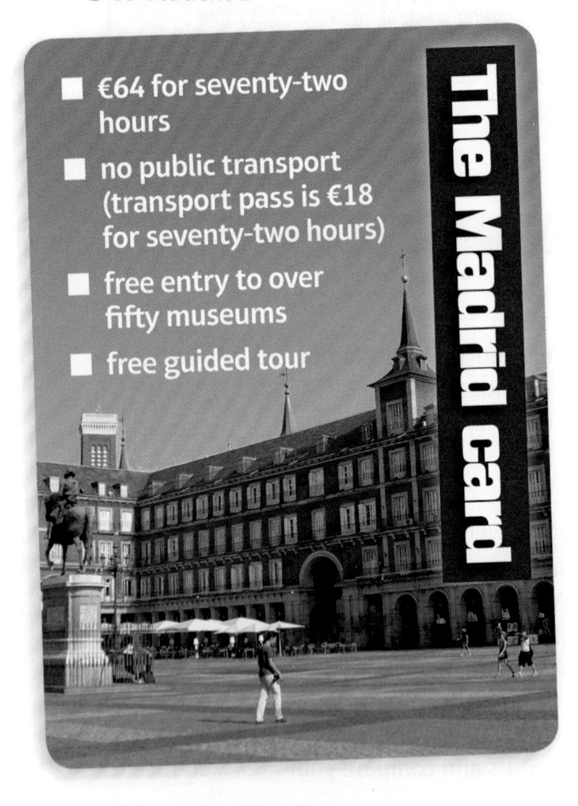

€64 for seventy-two hours
no public transport (transport pass is €18 for seventy-two hours)
free entry to over fifty museums
free guided tour
The Madrid card

Lesson 12.3

6 A Student B: Situation 1. You've lost your credit card. Call the credit card company and report the lost card.

B Situation 2. You missed the last train. You lost your mobile and almost all your money, so you call your friend from a phone box. First, ask him/her to call you back and give the phone number (it's ______). When he/she calls back, ask him/her to come and get you.

Lesson 2.2

8 A Student A: read the texts. Write questions to ask your partner for the missing information.

1 Where *does he work?*
2 When …
3 Where …
4 What time …
5 What time …
6 What …
7 When …

Dao is a window cleaner on high-rise buildings. He works in [1] ______. He gets up at 5a.m., leaves home at [2] ______ every day and starts work at seven. He doesn't have breakfast at home – he has coffee and a roll [3] ______. He usually cleans windows on one building for two or three days in a week – a typical high-rise has thousands of windows, and on hot days he has lunch on top of the building. He finishes work at [4] ______ and gets home for dinner, at seven.

Lisa is an acrobat and mother of three boys. She works in Switzerland at the National Circus. She gets up early and has breakfast at [5] ______ with her boys. She goes to the circus at 7a.m. In the morning she [6] ______ and practises her high-flying routine. On circus days, in the afternoon she goes to bed and then gets up and has a sandwich at 5.30p.m. She doesn't eat dinner before a show. The evening show starts at 7.30p.m. Lisa finishes work at about [7] ______ and gets home at 11p.m.

B Ask Student B about the missing information. Complete your text.

Lesson 4.2

5 D Student A: write the buildings on the map on page 41. Don't show your partner.

The museum is on the left of the pharmacy.
The theatre is next to the museum.

E Ask Student B about the places below. Write them on your map. Then answer Student B's questions.

- the school
- the park

Lesson 2.3

5 A Student A: you work at the Tourist Information Centre. Look at the information below. Answer Student B's questions.

	Start time	Finish time	Place	Price
Boat tour	9a.m.	11a.m.	Leaves from Pier 43, Fisherman's Wharf	$26
Bus tour	9a.m.	2p.m.	Leaves from Union Square	$44

B Change roles. Student A: now you are a tourist in San Francisco. Ask Student B questions and complete the notes below.

Excuse me. Can you give me some information about the … ?
What time does it … ?

	Start time	Finish time	Place	Price
Walking tour				
Rock concert				

Lesson 5.3

6 C Student B: you are the customer. Student A is the waiter. Look at the menu and order your food. Ask the waiter about the specials.

B: *Are you ready to order?*
A: *Can I ask about today's specials? What's the Spring special?*

MENU

Starter

Tomato soup	2.50
Italian-style grilled vegetables	3.50

Main course

Cheese, tomato and mushroom pizza	7.00
Cheese, tomato, mushroom, olive and ham pizza	7.50
Pasta of the day	8.00
Served with a side salad	3.00

Today's specials

Spring special	6.50
Fisherman's platter	7.50
Roman holiday	7.00

Dessert

Ice cream	4.00
Fruit salad	4.00
Three cheese plate	5.00

All prices in euros. Service not included.

Lesson 12.3

5 D Student A: work with other Student As. Draw a line between the numbers where you think a pause is good. Practise saying the numbers.

Sam	
Ahmed	5823031
Nina	
Chen	3662149
Simon	
Fatima	08701642513
Yuko	
Penny	00285955427

E Work in pairs. Student A: ask Student B for the telephone numbers. Answer Student B's questions.

A: *What's Sam's phone number?*
B: *It's … What's Ahmed's phone number?*
A: *It's …*

Lesson 5.2

4 B Student A

(The underlined answers are correct.)

1 a) about 300 times b) about 100 times
3 a) 750 litres b) 7,500 litres
5 a) about 2,000 b) about 7,000
7 a) 1,700 b) 940

Lesson 7.3

5 D Student B: listen to Student A. Use the information below to correct any mistakes.

1 Kris lives in North Avenue.
2 His house is ten minutes from here.
3 It's on the right.

Now check this information. Read it to Student A.

1 The bank's in West Street.
2 It's on the left.
3 Take the number five bus.

Lesson 1.1

5 B Check your answers to the quiz.

1 1C 2A 3E 4B 5D
2 1C 2E 3B 4D 5A
3 1E 2D 3C 4A 5B

Lesson 1.3

7 **Student B: answer Student A's questions. Then ask Student A the prices to complete your table.**

A: *How much is a muffin and a tea?*
B: *One seventy-five. How much is a sandwich and a juice?*

	tea	juice	coffee
muffin		2.25	2.00
burger	3.65		3.90
chips		2.45	
sandwich	3.25		

Lesson 4.3

6 A **Student A: You are a shop assistant in a sports shop. Look at the things in the list below. Write a different price for each. Then role-play the situation. Answer Student B's questions. Begin the conversation: *Good morning. Can I help you?***

- a football *€19.99*
- trainers
- a swimming costume
- walking boots

B **Now you are a customer in an electronics shop. Role-play the situation. Ask Student B questions and try to buy the things below. When you buy something, write the price.**

- a SIM card
- a memory stick
- headphones
- a tablet

Lesson 5.3

6 B Student B

TODAY'S SPECIALS

Chef's Sunday special –
Roast beef with potatoes and corn on the cob

Garden delight –
Rice with three different vegetables (peas, green beans, carrots)

Spring mix –
Salad and two kinds of meat: lamb and beef

Lesson 11.2

5 Student A

A **Read this list of ways of reducing stress. Put a tick (✓) for good ideas and a cross (✗) for bad ideas.**

Turn off your phone for one hour a day.
Sleep nine hours a night.
Do a karate class.
Take a five-minute break from work every hour.
Don't drink coffee.
Do something you enjoy, e.g. singing, twice a week.
Play video games.
Paint your walls green – it's a relaxing colour.

B **Work with other Student As and compare your ideas. Choose the top three good ideas.**

A: *Which ideas do you think are good?*

C **Work in pairs with a Student B and tell each other your top three ideas. Choose the best three ideas.**

A: *What are your top ideas?*
B: *Well first I think you should/shouldn't …*

D **Work with all the other students and choose the best three ideas.**

Lesson 5.2

4 B Student B

(The underlined answers are correct.)

2 a) about 50 times b) <u>about 15 times</u>
4 a) about 2,000 b) <u>about 7,000</u>
6 a) <u>200 bottles</u> b) 2,000 bottles
8 a) about 590 kilometres b) <u>about 950 kilometres</u>

Lesson 9.1

6 A Student A

€67 for seventy-two hours
all public transport
free entry to over twenty-five museums
free boat tour
The Amsterdam card

Lesson 8.1

6 Student A: ask and answer questions to compare your picture with Student B's. Don't look at Student B's picture. Find eight differences in the pictures.

What's Mike doing? What's he wearing?

Lesson 7.3

4 Student A: write directions for Liverpool James Street Station (B on the map) and to a Greek restaurant (J on the map). Then cover your directions and answer Student B's question.

You want to go to Tate Liverpool and you want to find a pharmacy. Ask Student B for directions.

Lesson 12.3

6 A Student A: Situation 1. You work in customer services for the credit card company. When the customer calls, ask three questions (e.g. 'Where did you lose it?'). Finally, tell them to call a different number (It's____________).

B Situation 2. Your friend calls and has missed the last train. You can't go and pick him/her up. Suggest alternatives: *taxi, bus, walking*.

Lesson 4.1

8 B Look at the picture below for fifteen seconds. Then turn back to page 39 and correct the sentences.

Lesson 12.3

5 D Student B: work with other Student Bs. Draw a line between the numbers where you think a pause is good. Practise saying the numbers.

Sam	9240473
Ahmed	
Nina	7886301
Chen	
Simon	04633739912
Fatima	
Yuko	00442816933
Penny	

E Work in pairs. Student B: answer Student A's questions. Ask Student A for the telephone numbers.

A: *What's Sam's phone number?*
B: *It's … What's Ahmed's phone number?*
A: *It's …*

Lesson 2.3

1 D Student B: ask and answer questions. Complete the times on the clocks.

B: *What's the time in number 2?*
A: *It's … What's the time in number 1?*
B: *It's …*

Lesson 2.2

8 A Student B: read the texts. Write questions to ask your partner for the missing information.

1 When *does he get up?*
2 What time …
3 Where …
4 Where …
5 What time …
6 What …
7 When …

Dao is a window cleaner on high-rise buildings. He works in Shanghai. He gets up at [1]__________, leaves home at six every day and starts work at [2]__________. He doesn't have breakfast at home – he has coffee and a roll on the bus. He usually cleans windows on one building for two or three days in a week – a typical high-rise has thousands of windows, and on hot days he has lunch on [3]__________. He finishes work at five and gets home for dinner, at seven.

Lisa is an acrobat and mother of three boys. She works in [4]__________ at the National Circus. She gets up early and has breakfast at 6a.m. with her boys. She goes to the circus at [5]__________. In the morning she does exercises and practises her high-flying routine. On circus days, in the afternoon she [6]__________ and then gets up and has a sandwich at 5.30p.m. She doesn't eat dinner before a show. The evening show starts at 7.30p.m. Lisa finishes work at about 10p.m. and gets home at [7]__________.

B Ask Student A about the missing information. Complete your text.

Lesson 11.3

6 B Student B

Problem 1
I'm really tired.

Problem 2
I can't see the whiteboard. It's too dark in here.

Problem 3
I'm really thirsty, but I haven't got any money for a coffee.

Lesson 9.1

6 A Student C

The Prague card
€36 for seventy-two hours
free entry to over fifty museums and sights
free guidebook
unlimited travel on Prague transport system for an extra €14

Lesson 7.3

5 D Student A: check this information. Read it to Student B.

1 Kris lives in North Road.
2 His house is five minutes from here.
3 It's on the left.

Now listen to Student B. Use the information below to correct any mistakes.

1 The bank's in East Street.
2 It's on the right.
3 Take the number nine bus.

Lesson 4.2

5 D Student B: write the buildings on the map on page 41. Don't show your partner.

The school is opposite the pharmacy.
The park is behind the sports centre.

E Answer Student A's questions. Then ask Student A about the places below. Write them on your map.

- the museum
- the theatre

Lesson 3.1

2 B Student A: read the text below. Circle the numbers in the box that are in the text. What do they refer to?

600	17	(16)	9	8	7	3	2	1

16 children in the Radford family

For Sue and Noel Radford, 'Big is beautiful' when you talk about families. They've got sixteen children – nine boys and seven girls. They are also grandparents, as their daughter Sophie has got a one-year-old daughter, Daisy.

The Radford family lives in a nine-bedroom house. Sue and Noel have got a bakery down the road from the house, and the family travels everywhere in their seventeen-seat minibus.

Life in the Radford house starts early. Noel goes to the bakery at 4.30a.m., gets home for breakfast at 7.30, takes the school-age children to school and then goes back to the bakery. At 3p.m. he brings the children home from school and then he cooks dinner every night – often spaghetti or homemade pizza.

So why do they have so many children? Sue smiles and says, 'I love having children around me. I like all the noise and activity.'

A family friend says, 'They're a lovely family and the children are really good kids. Sue and Noel are great parents.'

It's true, Sue and Noel don't have very much time alone. They don't go out to restaurants or to the cinema and they only talk about the children – there's no time to talk about other things.

But the children are happy. 'They've always got friends around them,' says Noel.

Lesson 8.1

6 Student B: ask and answer questions to compare your picture with Student A's. Don't look at Student A's picture. Find eight differences in the pictures.

What's Mike doing? What's he wearing?

Lesson 10.2

2 B Student A

How to stay safe near lightning

First, get down from the hill – high places are dangerous. Don't stand under trees because lightning often hits trees. In the open field, don't lie down on the ground. Put your feet together, then crouch down. Don't put your hands on the ground. Stay away from metal – never use a mobile phone or an umbrella when there is lightning near you. You'll be safe inside your car, if you can get to it – lightning goes around cars. But don't touch anything metal in the car.

What to do if you get stung by a bee

First, move away from the other bees – they might sting you too. When a bee stings you, don't pinch the sting with your fingers or it will get worse. Use a credit card and push the sting out. Then wash your arm with soap and water and raise it above your heart for a short time. You can put an ice pack on your arm and also take some painkillers. If you still have problems, go and see your doctor.

Lesson 8.1

2 D

The first writer is probably a woman in her thirties.

The second writer is probably a man in his twenties.

Lesson 11.3

6 B Student A

Problem 1
It's cold in here.

Problem 2
This computer doesn't work.

Problem 3
It's too noisy. The music's too loud and I can't concentrate.

Lesson 7.3

4 Student B: You want to go to Liverpool James Street Station and you want to find a Greek restaurant. Ask Student A for directions.

Write directions for Tate Liverpool, a famous art gallery (K on the map) and a pharmacy (I on the map). Then cover the directions and answer Student A's question.

AUDIO SCRIPTS

Lesson 1.1 Recording 1.1

Conversation 1

D = Dave J = Jenny A = Anthony O = Omar

D: Hi, Jenny. Hi Anthony. Good to see you.
J: Hi, Dave.
A: Hey, Dave. How are you?
D: Great, thanks. And you?
A: Good.
J: I'm fine.
D: Hi, erm …
J: Oh, this is Omar.
D: Hi, Omar. I'm Dave. Nice to meet you.
O: And you.
D: Can I join you?
J: Sure, come and sit down.
D: Are you in Jenny's class?
O: No, we're friends. I'm not a student.
D: Oh, so are you friends from school?
J: Yes, we are. We're old friends from school. We …

Conversation 2

M = Marie K = Ken C = Chris

M: Hey, Ken, how are you?
K: Oh hi, Marie. Good to see you. I'm OK. How are things?
M: Not bad. Busy.
K: Yeah, me too. Hi, I'm Ken.
C: I'm Chris. Nice to meet you.
M: Oh sorry, yes, Ken, this is Chris, Chris this is Ken.
K: Pleased to meet you, Chris.
M: He's here from the UK.
K: Really? First time in Hong Kong?
C: Yeah. First time.
K: What do you think?
C: It's fantastic. Beautiful.
K: Great. Hey, nice to meet you.
C: You too.
K: And good to see you, Marie.
M: Good to see you too. Goodbye …

Conversation 3

R = Rita A = Andrea L = Liz M = Mark

R: Good morning, everyone. This is Andrea. Andrea, this is Liz and Mark.
A: Pleased to meet you.
L/M: Good to meet you/Nice to meet you.
L: Sorry, is your name Andrew?
A: No, it isn't. It's Andrea. It's an Italian name.
L: Oh, are you from Italy?
A: My mother is, but no, I'm British.
M: Coffee, Andrew, Andrea? Sorry, I'm bad with names.
A: No, thanks.

Lesson 1.2 Recording 1.6

Conversation 1

S = Security guard W = Woman

S: Is this your bag?
W: Yes, it is.
S: Could you open it, please?
W: What's the problem?
S: This is the problem.
W: That's my shampoo.
S: Sorry, it's over a hundred millilitres.
W: Oh, sorry … I forgot.
S: Have a good day.

Conversation 2

S = Security guard M = Man

S: Come through, please.
M: OK.
S: Come over here, please. What's that in your pocket?
M: Ah, sorry, these are my keys.
S: OK, go ahead.

Conversation 3

M = Man W = Woman

M: Excuse me, those are my friend's bags. Can I … ?
W: Sorry, that's my bag. The black one in your hand.
M: No, this is my friend's.
W: Look, my name's on it. It's mine.
M: Oh, sorry. You're right. It's yours.

Lesson 1.3 Recording 1.10

Conversation 1

T = Tourist SA = Shop assistant

T: Excuse me. Do you speak English?
SA: Yes. Can I help you?
T: Can I have one of those, please?
SA: One of these batteries? For your camera?
T: Yes, that's right.
SA: OK. That's eleven euros, please.

Conversation 2

T = Tourist W = Waiter

T: Can I have a sandwich and an apple juice, please?
W: That's six euros.
T: Ah, I only have five euros. How much is the sandwich?
W: Four euros fifty. And the apple juice is one fifty.
T: OK. Could I have the sandwich, but no juice?
W: Yes, of course. That's four fifty.
T: Thank you.

Conversation 3

T = Tourist TS = Ticket seller

TS: Can I help you?
T: Could I have a single to Sydney, please?
TS: Today?
T: Yes.
TS: That's twenty-five dollars.
T: Here you are. Which platform is it?
TS: Platform three.
T: Thanks.

Lesson 1.3 Recording 1.12

1 Can I have a sandwich, please?
2 Can I have a sandwich, please?
3 Can I have one of those batteries, please?
4 Can I have one of those batteries, please?
5 Could I have a single to Sydney, please?
6 Could I have a single to Sydney, please?

Lesson 1.3 Recording 1.13

T = Tourist W = Waiter

T: Can I have a sandwich and an apple juice, please?
W: That's six euros.
T: Ah, I only have five euros. How much is the sandwich?
W: Four euros fifty. And the apple juice is one fifty.
T: OK. Could I have the sandwich, but no juice?
W: That's four fifty.

Lesson 1.3 Recording 1.14

M = Man W = Woman

1 **M:** How much is an apple juice, please?
W: It's two euros twenty.
2 **W:** A single ticket is four euros eighty and a taxi is thirteen euros.
3 **M:** That's two euros fifty for the coffee, and another three seventy-five for the sandwich and a bottle of water – that's one thirty. That's seven euros and fifty-five cents altogether.

Lesson 1.4 Recording 1.15

R = Receptionist G = Guest

R: Good evening. Can I help you?
G: Good evening. Yes, I have a reservation. My name's Baumann.
R: Ah, yes. Mr Baumann. For two nights?
G: That's right.
R: Could I ask you to complete this form?
G: Oh, I haven't got my glasses. Can you help?
R: Certainly. What's your surname?
G: Baumann.
R: Could you spell that?
G: B-a-u-m-a-n-n.
R: Is that double 'n'?
G: Yes, that's right.
R: Your first name?
G: Jeff.
R: And what's your phone number?
G: 212 4742 285.
R: OK. You're in room 407. That's on the fourth floor. The lift's over there.
G: Room 407?
R: Yes, and this is your keycard.
G: Thank you. What's the WiFi code?
R: It's PI936.
G: Thank you. What time's breakfast?
R: From seven to ten.
G: And where is it?
R: In the restaurant, over there.
G: Thank you.
R: Have a good stay.
G: Thanks.

Lesson 2.2 Recording 2.2

P = Presenter G = Gonzales E = Emma

P: And today on Radio 99 we talk to some high flyers – men and women who work in very high places around the world: high buildings or high mountains or planes. Our first guest is from the United States. His name is Gonzales Delgado and he has a great job. He works on bridges. Welcome, Gonzales.
G: Good morning.
P: So, tell us about your job.
G: Well I'm a painter and I work on bridges. Now I'm at the Mackinack Bridge, in Michigan.
P: Oh yes. I have a photo of you … on that bridge. It looks dangerous.
G: Yeah, maybe, but I like it.
P: What do you like about it?
G: Well, I leave home at four in the morning and start work at five and it's quiet, no people, no cars, just me. I love the fresh air. It's great being outside. I like all that … the only problem is the wind and the cold …
P: Yes.
G: … and then I finish work at two and get home at three and that's great!
P: Yes. And do you come down to have lunch?
G: No, I have a sandwich up on the bridge.
P: And what does your family think about it?
G: Oh well, my wife doesn't like it. She thinks it's dangerous. But she loves the money, it's very good money.
P: I'm sure! Anyway, thanks, Gonzales. Please don't go because our next guest is another high flyer. She's a pilot in Canada. Good morning, Emma. Can you hear me? Emma?
E: Yes, fine. Hi.
P: Where are you now?
E: In Ottawa, Canada, at the airport.
P: So, do you fly from Ottawa?
E: Well, I live in Ottawa. But mostly I fly between small towns. I take food, post and other things out to small towns in Canada.
P: Is that a lot of flying?

E: Yes, it's erm … four or five hours from one town to another.
P: That's a lot of time. When do you eat?
E: Oh, I don't eat on the plane. I have dinner in the towns, with friends.
P: And you fly every week?
E: Yeah. I leave home on Monday morning and I get back home on Thursday.
P: Do you like your job?
E: Oh yes, yes, I do. I love the mountains. They're … they're beautiful …
P: Yes.
E: … really beautiful.
P: And what does your family think about your job?
E: Hmmm. So-so. I'm not home for three days a week so that's a problem for my eight-year-old girl.
P: Ah. What's her name?
E: Her name's Alice.
P: Does she want to be a pilot?
E: No, Alice doesn't like flying. She wants to work with animals – she watches animal programmes on TV all the time.
P: Thanks, Emma. Have a safe journey.
E: No problem. Thank you.
P: So, Gonzales, do you …

Lesson 2.2 Recording 2.3

works, has, loves, watches

Lesson 2.2 Recording 2.4

gets, leaves, phones, teaches, starts, likes, goes, wants, sees, finishes, stops

Lesson 2.3 Recording 2.7

1 half past twelve
2 quarter past four
3 twenty to seven
4 twenty-five to five

Lesson 2.3 Recording 2.8

A = Tourist B = Tourist C = Tour guide

A: Oh look, Tourist information. We can ask there.
B: OK. You ask.
A: No, you ask. My English isn't very good.
B: You speak English very well. You ask.
A: No, you ask.
B: No, you ask.
A: OK … Excuse me. Do you speak English?
C: Yes, can I help you?
A: Yes, thank you, my friend has a question.
B: Nooo … ohhh … uh … OK … We want to take a tour.
C: OK. Which tour is that? The Hop-on-Hop-off bus tour, the Golden Gate boat tour or the Chinatown walking tour?
B: I don't understand anything
C: She asked which tour.
B: Oh, the Golden Gate boat tour.
C: Ah, the boat tour, good choice, and I think we have a couple of places left on the tour tomorrow morning if you're interested in that one …
B: Thank you, goodbye.
C: Oh. Goodbye.
A: What's the problem?
B: I don't understand her. She speaks too fast!
A: Oh, come on! Let's go back.
B: No, I don't want to. I feel sooo stupid!
A: Oh, come on.

Lesson 2.3 Recording 2.9

1 What time does it start?
2 Where does it leave from?
3 When does the tour finish?
4 How much does it cost?
5 Do you take credit cards?

Lesson 2.3 Recording 2.10

A = Tourist B = Tourist C = Tour guide

A: Hello. We're back.
C: Hello again! So, do you want the Golden Gate boat tour?
A: Er. Could you speak more slowly, please?
C: Of course. Would you like the Golden Gate boat tour?
A: Yes, tomorrow.
C: Would you like the morning or afternoon tour?
A: Tomorrow morning. What time does it start?
C: At ten o'clock exactly.
A: Excuse me, ten o'clock … ?
C: Yes, at ten.
A: And where does it leave from?
C: From Pier forty-three. Or the minibus to the boat leaves from the front gate at nine forty-five.
A: Sorry, could you repeat that?
C: The minibus bus to the boat leaves from the front gate.
A: The front gate? Here? Outside?
C: Yes, just over there. Do you see the sign?
B: Yes, I can see the sign. I can see it!
A: Nine forty-five.
B: Nine forty-five. OK. And when does the tour finish?
C: The boat arrives back here at 1p.m.
A: One p.m. OK. How much does it cost?
C: Twenty-six dollars per person.
A: Twenty-six dollars. So, fifty-two dollars for two.
C: That's right.
A: OK, that's good. So could we have two tickets for tomorrow morning, please?
B: Er, do you take credit cards?
C: Yes, of course …

Lesson 2.3 Recording 2.12

Could you speak more slowly, please?
Excuse me, ten o'clock … ?
Sorry, could you repeat that?

Lesson 2.3 Recording 2.13

M = Man W = Woman

M: What do you think? What does a good guest do?
W: Erm. Well he …
M: Or she …
W: Yes, let's say he …
M: OK.
W: He doesn't arrive early.
M: For example?
W: For example, he says seven o'clock and then he arrives at six o'clock. One hour early, and I'm not ready.
M: Yes, I agree. That's bad.
W: So, number one a good guest doesn't arrive early.
M: Not too early, not too late.
W: Yes, that's good. What else?
M: Erm … what about money?
W: Hmm … I don't know, what do you think?
M: Well I think it's important to give some money for your food.
W: Oh no, I don't agree.
M: Well maybe you have dinner at a restaurant one evening and you pay.
W: It depends. Not for one night.
M: OK, when a guest stays three nights, he pays for dinner at a restaurant.
W: I think that's strange, but OK.
M: And language? Maybe the guest speaks a different language.
W: Yeah. Well, then …

Lesson 3.2 Recording 3.2

Conversation 1

H = Hakim M = Man

Hakim from Indonesia
H: I know a lot of people but I haven't got many close friends. Do you know Tomi?
M: Yes … he works in your office …
H: That's right. Well, we like doing the same things, sport, cinema, you know.
M: Uh huh.
H: Well, at the weekends we usually play football or go running together … but I never talk about home life or personal things.
M: Yeah. I know what you mean.
H: I talk to Padma, my wife … Yes, Padma is my best friend. I don't need other people. I'm happy with my family.

Conversation 2

B = Bridget W = Woman

Bridget from Scotland
B: I've got, erm, thirty-five online friends and I know them all. They're people in my family and my friends in real life.
W: Really?
B: But my son, Mark, has got about one thousand five hundred friends! I mean, one thousand five hundred friends!
W: He doesn't know one thousand five hundred people!
B: Of course not. He meets people at parties, and he adds them to his friends or he meets them online.
W: But they aren't real friends.
B: I don't think so … but Mark is sometimes on his computer for eight hours or ten hours. Not every day, but two or three times a week.
W: It's crazy …
B: Yes, I think so.

Conversation 3

J = Jane W = Woman

Jane from New Zealand
J: I think my sister is one of my real friends.
W: Your sister, Diana?
J: Yes, I think she's my best friend. She phones me every day and we talk about everything … our problems and our good times, everything.
W: You're lucky. I haven't got any brothers or sisters.
J: I know. She always listens to me and we often visit each other.
W: That's nice.
J: And then I've got a really good friend from school. Her name's Julie. We hardly ever see each other, erm, maybe three or four times in the last five years, but we often email or text each other.
W: Yeah, I have a friend like …

Lesson 3.3 Recording 3.5

M = Max R = Ron

M: Hello?
R: Hi, Max. It's Ron.
M: Oh, hi. How are you?
R: Fine, thanks. And you?
M: OK.
R: Uh, well, I'm at my new office, you know I've got a new job … Uh, the people are very friendly … Hello, are you there?
M: Yes. Yes, I'm still here.
R: … and the work's really interesting … er … Hello, are you there?
M: Yes.
R: Oh … and, well, it's not perfect. I haven't got my own office and my manager isn't very friendly … Are you there?

M: Yes, I'm here.
R: Anyway, are you free tonight?
M: Yeah, I think so.
R: How about going to the cinema? I'd like to see the new Jennifer Lawrence film.
M: Jennifer Lawrence … ah, wait, I'm busy. Sorry …
R: Oh … OK, well, maybe next time.
M: Yeah, see you.
R: Bye.

Lesson 3.3 Recording 3.6

A = Amy R = Ron

A: Hello?
R: Hi, Amy. It's Ron.
A: Oh, hi. How are you?
R: Fine, thanks. And you?
A: I'm OK. How's your new job?
R: Good. The people are very friendly …
A: Uh-huh.
R: … and the work's really interesting.
A: That's great!
R: It's not perfect. I haven't got my own office and my manager isn't very friendly.
A: Oh, that's a shame!
R: Yeah. Anyway, are you free tonight?
A: Yes, I think so. What would you like to do?
R: How about going to the cinema? I want to see the new Jennifer Lawrence film.
A: Sounds good. Where's it showing?
R: At the ABC in town.
A: OK. What time does it start?
R: Let me look. The film's at six o'clock and at half past eight. What time's good for you?
A: I finish work at five. So six is good.
R: Right. How about meeting at … er … half past five at the cinema?
A: Yes, that's fine.
R: Great! See you there.
A: Yeah. Oh, how about asking Max?
R: Hmm. You call him!
A: OK. Bye.
R: Bye.

Lesson 3.3 Recording 3.8

1 I've got a new job!
2 I haven't got any money.
3 I've got a new boyfriend …
4 … and he's a very nice person.
5 Oh, look – rain!
6 My English teacher is great!

Lesson 3.4 Recording 3.10

C = Christine J =James

C: What's a special occasion in your country?
J: Hogmanay.
C: Hog … er … man … ?
J: Hog-man-ay. Let me tell you about it. OK … Hogmanay happens in Scotland on New Year's Day. In our families, on the day before Hogmanay, we always clean the house – all day – because it's important to start the New Year in a clean house. Then, in the evening, we usually have a big party with friends and family. At midnight we stand in a circle, join hands, sing 'Auld Lang Syne' … you know. I think people sing this in a lot of countries now. We also have a special custom. After midnight, the first person who visits the house gives presents to the family, usually shortbread or coal. This brings good luck. Then we eat and drink. The party often goes on all night. I like it because all our friends and family come together and it's a great start to the New Year!

Lesson 4.1 Recording 4.1

a sofa, an armchair, a carpet, a cupboard, a shower, a wardrobe, a table, a bedroom, a bathroom, a kitchen, an office, a terrace

Lesson 4.1 Recording 4.2

J = Jamie R = Renée

J: Hi, it's Jamie …
R: Oh hi, you got my email.
J: Yeah, is it OK to talk now?
R: Yes, that's fine.
J: I've got two or three questions.
R: Go ahead.
J: So there's a roof terrace …
R: Uh huh.
J: So we can sit and enjoy the sun …
R: Erm … yes … but it's very hot in the daytime. Erm … very hot, but it's good for the evening.
J: Oh, to have dinner, that's good.
R: Yeah, there are chairs and a table on the terrace.
J: Right. There's no information about cooking. Is there a kitchen?
R: Yes, oh yes, you're welcome to use our kitchen any time.
J: Oh, so we share the kitchen.
R: That's right. There isn't a separate kitchen.
J: Oh. OK. And you say Valletta is only thirty minutes away.
R: Er, yes, well maybe forty minutes by bus.
J: And are there buses at night?
R: Erm, well, there aren't any buses late at night.
J: I see.
R: But they're good in the daytime. And the early evening.
J: Uh huh. But there are lots of restaurants near the apartment, right?
R: Yeah, some really good Italian and Greek restaurants on the seafront.
J: OK … Great … Well, two minutes from the sea, that sounds amazing. Great for my morning swim.
R: Well, it's not really a swimming beach. But it's nice, the sea. We often walk there in the evening.
J: Oh. Is there a good swimming beach somewhere?
R: Erm, well there's a swimming pool in a hotel about ten minutes away. The name …

Lesson 4.2 Recording 4.6

1 You can't borrow DVDs.
2 You can watch short films there.
3 Can you buy medicine here?
4 You can't swim there.
5 Where can I change money?
6 We can't eat lunch here.

Lesson 4.2 Recording 4.7

The supermarket is opposite the art gallery.
The cinema is on the right of the art gallery.
The post office is opposite the cinema and on the left of the supermarket.
The sports centre is near the post office.

Lesson 4.3 Recording 4.9

Conversation 1

A = Assistant C = Customer

A: Can I help you?
C: Yes, how much is this sweater?
A: Erm, let me look. It's nineteen ninety-nine.
C: And where are the changing rooms?
A: Over there. Next to the mirrors.
C: Thanks.
A: How is it?
C: Hmm. It's too small. Have you got it in large?
A: Sorry, no.
C: Mmm. It really is too small … No, it isn't right. Thanks anyway.
A: No problem.

Conversation 2

C: Uhhh … Excuse me.
A: Yes, can I help you?
C: I need one of these for my mobile. Mine doesn't work in England.
A: Let's see. What type is that?
C: Uhh … let's see … Well, it's a normal SIM card, I think.
A: Here you are.
C: How much is it?
A: It's eight ninety-nine. The PIN code is on the back. And the phone number is here.
C: Does it work on my phone?
A: Yes, it does. You can make local calls with it.
C: That's fine. I'll take it.

Conversation 3

A: Can I help you?
C: Yes, can I try these trainers?
A: What size are you?
C: Thirty-eight.
A: These are size thirty-eight. How are they?
C: Yes … er … good, thanks. How much are they?
A: One hundred and twenty euros. Would you like to buy them?
C: One hundred and twenty? Er … I'm not sure. I need to think about it. Thanks.
A: Fine. No problem.

Conversation 4

A: Can I help you?
C: No, thanks. I'm just looking.

Lesson 4.3 Recording 4.11

1 Can I help you?
2 C: Have you got it in large?
A: Sorry, no.
3 C: How much are they?
A: One hundred and twenty euros. Would you like to buy them?

Lesson 4.4 Recording 4.12

One of my favourite places in the world is Lake Titicaca. It's between Bolivia and Peru and is, oh, about 4,000 metres above sea level. The water is always very, very cold. I go there every year with my family and we stay in a small town near the lake. When I'm there, I usually go out on the lake in a boat, and sometimes I visit one of the small islands. Sometimes there are big waves on the lake, but it's usually very quiet. So why do I like the lake? Well, I love its deep blue colour and it's a great place to relax.

Lesson 5.1 Recording 5.2

I travel around the world and I usually stay with friends, not in hotels. I always take photos of my friends, and last year I started taking photos of their fridges, too. It's amazing what a fridge can tell you about a person. Look at this picture … You can see right away it's a single person, probably lives alone. There isn't much food in this fridge, and maybe he doesn't like cooking. There's some takeaway food here, Chinese takeaway. There's not a lot of food, but he's got some broccoli, some peppers and an apple up here. Oh and some garlic. I know he's a big meat eater … let's see, has he got any meat? OK, in this photo he hasn't got any meat, but I know he likes meat.

Look at all these vegetables and fruit – I mean he tries to be healthy. And I know him well. His name's Vinnie and he lives in New York City. He's single, a businessman, a quiet, serious guy. He buys fruit and vegetables, but he doesn't often cook; he often has takeaway food or goes out to restaurants.
Look at this one. All this food – they've got some fish here, some chicken – a roast chicken, ready to eat – and there's a big pasta salad, and some really nice cheese. They've got all this water because they do a lot of exercise and they like having water with them when they go running or play tennis. You can see they try to be very healthy – just look at all that fresh food. But the main thing is all this food is ready to cook. That tells me that these people are friendly; they like having friends for dinner. And it's true, Mike and Liz are really friendly, and I love staying with them because they're funny and intelligent and there are always lots of people around in their apartment. I stay with them every time I go to Lisbon.

Lesson 5.3 Recording 5.6

WT = Waiter M = Man W = Woman

WT: Good evening. A table for two?
M: Yes, please.
WT: By the window?
M: That's fine.
WT: Can I take your coats?
M: Thank you.
WT: Would you like something to drink?
W: Er … yes, please. Could I have an orange juice, please?
M: And I'd like a cola, please and er can we have a bottle of mineral water, please?
WT: Certainly. The menu …
M: Thank you.
WT: Tonight's special is Chicken à la Chef de Saint Germaine de Paris Rive Gauche.
W: What's that?
WT: It's grilled chicken with potatoes and green beans.
W: Is it French?
WT: Not really …
W: But it has a French name.
WT: Well, that's true … it's very good …
WT: Are you ready to order?
M: Yes, I'd like some soup and the special.
W: The same for me, please.
WT: Thank you.

Lesson 5.3 Recording 5.8

1 Could I have an orange juice, please?
2 Could I have an orange juice, please?
3 Can we have a bottle of mineral water, please?
4 Can we have a bottle of mineral water, please?
5 I'd like some soup, please.
6 I'd like some soup, please.
7 The same for me, please.
8 The same for me, please.

Lesson 5.3 Recording 5.10

M = Man W = Woman

M: Afternoon, what can I get you?
W: Uhhh … the Jackpot special, please.
M: Is that eat in or take away?
W: Take away.
M: Large fries with that?
W: No, medium …
M: Something to drink?
W: A cola.
M: Small, medium or large?
W: Small.
M: Anything else?
W: No thanks.
M: That'll be nine ninety-five.
W: OK.

Lesson 5.4 Recording 5.12

One of my favourite dishes is American pancakes. I like them because they're easy to make and not too sweet. Americans often eat pancakes for breakfast, but I like eating them at any time, hot or cold.
So, you need some flour, some sugar and a bit of salt, some baking powder, a cup of milk, an egg and a little oil. Mix together the milk, egg and oil in a big bowl. Then add the flour, sugar and salt. Stir everything together.
After that, you put a little oil in a frying pan and heat it, but not too hot. Put some of the pancake mix into the pan. After about one minute turn the pancake over, and then wait about two minutes. Take it out and make some more.
Pancakes are really good with butter and honey, or with lemon and sugar, but some people like them plain, with nothing on them.

Lesson 6.1 Recording 6.2

1 She's very kind.
2 She was very kind.
3 They were my friends.
4 They're my friends.
5 It isn't very funny.
6 It wasn't very funny.
7 We were very happy.
8 We're very happy.

Lesson 6.1 Recording 6.6

M = Man W = Woman

M: Do you know all the dates?
W: Let's check. OK. Christmas Day is the twenty-fifth of December. Everyone knows that.
M: And New Year's Day is January the first.
W: Valentine's Day – well, you always forget – that's February the fourteenth. Halloween is the thirty-first of October …
M: And International Women's Day?
W: I don't know. Let's do the next one.
M: OK, but I know that one. Independence Day in the USA is the fourth of July.
W: So International Women's Day is … ?
M: March the eighth
W: Bingo. Well done!

Lesson 6.3 Recording 6.9

A = Ahmed I = Isabel J = Jane

Conversation 1

A: Hi, Isabel!
I: Hi, Ahmed. How was your weekend?
A: Good. And yours? What did you do?
I: On Saturday I went for a walk. It was really good. Nice weather.
A: Yes it was lovely. Where did you go?
I: Down by the sea. It was really beautiful.
A: That sounds nice.
I: And you? What did you do?
A: Nothing much on Saturday but on Sunday we went running.
I: Oh, who did you go with?
A: Some old friends of mine from school. And then we saw a film in the evening.
I: Oh, what was it?

Conversation 2

A: Oh look, there's Jane.
I: Jane, hey, come and sit with us.
J: Hi, guys.
A: Did you have a good weekend?
J: Weekend? Yes, it was OK.
I: What did you do?
J: I slept.
I: You slept? You stayed in bed? All weekend?
J: Yeah, well, on Saturday. I was very tired. Oh, I saw some friends on Sunday afternoon, yesterday afternoon. We went into town and had a coffee.
I: That sounds good.
J: How about you? What did you do?
I: Oh I went for a walk …

Lesson 6.4 Recording 6.11

I = Interviewer F = Fernanda

I: Thank you for joining us today and welcome to the programme, Fernanda.
F: Thank you.
I: We are all very interested to know more about your work. But, first of all, let's start from the beginning … erm, where were you born?
F: I was born in San Pedro in Honduras in nineteen seventy-three.
I: Can I ask you about your childhood?
F: Yes, of course. I was the fourth child in a very big family – there were eleven of us. My father was a teacher and my mother cleaned houses for rich people.
I: Did you go to school?
F: Yes, I did. Education was very important to my parents.
I: When did you decide to work with poor children?
F: When I was in school, one of my friends lost his parents. He had no family … no living grandparents, so he moved to a house for orphans. I visited him and when I saw his life there I decided to work with orphans, children with no parents or children who lost their parents.
I: When did you open your orphanage?
F: We opened it in two thousand and six.
I: We?
F: Yes, my husband and I. We got married in two thousand.
I: And who's your hero?
F: I'm glad you asked that – it's Mother Teresa. I often think about her words: 'I can do no great things, only small things with great love.'
I: That's very true. So how many kids are there at the orphanage?
F: At the moment we have about two hundred and fifty. We usually have between two and three hundred.
I: You're very busy, then!
F: Yes, I am.
I: Do you ever have time to relax?
F: Not much, but when I have time, I like to read.
I: Ah, so what's your favourite book?
F: Let me think about that. I like many books but *Long Walk to Freedom* is one of my favourites. It's the story of Nelson Mandela's life in his own words.
I: That sounds interesting, thank you. OK … now, it's time to ask the audience for questions. Are there any questions for Fernanda … ?

Lesson 7.1 Recording 7.2

M = Man W = Woman

M: So, on holiday, how do you like travelling? By plane, train or car?
W: Well, I don't like airports, so put train. I hate travelling by car.
M: Me too. I put 'plane' because well, planes are faster than trains.

W: Not always! OK, number two. It says 'I like staying in a) a hotel, b) a self-catering apartment or c) a tent'.
M: Forget the tent! Erm In an apartment. And you?
W: In a hotel.
M: Really. A hotel's more expensive than an apartment!
W: Yeah, but it's more comfortable. Hmm … next question. Do you prefer: relaxing on a beach, doing something sporty or going sightseeing?
M: What does it mean … something sporty?
W: Erm … playing tennis or maybe golf.
M: No, thank you! Not on holiday. But I hate staying on the beach all day. Boring!
W: OK – there's one we answered the same. So we agree about that.
M: Yeah, sightseeing's definitely more interesting than the beach!
W: Right. When do you like going on holiday: in spring, summer or winter?
M: In spring – I never go on holiday in winter, but I don't really like very hot weather. Tourist places are more crowded in summer.
W: True. But the weather's better. Summer's hotter than spring. I love hot weather.
M: Well, we don't agree there. Anyway, next question. What do you like eating: local dishes, the food you usually eat or fast food?
W: Local dishes, I think. You?
M: Definitely!
W: Hmm, interesting. Next … In the evenings I like going for a walk, going to a restaurant or going to a nightclub.
M: Erm, going to a restaurant.
W: Oh, good. Me, too. I don't like noisy places.
M: Yes, I agree. Restaurants are quieter … more relaxing. But I like going for a walk too, sometimes, so I'm not sure. OK, let's say going to a restaurant.
W: And the last question … how long is your perfect holiday?
M: Three months.
W: You can't have three months! The answer is a weekend, a week or a month.
M: OK, a month then.
W: Me, too!
M: Maybe we can travel together …

Lesson 7.2 Recording 7.5

I = Interviewer J = Jeff

I: So Jeff. A few questions about the trip. What was the coldest place you visited?
J: The coldest place was in the mountains in Kyrgyzstan. There was lots of snow, too.
I: Really? And what was the hottest place?
J: Well, it was Turpan, China. I think it was over fifty degrees centigrade.
I: Ah, was it? And what was the friendliest place?
J: That's an impossible question. I can't say. We met so many fantastic people. I think Iran; the people there were so kind. Perhaps that was my biggest surprise.
I: OK. What was the longest you travelled in one day?
J: One day we travelled about a hundred and fifty kilometres in western China. That was a long day!
I: Very! So, what was the most beautiful building you saw?
J: There were some great ones in all of the countries but my favourite building was the Bibi-Khanym Mosque in Uzbekistan. I think it's the most beautiful building in the world.
I: Wow. So, what was the most amazing experience of the journey?
J: Arriving in Istanbul after twelve thousand kilometres. A-ma-a-a-zing!

Lesson 7.3 Recording 7.7

W = Woman M = Man

Conversation 1

W: Excuse me.
M: Yes.
W: Can you tell me the way to the Beatles Story?
M: Yeah. You go straight on here and can you see those traffic lights?
W: Yes.
M: Well turn left at the traffic lights.
W: Turn left?
M: Yes. Then you go past some water, that's Salthouse Dock, and you come to some big red buildings. That's Albert Dock. You can't miss it.
W: OK.
M: There are always a lot of tour buses there. Go straight on for about a hundred metres and the Beatles Story is on your right.
W: Thanks. So, it's left at the traffic lights and then past some water and then it's on the right, at Alba … ?
M: Albert Dock.
W: Albert Dock. Right, thanks.
M: No problem.

Conversation 2

W: Excuse me. Is there a cinema near here?
M: Erm. Let me think. Yes, there's a cinema in Liverpool One, the big shopping centre, but it's not very near.
W: Can you tell me the way?
M: I think the easiest way is … erm … OK, go straight on here and then turn right at the traffic lights. The name of the road is Liver Street.
W: Liver Street.
M: Yes, and keep walking. Go past the big car park on the left. There are traffic lights at Hanover Street. Go straight on at the traffic lights. There's a pedestrian street. I think it's called Paradise Street.
W: Paradise Street. OK.
M: Go straight on. The cinema is on the left. You can't miss it. It's really big.
W: Can I just check the first part? So straight on here, then turn left at the traffic lights.
M: No, turn right.
W: Turn right and go straight on.
M: Yes.
W: Erm … can you repeat the last part.
M: OK, at the traffic lights at Hanover Street, don't turn left or right, just go straight on.
W: OK, and then the cinema's on the left.
M: Yes.
W: How far is it?
M: Oh, about ten minutes from here.
W: Thanks very much.
M: You're welcome.

Lesson 7.4 Recording 7.11

OK, so this place is in London. It's in the north of London and most tourists don't know about it. It's called Little Venice, Little Venice because it's next to the water, there's water everywhere. There are lots of boats, houseboats – people live in them. There are lots of good restaurants and cafés next to the water. I like it because I can sit there, have a coffee and watch people on the boats or by the water. Little Venice is a lovely place in the daytime or at night. And it's one of the best places to take photos. You can take a photo of the houseboats or the water or the people. Some of the people are very interesting. I think the best time to take a photo is in the early morning or in the early evening because it's really quiet and the light is beautiful.

Lesson 8.2 Recording 8.3

Conversation 1

W = Woman M = Man

W: Amazing.
M: What are you reading?
W: Look at this.
M: Who are they? Oh, that's Christian Bale, yeah?
W: Yup, in one of the Batman films. And this?
M: I don't know.
W: It's the same actor. Christian Bale. All three of these.
M: Wow, that is amazing. He's so … different. He's a lot bigger here and he's got glasses.
W: Yeah, and longer hair.
M: Which film is that from?
W: *American Hustle*.
M: Oh yeah, I remember now. And this one?
W: That's him too, in *The Machinist*. He lost twenty-nine kilos for that film.
M: Unbelievable. How did he do it?
W: Let me see. Erm. He just had one apple and a cup of coffee every day. And water. And he ran a lot.
M: That's not very healthy …
W: Then he put on fifty kilos for the next Batman film.
M: Crazy.
W: I think he's great, though. He always changes his appearance for each film.
M: A lot of actors do that.
W: Yeah, that's what this article is about. Look at these.
M: That's erm, don't tell me, don't tell me … erm … I saw the film… ah *Bridget Jones's Diary*. I liked it. Oh … what's her name?
W: Renée Zellweger.
M: That's right. That's an old film and how old is she now?
W: In her forties I think. But she was in her early thirties when she was in Bridget Jones.
M: I think she looks nice.
W: Yeah, and look. This is her, too.
M: Wow!
W: This is her in *Leatherheads*. It came out in 2008.
M: How did she do that?
W: Erm … it says she put on ten kilos for Bridget Jones. Pizza, chocolate, doughnuts. And then she lost it. But she doesn't look so different.
M: No, just thinner, really. And she's wearing black in this picture, so she looks thinner. Her face is the same. I actually think she looks better like this, in Bridget Jones.
W: I know what you mean. Oh this is interesting.
M: What?
W: Zellweger ate doughnuts to put on weight. And what's the first thing Christian Bale ate when he wanted to put on weight?
M: Doughnuts?
W: Yup. Now I'm hungry.

Lesson 8.3 Recording 8.4

W = Woman M = Man

Conversation 1

W: Is it a man or a woman?
M: A woman.
W: What does she look like?
M: I think she's in her thirties. She's got straight blonde hair. She's a little overweight. She's reading something.
W: Oh, it's Renée Zellweger in …

Conversation 2

W: Is it a man or a woman?
M: A man.
W: What does he look like?
M: He's got short brown hair. He's very thin.
W: Oh, I know … it's Christian Bale in …

Lesson 8.3 Recording 8.7

Conversation 1

P = Phil H = Harry

H: … and we had a great time. Hey, Phil.
P: Yeah?
H: I've got a long train journey next week. I'm off to Edinburgh. Can you recommend a good film? For the journey?
P: Erm … let me think. What kind of films do you like?
H: Well, action films and er … dramas, that kind of thing.
P: Erm … How about *Gravity*?
H: Oh that film with er … oh, who's in it?
P: Sandra Bullock and George Clooney. It's very good.
H: Mmm. I don't really like sci-fi films.
P: I don't either but this one is good … it's got a lot of drama and the acting is great. Sandra Bullock is amazing.
H: What's it about? It's two astronauts, yeah?
P: Yes, it's about two astronauts and they have an accident in space and they try to get back home. That's all. But it's fantastic. The photography is great. I think you'd like it.
H: OK. Sounds good. Thanks.
P: No problem.

Conversation 2

C = Clara R = Rachel

R: Hey, Clara. Can you recommend a good film?
C: At home or at the cinema?
R: At home.
C: What kind of films do you like?
R: Erm, different kinds, er, comedies, dramas, romantic films …
C: Do you want a new film?
R: No, it can be new or old.
C: What about *Let the Right One In*? It's a kind of love story.
R: Mmm. I saw that on TV last year. It's more of a horror film. I don't really like horror films.
C: Let me think … Do you know *Happy-Go-Lucky*?
R: No, I don't think so.
C: Well, it's a comedy but also a drama. I really liked it. And I laughed a lot.
R: What's it about?
C: Erm, it's about a teacher in London. Her name's Poppy; she's really kind to everyone and she's always happy. It's about her life. Erm … she takes driving lessons and there are problems at her school and … anyway, I think you'd like it.
R: Sounds good. Who's in it?
C: I don't know their names. But the actress playing Poppy is fantastic.
R: OK. Thanks. I'll try it.

Lesson 8.4 Recording 8.11

W = Woman M = Man

W: Can I ask you a few questions?
M: Sure.
W: Do you often go to music festivals?
M: Oh, yes. I love festivals, not just music but all types. I started going to music festivals when I was very young.
W: Really? What kind of festivals do you like?
M: I like all kinds.
W: For example?
M: Rock festivals, folk festivals, theatre, literature …
W: Oh, so you really do like all kinds of festivals. Do you think festivals are very different now?
M: Compared to years ago? Oh, yes.
W: How are they different?
M: Well, lots of ways.
W: OK, I'll say something about festivals, you tell me how it's different now.
M: OK.
W: Price?
M: More expensive. Much more expensive.
W: OK. What about er security?
M: Well, security is much better now. Sometimes it's too good! They check your bag when you go in and it takes a long time.
W: Mmm.
M: And there are more security people around. But it feels safer at these big festivals now.
W: That's interesting. Erm … how about what people wear? You know, fashion at festivals.
M: Oh, I don't know. It depends on the festival.
W: That's OK. One more thing: technology.
M: Oh, that's a big change. Years ago you couldn't always get information on the internet. Or buy tickets.
W: Wow. I can't imagine that.
M: And a simple thing like mobile phones. Not everybody had one. So, when you wanted to find your friend at a big festival, it was really difficult.
W: That's really interesting. Thanks for your time.
M: That's all right.

Lesson 9.2 Recording 9.3

W = Woman M = Man

W: We never travel long distance. It's too expensive. And I hate travelling by plane.
M: Really? What about trains or cars?
W: Well, I like travelling by train and I love going by car, because you can stop anywhere. But they're all too expensive now.
M: Mmmm … not really. You can travel for free.
W: Sure, if you go by bike or on foot.
M: No. Last year I was on holiday in the US, and I drove across the country for free.
W: How?
M: I had a Driveaway car.
W: A driveway?
M: No, drive-A-way. Driveaway. It's a company.
W: How does it work?
M: Well, there was a family in New York, and they wanted to go to Los Angeles but they didn't want to drive there. It's almost five thousand kilometres. But they needed their car in Los Angeles. So they went by plane, and I drove their car to Los Angeles, to their hotel in the city centre. I had a week to get there. I stopped in the Grand Canyon on the way. It was the best journey ever – I love driving and I love cars.
W: That's amazing. And it's free?
M: Yeah, I just paid for petrol.
W: And did you have time to stop?
M: I had a week, so I stopped in a few places. St Louis – I have friends there – the Grand Canyon.
W: That sounds great.
M: It was wonderful. Not good for everybody. You can't choose the date or the place you want to go. But good for me.
W: Yeah … and is that the longest journey? The longest you travelled for free?
M: Erm, let me think. I once travelled about fourteen thousand kilometres for free … by ship. I was in Mombasa.
W: Where's that?
M: It's a city in Kenya.
W: And?
M: Well, it has a lot of big container ships. I found a ship that went to Indonesia.
W: For free?
M: Well, I worked on the ship.
W: Oh, that sounds hard.
M: Not really. Well, long days, yes. But I learnt a lot. And I loved the slow life. In the evenings I loved watching the sun go down.
W: Was it difficult to find a ship?
M: It wasn't easy. But if you have time, it's possible.
W: That's the problem, isn't it? When I was younger, I had more time.
M: Do you want to travel with me next summer?
W: Where to?
M: Around India.
W: Mmmm. Maybe not.

Lesson 9.3 Recording 9.7

K = Kama V = Val

K: Hey, Val. Did you stay in bed too long this morning?
V: Ha-ha! It's these trains – they're terrible!
K: Why? What happened this time?
V: Well, first of all, the train was late leaving the station, but only about a quarter of an hour or so. After that, it just went at walking speed – all the way to London. Really! There was a guy on a bicycle on the road next to us … I think he got to London before we did!
K: Well, you're two hours late … and the boss wants to see you.

K: Hey, Val. The boss wants to see you. Whoa! What happened to you? You're all wet!
V: Believe me, it's a long story. First of all, I got up late because I didn't hear my alarm, so I only woke up at eight thirty. I ran to the train station – usually I walk – but I missed the train by two minutes! Then I waited for the next train, the nine fifteen, and everything was fine until we just stopped – just stopped – in the middle of nowhere. The guard said that there was a signal problem. After that, the air-conditioning stopped working. It was like an oven – at least a thousand degrees! Finally, after forty minutes, we started moving … very, very slowly. What could I do? Uh-oh, there's the boss.
K: Yeah. She's not happy. Two and a half hours late, Val … Good luck!

Lesson 9.4 Recording 9.9

A = Attendant P = Passenger

A: Your meal, Sir.
P: Thank you. Erm, excuse me.
A: Yes, can I help you?
P: Hope so! I'm sorry, but there's a small problem here … I ordered a vegetarian meal – but this is meat.
A: Oh, just a moment … I checked and we don't have a record of your order.
P: What?! But I always order vegetarian. I'm a frequent flyer.
A: I understand, sir, but we don't have any more vegetarian meals.
P: I don't believe it! You always have extra meals in business class.
A: Yes, but this is economy class.
P: You don't understand. Let me explain one more time. I don't eat meat. I ordered vegetarian. I can't fly to Tokyo without dinner. It's your job to bring me a meal. A business class vegetarian meal is fine.
A: Just a moment. Here you are, Sir. A vegetarian meal.
P: Thank you … but this is already open. And it's cold. Erm, can I speak to the person in charge, please?

Lesson 10.1 Recording 10.1

I = Interviewer J = Jean M = Martin

I: Jean and Martin, the luckiest couple in Australia today … welcome.
J/M: Thank you.
I: So Jean, When did you find out.
J: Martin phoned me at work. I didn't believe him at first.
M: She said 'You're lying!' I said I didn't believe it myself.
J: Yeah.
I: And is it true that you're not going to stop working?
J: That's right. We enjoy our jobs.
M: Yes. People think gardening work is hard and boring … but it isn't. I work outdoors, and I enjoy it. So yes, I'm going to stay in my job.
I: So what are you going to do with the money?
M: First thing, we plan to give some money to Jean's parents in England.
J: They're retired and they need a little help.
I: That's nice. And how about for yourselves? Any plans?
M: Well, we got married last year, but we didn't have a big party. So we're going to have a party and invite all our friends and family.
I: Nice.
J: And we'd like to move. At the moment we're living in a small apartment. So we're going to look for a house near the beach.
M: Yes, maybe near the beach, or …
I: And are you going to take a break? Travel round the world?
J: Not a big break, just a short holiday … to Thailand.
M: I'm not sure about Thailand.
I: Oh, what would you like to do, Martin?
M: I'd like to go to Greece.
I: Fabulous. And do you want to buy anything else? Maybe a new computer … or … ?
M: Well, I want to buy a plane. Just a small one, a small plane.
I: Oh. Do you fly?
M: No I …
J: He doesn't fly. The plane is a kind of dream.
M: Well, I'd like to learn to fly.
I: Sounds wonderful. Thanks very much for talking to us today. Oh, just one last question … You get the money tomorrow, yeah? What's the first thing you're going to do?
J: He's going to buy a new car, of course! The old car didn't survive that tree.

Lesson 10.3 Recording 10.5

W = Woman M = Man

W: Hey, let's do something new this weekend.
M: That's a good idea. Erm …What do you mean … new?
W: I mean something we don't usually do. Something … different. OK … AlternativeCity. Hey, look at this.
M: Silent disco, what's that? Dancing with no music?
W: No, it's … You get headphones, wireless headphones, and you can hear the music and you dance.
M: I don't understand. Why?
W: Well, there's different music and you can choose. So you dance to your favourite music, with headphones. Shall we try it?
M: No. I don't feel like doing that. What's this one?
W: Blind date cinema. That's … Oh, we book a cinema ticket but … they don't tell us the film.
M: That doesn't sound very good. Fine if it's a good film, but if it's a bad film?
W: No, it's OK. If we don't like the film, at the end they give us our money back.
M: Mmm. No. It's not for me.
W: OK, so how about going to the theatre?
M: That's not new.
W: No, playback theatre. It's a very small theatre. And people in the audience tell stories about their lives. The actors act out the stories.
M: Oh. Do I have to tell a story?
W: No, you can just watch. It says it can be very funny or more serious.
M: OK. That sounds interesting.
W: I'd like to go. Let's do that.
M: Cool!
W: OK, that's tomorrow evening at seven. And why don't we go to the museum in the afternoon?
M: For … museum meditation? What's that?
W: Listen to this. You go with a small group into one of the rooms and meditate for an hour.
M: Meditate. Do you look at the paintings or statues?
W: I don't know. Maybe you close your eyes.
M: Oh, THEN you look at the paintings.
W: Mmmm, yes, and then talk about them.
M: Brilliant! So … shall we go to the theatre in the evening and the museum in the afternoon?
W: Sounds great. And for dinner?
M: Let me see. Dinner in the dark?

Lesson 10.4 Recording 10.8

In Dublin today, it'll be hot and sunny with temperatures up to twenty-five degrees Celsius. Tomorrow will be cloudy, but warm, with a high of twenty. Things will change on Friday night: it'll be a wet night with rain from midnight to early next morning. The temperature will fall to ten so it'll feel cool, but the rain will stop, so we'll have a dry day all Saturday. Sunday will be windy and cloudy … and very cold, so make sure you wear your winter coat!

Lesson 10.4 Recording 10.9

I can remember the sirocco very well. I was in Pisa, in Italy about five years ago. I worked there as a teacher for two years. I love hot, sunny weather and the summers were wonderful. I remember my first summer. It was very hot, but then one day the weather changed. It got hotter. I woke up one morning and everywhere was white, there was white sand over all the cars and the streets. And everything was dry, your eyes, your mouth. Everything. The car was like an oven … the metal of the car door was really hot. It was difficult to breathe. People told me it was the sirocco. The sirocco is a strong wind from Africa, from the desert. At work everyone got very tired. Me too. I was glad when it was over.

Lesson 11.1 Recording 11.2

P = Presenter Dr H = Elizabeth Harper

P: And this week in *Health Matters*, we're talking about colds and flu. What's the difference, and more importantly, what should you do when you have a cold or flu? With me in the studio is Dr Elizabeth Harper.
Dr H: Hello.
P: Dr Harper … First, can you tell us … how is flu different from a cold?
Dr H: Well one big difference is how they start. Flu starts very suddenly. One minute you're fine, you're OK, the next minute you feel terrible. You've got a headache – often a very bad headache – and sometimes a cough. You have a sore throat and your arms and legs hurt. You feel awful.
P: OK. And do you usually have a temperature?
Dr H: Yes, you get very hot. Usually you have a temperature of over thirty-eight degrees centigrade and you're too ill to do anything. You can't work. You just want to go home and go to bed.
P: So it's serious.
Dr H: Yes. Don't try to work. You should go to bed. Get lots of sleep. Sometimes you have to stay in bed for a week or more. You shouldn't go back to work too soon.
P: Anything else?
Dr H: Yes, you should drink lots of water.
P: Right. And what about a cold? How is a cold different from flu?
Dr H: Well, a cold starts slowly. Maybe it takes two or three days to start. It's a cold when you've got a bad throat … or a cough and a runny nose and you don't feel very well. But – and here's the big difference – if you can get up and go to work, then you've probably got a cold, not flu.
P: So should you go to work with a cold?
Dr H: Er, it depends. You don't want to give your cold to other people at work, so some people take two or three days off work or work from home. But, yes, you can usually work and after a week you usually feel better.
P: And after flu?
Dr H: After flu, you often feel very tired for a very long time, maybe three or four weeks.
P: Should you rest a lot?
Dr H: Well, it depends, but be careful. For example, don't do too much sport or hard exercise until you feel better.
P: Another question about colds and flu. What do you think about antibiotics?
Dr H: Well, you shouldn't take antibiotics with a cold and …

Lesson 11.3 Recording 11.5

W = Woman M = Man

Conversation 1

W: Oh, no.
M: Here, let me help. What a mess!
W: Thank you very much. It's my leg. It's difficult …
M: … Oh, don't move. I'll do it.
W: Thanks a lot.
M: No problem.

Conversation 2

W: Er … Excuse me?
M: Yeah.
W: You dropped this.
M: Oh. Thanks so much.
W: That's OK.

Conversation 3

W: Can I help you?
M: Oh, thanks.
W: The traffic's really bad here.
M: Yes.
W: Shall I carry your bag?
M: No, no, it's fine, thanks.
W: Here you are.
M: Thanks very much. That's kind of you.
W: You're welcome.

Lesson 11.4 Recording 11.9

S1, 2, 3 = Students D = Doctor H = Hilary

S1: I've got a question for the doctor.
D: Yes? What's your question?
S1: Do you think these diets are dangerous?
D: What do you mean?
S1: Well, is it dangerous to eat only sugar or only fat?
D: Yes, well, this was an experiment. You shouldn't go on a sugar or fat diet for a long time.

S2: Hilary, do you agree with him?
H: Yes, of course. These are not healthy diets.
S2: So what do you recommend for people to eat and not eat?
H: That's a very good question. The answer is complicated.
S2: Well, should we stop eating anything?
H: Well, some foods are bad for you.
S2: Could you give an example?
H: Well, we know that processed foods are bad for you. So try to eat less processed food.
S3: How do we know what's processed?
H: In the supermarket, look at the label. And of course, we should eat lots of fresh food, fruit and vegetables.
S3: I see. Erm, I've got a question for Chris. Can I ask you about your diet? What was the worst thing about it?

Lesson 12.1 Recording 12.1

I = Interviewer M = Man

Conversation 1

I: Excuse me. Do you have a second? We're asking people about great experiences, unforgettable experiences …
M: Oh … Er, yes, if it's quick.
I: Great! Could you look at this list? Have you done any of these things?
M: Hmm … Yes, yes, I have. I've been to a karaoke bar, in Japan. I sometimes go to Tokyo on business.
I: How was it?
M: Scary! I like singing, but I'm not a very good singer. Or my wife tells me I'm not a good singer. But at a karaoke bar in Japan, you have to get up and sing. Everyone does …
I: And you did too.
M: Yes. And it was amazing. Unforgettable. *My Way*. It's my favourite song. You know. Do you want me to sing it?
I: Er, no, no. That's fine. Have you done anything else on the list?
M: No, no, I don't think so. Sorry, I have to run …

Conversation 2

I = Interviewer W = Woman

I: Excuse me …
W: What?
I: Have you ever ridden an elephant?
W: What? Why? Uh, no. No, I haven't …
I: We're doing a survey on unforgettable experiences. Can I show you this list? Have you done any of these activities?
W: Oh, OK. OK. Let's see … Er … No, no, no, no. Oh, I've watched the sun rise. Over Istanbul … so that's one thing. I never get up early, but I was with my husband on vacation and he was ill, so we were awake all night. So we saw the sun rise.
I: Sounds great.
W: Well, I enjoyed it more than my husband did. It was amazing, really. Unforgettable.
I: And anything else on the list?
W: Well I've seen a volcano in Indonesia. And yes, I've climbed a volcano. In Italy, on vacation. I got very tired but it was awesome.
I: Really? Where was that?
W: Well it was …

Conversation 3

I = Interviewer W = Woman

I: Excuse me. We're doing a survey … about unforgettable experiences.
W: Right …
I: Two minutes. Could you just look at this list? Have you done any of these things?
W: OK. Well … I'm not really an outdoor person, so … I haven't slept outside. Or climbed a volcano. And I've never watched the sun rise. Mmm … I've never done a bungee jump. I'd like to try it. It looks fun but scary! But I've never done that.
I: And the other things?
W: Hmm … oh yes, I've been in a film. I'm not a very good actor. In fact, I'm a terrible actor.
I: Is it a famous film?
W: Well, no, it was a short video, a little drama. My friend makes short videos and once she asked me to act in one. It's on YouTube. It got over ten thousand hits. That was amazing.
I: Wow! That's interesting. What was it about?
W: Well, I played this woman and she was …

Lesson 12.3 Recording 12.4

Conversation 1

S = Sean D = Debbie

S: Hello.
D: Hi, Sean. It's Debbie.
S: Hi, Debbie. What's up?
D: Is Kevin there?
S: No, he's not. He went out about ten minutes ago.
D: Oh …
S: What's up?
D: Well, I locked the keys in the car. Kevin has the spare key.
S: Oh, what a drag!
D: Could I leave a message for him?
S: Of course.
D: Just ask him to call me.
S: On your mobile?
D: No, that's in the car … I'll give you a number.
S: Hold on … OK, go ahead.
D: OK, let's see … It's 3-double 2, 6-3, 2-8.
S: Got it. I'll tell him.
D: Thanks, bye.
S: Bye.

Conversation 2

C = Customer O = Operator CS = Customer services

O: Berkley Bank.
C: Hello. Could I speak to customer services, please?
O: Just a moment.

CS: Customer services.
C: Hello. This is Alan Simpson. I've got a problem. I think I've lost my credit card.
CS: I see. I'm sorry, this line is very bad. Where are you calling from?
C: I'm in Madrid, actually. In fact, I'm calling from a public phone and I've only got one minute on this card. Could you ring me back?
CS: Of course. Could you give me the number there?
C: Just a moment … It's 34 for Spain, 91 for Madrid, then 308 5238.
CS: Let me check that. 34 91 308 5238.
C: That's right.
CS: Fine. Now hang up – I'll call you back straightaway.
C: Thank you.

Conversation 3

W = Woman M = Man

W: Hello?
M: Oh, thank goodness. Hello, uh … Who's this?
W: My name's Marianne.
M: Thanks for picking up.
W: Well, the phone rang so I picked it up.
M: Yes, well, that's my cell phone. And you found it.
W: Oh, OK … It's yours. Do you want to get it back?
M: Yes, thanks. Where are you?
W: Central Park, by the fountain. It was here in the grass.
M: Ah, yes … I thought it might be.
W: So where are you?
M: Not far away. I can be there in ten minutes.
W: OK, I'll wait here.
M: Great. Thanks a lot!

Lesson 12.4 Recording 12.8

This happened in Australia … when I was about twenty-five. I spent a few days at a hotel in Alice Springs and went to Ayers Rock and … well, anyway, one day, I went out for a walk … in the outback. It was a lovely day so I walked and walked … and then I realised I didn't really know where I was. I was a bit stupid, really… because I decided to go further … I guess I thought I'd find the way back. Erm … anyway, after that I heard some dogs. First I heard them barking, and then I saw them … there was a group – maybe five or six dogs, wild dogs, coming towards me. I felt really frightened, but I remembered some advice I, er …, I read in my guidebook: Don't move, and don't look at the dogs. So I froze, like a statue … I didn't move … and I looked at a tree, not at the dogs, and didn't move my eyes. The dogs were all around me, jumping and barking … I thought they were going to bite me. Then one dog did bite my arm, just a little, but still I didn't move. In the end, after about twenty minutes, the dogs went away. I stayed there for a few more minutes and then luckily found my way back to the hotel. It was the most frightening experience I've ever had!